CINEMA

Key Texts in the Anthropology of Visual and Material Culture

Editor: Marcus Banks

Key Texts in the Anthropology of Visual and Material Culture is an innovative series of accessible texts designed for students. Each volume concisely introduces and analyses core topics in the study of visual anthropology and material culture from a distinctively anthropological perspective.

Titles in this series include:

Cinema: A Visual Anthropology

Forthcoming titles:

Museums: A Visual Anthropology

CINEMA
A Visual Anthropology

Gordon Gray

Oxford • New York

English edition
First published in 2010 by
Berg
Editorial offices:
First Floor, Angel Court, 81 St Clements Street, Oxford OX4 1AW, UK
175 Fifth Avenue, New York, NY 10010, USA

Berg is the imprint of Oxford International Publishers Ltd.

Library of Congress Cataloging-in-Publication Data

Gray, Gordon
    Cinema : a visual anthropology / Gordon Gray. — English ed.
      p. cm. — (Key texts in the anthropology of visual and material culture)
    Includes bibliographical references and index.
    ISBN 978-1-84520-793-9 (cloth) — ISBN 978-1-84520-794-6 (pbk.)
  1. Motion pictures in ethnology. 2. Visual anthropology. I. Title.
    GN347.G723 2010
    301—dc22

                                        2009045269

British Library Cataloguing-in-Publication Data

A catalogue record for this book is available from the British Library.

ISBN 978 1 84520 793 9 (Cloth)
         978 1 84520 794 6 (Paper)

Typeset by JS Typesetting Ltd, Porthcawl, Mid Glamorgan
Printed in Great Britain by the MPG Books Group, Bodmin and King's Lynn

www.bergpublishers.com

CONTENTS

List of Illustrations — vii

Introduction — ix

Suggested Further Reading — xvii

1 The History of Cinema — 1
Introduction — 2
Precursors — 3
Early Cinema — 5
The "Golden Era" of Fiction Film — 15
Auteurs, Independents, and Global Blockbusters — 28
Suggested Further Reading — 33

2 Film Theory — 35
Introduction — 36
Early Film Theory — 37
Critical Film Theories — 45
Suggested Further Reading — 73

3 Context of Production, Distribution, and Exhibition — 75
Introduction — 76
Context of Production — 77
Third Cinema — 88
Contexts of Distribution and Exhibition — 96
Social and Cultural Contexts – Anthropology of the Cinema — 99
Suggested Further Reading — 107

vi contents

4   Context of Reception   109
    Introduction   110
    Reception and Audience Studies   112
    Suggested Further Reading   133

Conclusion   135
Notes   143
Bibliography   147
Index   157

LIST OF ILLUSTRATIONS

I.1   Local cinema in the Asakusa district of Tokyo, Japan.   ix

1.1   Toshiro Mifune and Machiko Kyo in a scene from *Rashomon*.   1

1.2   Scene from *Le Voyage dans la Lune* [Voyage to the Moon]
(G. Méliès 1902).   7

1.3   George Siegmann and Lillian Gish in a scene from *The Birth of a
Nation* (D. W. Griffith 1915).   8

1.4   Max Schreck in a scene from *Nosferatu* (F. W. Murnau 1922).   12

1.5   Actress Aishwarya Rai in a Bollywood song and dance number from
Bride and Prejudice (G. Chadha 2004).   18

1.6   Filming *Casablanca*. Humphrey Bogart and Ingrid Bergman
(M. Curtiz 1942).   19

1.7   An example of the Golden Age "Picture Palace" – the Eros Cinema
Mumbai, India. Built in 1938.   20

1.8   Robert De Niro in *Taxi Driver* (M. Scorsese 1976).   27

1.9   Movie poster for *Terminator 2: Judgment Day* (J. Cameron 1991).   31

2.1   An art-house cinema in Nagoya, Japan.   35

2.2   Orson Welles in a seminal scene from the expressionist influenced
The Third Man (C. Reed 1949).   40

2.3   Director Orson Welles and cinematographer Gregg Toland filming
Citizen Kane (O. Welles 1941).   48

2.4   Palace Talkies theatre Mumbai India. Built for millworkers.   51

2.5   Some Bollywood codes on display – hand-drawn movie posters on
a wall in Bangalore, India.   57

2.6   Stall selling Nigerian VCDs at the multicultural Kwakoe festival in
the Bijlmermeer district of Amsterdam, the Netherlands.   65

2.7   Projectionist checking the equipment at the Elgin Talkies movie
theatre (built in 1896) Bangalore, India. The equipment is from
the 1930s.   71

3.1   Cinema in Marrakesh, Morocco.   75

3.2 Partially hand drawn poster advertising Jean-Claude Van Damme in *JCVD* (El Mechri 2008) – Nagoya. Japan. 78

3.3 Inside the Elgin Talkies cinema hall (built in 1896) Shivaji Road in Shivaji Nagar district of Bangalore, India. 80

3.4 Cinema in Gunung Sitoli, Nias Island, Indonesia. 82

3.5 Facade of the colonial-era Elgin Talkies cinema hall building (built in 1896) in Bangalore, India. 87

3.6 Sign outside the abandoned Cine Oriente in the center of Santiago de Cuba, Cuba. 91

3.7 While cineplexes exist throughout Africa, films are also viewed in unexpected places, such as this cinema in Gambia. 106

4.1 Cathay Cinema in Shanghai, China. 109

4.2 Cinema-goers at the entrance of the Elgin Talkies cinema in Bangalore, India. 111

4.3 Films are not only watched in cinemas, the Special Video Club, Gambia. 122

4.4 Nollywood VCDs on display at a stall at the multicultural Kwakoe festival in the Bijlmermeer district of Amsterdam, the Netherlands. 127

4.5 Close-up of Nollywood VCDs on display at a stall at the multicultural Kwakoe festival in the Bijlmermeer district of Amsterdam, the Netherlands. 128

C.1 Cineplex in Japan. 135

INTRODUCTION

Figure I.1 Local cinema in the Asakusa district of Tokyo, Japan. Photograph by Erik Katerborg, 2008.

So in viewing *Rashomon* we cognitively "know" and affectively "feel" in relation to a series of events that never took place, that are not real, that are "only a film." Furthermore, as the very first philosopher to write about film, Hugo Munsterberg, argued, we experience and feel the film world all the while knowing it is not real; knowing that its apartness from our world is absurd, yet enjoying it. We are not fooled. How can this be, and what is the nature of the suspension of credibility that allows cognition and affect to work, but not so as to deceive us into mistaking the film's world for real?

Jarvie, Philosophy of the Film: Epistemology, Ontology, Aesthetics

For many people the words "anthropology" and "cinema" go together like bread and gasoline. This is unfortunate as they have a substantial amount to offer one another. One of the principal reasons for this book is to make the case for changing our perceptions of that relationship. To that end, this book will provide students with fundamental tools with which to engage one of the most interesting and vibrant of media – the cinema.

Before getting too far into this Introduction, this may be an appropriate place to raise an important issue – namely what *the cinema* means. On the face of it, this may seem like a strange thing to query, as we all know what we mean when we say "the cinema" – but we do not always mean the same thing, and we do not necessarily mean what someone else may think we mean by the same phrase. Cinema is a term that is used both frequently and casually, typically without much effort made to ensure that we are clear about what we actually mean. *Cinema* can be taken to mean very different things at different times –a physical space ("I am going to the cinema."), a medium of entertainment ("Casablanca is a cinema masterpiece!"), or even an entire industry with all the connections and entanglements that entails ("I am studying Bollywood cinema."). Further, that third usage, as an industry, may *or may not* include the prior two usages. One of my goals in this book is to excavate that term through looking at the different levels of meaning ascribed to the term, from narrowest to most inclusive. In doing so, we should arrive at some important answers to the question of what cinema is and how we understand it, and the strengths and weaknesses of various approaches to engaging with this tricky term.

Beyond disentangling the various meanings of the term itself, the study of the cinema has other benefits to offer. Understanding and experiencing the pleasures of watching a great film, or conversely the disappointments and frustrations of watching a poor film, adds immeasurably to the experience of cinema-going. Further, the study of cinema can provide us with significant insight into areas of a society of a different time or place that might otherwise be difficult, or even impossible, to access. Cultural producers are often crucially important in terms of their influence on issues such as fashion, aesthetics, and styles. Cinema can provide insights into the historical changes of those same styles and aesthetics, as well as providing information on the ideas and prejudices of a particular time and place, again particularly of the culture-producing class.

An issue that may be of even more importance than the pragmatic information mentioned above is that cinema has a power to move people. Some of the earliest theoretical approaches to mass media were highly critical of this very aspect of media such as cinema. As will be discussed in various places in the book, cinema has been a very successful medium in global terms, with not only a global reach but a rapid adoption across the globe as well. In other words, cinema has entertained and influenced people in places as diverse as New York, Berlin, Jakarta, Madras, and Tokyo. Understanding how cinema "works," then, how it can have affected so many people over such a long period of time, is also important as it can provide insights into areas like socialization and enculturation, not to mention globalization of culture and how people are making sense of the messages within the films they are watching. As such, fictional feature film (fiction film for short) can also act as a guide to cultural constructions of everyday life, to symbolic and metaphoric communication, and to political and economic forces. Fiction film can also give us insight into popular reactions to the issues and events of a particular time or place.

A further intention for the book is that while it is written by an anthropologist it engages students outside of anthropology. To accomplish this goal, the book uses examples of both Western and non-Western fiction films, and also outlines theories, ideas, and approaches both from within and outside of anthropology to further students' knowledge of and interest in fiction film. Case studies highlight and exemplify important issues, and there will be suggested further readings for each chapter to aid students who wish to pursue particular issues, topics, or individuals.[1] One of the historical limitations to much film theory is its focus upon the Western cinemas, although some areas of film theory have attempted to address non-Western cinemas. Therefore, while films from the USA, the UK, and continental Europe will be featured, an important focus will be the study of fiction film from around the world. Aside from the USA and the UK, the films of India, Japan, Indonesia, and Nigeria will be used to exemplify the ideas, methods, and approaches discussed throughout the book.

The historical limitation on non-Western films in much of American and European film studies (not just film studies the discipline) has had a further effect than simply a paucity of African or Indonesian films on film class syllabi. There has been a history of certain inequities in how Western and non-Western films are discussed within different forms of film studies, with Western films being analyzed through film theories such as those discussed in Chapter 2, whereas non-Western films tend to be analyzed as products of national industries, with perhaps some particular filmmakers being treated differently (Akira Kurosawa would be an instance). Further, while there have been attempts to get beyond this disjuncture in treatment of different cinemas, and this appears to be an area of increasing interest within film studies, the foundations of that understanding may not as yet be very strong. Chow (1995) and Shohat and Stam (1994) in particular have made appeals for a more sophisticated knowledge of the social and cultural *contexts* of film production, especially for cinemas less familiar to a Western audience, or indeed Western researchers. Indeed, Chow specifically calls for an anthropology of the cinema. Over the course of this book I will piece together what an anthropology of the cinema might involve.

Whereas cinema is a well-known but not always well-defined term, anthropology is well-defined, but not so well-known. Simply put, anthropology is the study of human beings. As such, the aspects of humans that anthropologists study are likewise vast – from genetics to gentrification to globalization. Anthropology is distinguished from other social science disciplines by its methodology, its emphasis on *cultural relativity* (understanding a particular culture in that culture's own terms), and its emphasis on context (sometimes referred to as *holism*). In general, anthropology investigates people and how they live their lives. That might include any number of activities, such as looking at kinship, gender, politics, economics, ritual and re-ligion, or even things like violence, warfare, and aggression. Field research in anthropology typically means *participant-observation.* Participant-observation is the somewhat awkward term used to refer to a set of qualitative research practices that are fundamental to the discipline of anthropology. The elements of these practices include: research usually takes place over an extended period of time (from months to years); speaking the language of the people you work with; and engaging as much as possible in the daily life of the people you are working with. One benefit of this approach is that anthropologists gain a great deal of access to what people "do" as opposed to what they "say." This is sometimes referred to as "official" versus "practice," e.g. people may have "official" marriage rules, but in practice only one son/daughter may marry in this way, while the others marry people other than "official" marriage partners. This is not to imply that people are lying about what they are doing, but that what they do is so normal that they do not consciously think about what they are doing or why they are doing it. As we will see in Chapters 3 and 4, anthropology with its emphasis on context and the daily life of the people they work with can extend the ways we have for understanding the cinema.

I mentioned at the beginning of this Introduction that anthropology and cinema tend not to go together in most people's minds. However, there is one form of film with which anthropology has had a generally positive relationship and that is a particular form of documentary cinema known as ethnographic film.[2] As a documentary filmmaker it pains me to say that I will not be expressly discussing ethnographic film, though in Chapter 3 I do discuss a form of fiction film that overlaps with ethnographic film – indigenous media and specifically indigenous fiction film, such as *Atanarjuat – The Fast Runner* (Kunuk 2001). I will be omitting ethnographic film, not to mention documentary film, for several reasons. Most pragmatically there have to be some boundaries on the content of the book, and distinguishing fiction from non-fiction is a well-rehearsed distinction – one that you will see in libraries or when browsing the DVD racks for new releases. There are other reasons to make the distinction, however. The very nature of the two genres requires very different ways of engaging with the final product as well as with the modes of their production. While fiction filmmakers do not have to limit themselves to telling a truthful account or depiction of a real situation or events (to as great an extent as possible), they have a different set of obligations and interests. Most of those obligations are discussed throughout this book, especially in Chapter 2 where film theory is discussed. The role of the filmmaker is different in the two genres, and the palette of possibilities regarding the way that they tell their stories likewise are very different. There are exceptions to these generalizations, as there are works like *Super Size Me* (Spurlock 2004) and filmmakers like Michael Moore who arguably do not fit the model I just described, but overall the two genres require different approaches, one of which I will not undertake in this book. Bearing that in mind, I would now like to return to what will be undertaken in this book

CHAPTER 1: THE HISTORY OF CINEMA

The book begins by providing an overview of the development of fiction film, both in Europe and America as well as in countries such as India, Japan, Nigeria, and Indonesia. To understand something, such as fiction film, it is important to understand where that something has come from – what historical changes and developments have that something undergone, and what epistemological developments have occurred. Fiction film is no different. This chapter will introduce students to some of the key developments and characters in the history of fiction film, such as the Lumière Brothers (French cinema pioneers, generally credited with inventing cinema), D. W. Griffith (an early and famously innovative American film director), and the Hollywood studio system. While much of this chapter will focus upon incidents in Europe and the United States, developments in other countries around the world will also be highlighted.[5] The case studies will begin to introduce some the issues that will be highlighted in later chapters, such as how exhibition, distribution, and censorship are crucial to the development of film around the world. Case studies include the aforementioned D. W. Griffith and F. W. Murnau (another early film director and innovator), as well as examples from the early development of cinema industries in India and Japan. These case studies will introduce students to the histories of film in different countries.

CHAPTER 2: FILM THEORY

In this chapter, the development of various critical approaches to understanding fiction film will be outlined. This will include attempts to understand the *content* of fiction film, such as approaching film as art. Students will also be introduced to the historical development of film theory and to some of the most influential of these theories. Given the antipathy that frequently exists between theory and practice in the study of film, it is ironic that the development of fiction film and the development of film theory are inextricably intertwined. Several of the key figures in the history of fiction film are also fundamental to the development of film theory. This reason alone makes understanding that latter development an important goal, but there are other reasons as well. Understanding how film works, one of the key strands in film theory, provides students with important tools for understanding film more generally, as well as a way to discuss that understanding. This chapter will summarize some of the important film theories from the 1920s onwards, such as theories on montage and *mise en scène* or perspectives that promoted film as an art form. Several important theoretical developments from outside the film world were incorporated into the film theory canon, such as approaches that interrogated cinema in terms of how it transmitted and promoted the ideologies of the state and elites (Marxism), theories that investigated the building blocks of film narrative and how they were employed to tell a story effectively (structuralism and semiotics), and theories that dealt with the relationship between film and our unconscious needs and desires (psychoanalysis-derived theories). These theoretical models will also be summarized. The crucial turn to approaches that treated films as texts, to be analyzed similarly (e.g. critical literary theory) in the latter part of the twentieth century will also be addressed. Further, this chapter will introduce theories, such as reception studies, third cinema, national cinema, and an anthropological approach to the study of cinema, which will have a larger role in later sections of the book. Case studies will include examples that students will likely already be aware of, such as Hitchcock, though not necessarily in the manner being discussed – understanding his films through psychoanalysis. Also included are examples that students may find less familiar, such as the early Soviet director and theorist Sergei Eisenstein and montage or globalized cinemas and the influential literary theories of Mikhail Bakhtin.

CHAPTER 3: CONTEXT OF PRODUCTION, DISTRIBUTION, AND EXHIBITION

While understanding the *content* of film – the actions, ideas, and activities shown or represented in the film – is important, understanding the *context* of film – everything else that goes into you watching that film – is also critically important. Therefore, while content-oriented approaches to film will be an important part of my argument in this book so too will context-oriented approaches, such as attempts to understand the influences of the nation and the cultural contexts in which a particular film or set of films are produced within. Although less numerous than studies of the context of viewing (discussed in Chapter 4), studies that analyze the context of fiction film production, distribution, and exhibition exist and provide useful and original insight into understanding the cinema. Although the idea of understanding the context in which films are produced goes back to the 1920s, two of the main approaches to analyzing that context are more recent – those of national cinema and third cinema (sometimes also known as Third World cinema). Bringing this discussion up to date, we will look at an offshoot of third cinema – indigenous media and specifically indigenous cinema. All of these approaches share an interest in the *ideological* aspect of the cinema. Often overlooked in the analyses of production is the role that distribution and exhibition have played within the cinema. This arena brings in political economies of cinema industries and in certain cases also involves nationalist agendas (detrimental duties placed upon the import of films from other countries in order to protect national film production for instance). Independent and amateur filmmakers have, through non-official channels such as the Internet and independent film festivals, circumvented the politics and economics of film distribution and exhibition with varying degrees of success. This chapter will begin to specifically delve into just what an anthropology of the cinema might look like and what it would have to offer, particularly but not only, in relation to non-Western cinemas. Again, in this chapter the majority of examples will be of non-Western cinemas. Case studies in this chapter will include an analysis of how Indonesian political upheaval "framed" Indonesian cinema output, how postcolonial ideologies manifest in African cinema, and of the social and cultural context of American cinema in the 1980s. These case studies will aid students in conceptualizing how aspects of our lives, which we normally do not associate with film (particularly in terms of America or Europe), do indeed have effects upon the films we enjoy.

CHAPTER 4: CONTEXT OF RECEPTION

A further context is that of the viewer and approaches that address that context, such as audience and other reception studies. Audience/reception studies is the one area of fiction film that anthropologists *have* tackled. However, anthropology is not the only discipline to have done this type of study, and this chapter will outline both non-anthropological and anthropological approaches to the audience. Practitioners of film studies had certainly tried to understand how films "work" vis-à-vis the viewer – psychoanalytical approaches in particular highlighted the audience – whereas media and communication studies were among the first to try to understand how "real world" audiences make sense of the content of fiction film. The focus within the cultural studies paradigm tended towards how the medium and/or the message was appropriated or subverted by the audience. As mentioned above, audience study is where anthropology has engaged with fiction film the most frequently. Anthropological audience studies are also interesting for being almost exclusively focused upon non-Western audiences and typically upon non-Western media as well. Therefore, although some of the examples given will be from the USA or UK, most will be from non-Western cinemas and/or cinema audiences, such as India. Case studies will include how Bollywood films are "read" outside of India and cinema-going in Nigeria. These case studies will illustrate the ways in which audiences understand films, sometimes concurring with the attentions of the filmmakers and sometimes making sense that is vastly different from what was intended.

A unique contribution that *Cinema: A Visual Anthropology* will make to the study of fiction film is twofold: for anthropology students, this book not only introduces them to theories and approaches outside of the anthropological canon but demonstrates the value in engaging in this fascinating medium; for non-anthropology students, this book will introduce them to an anthropologically informed approach to understanding fiction film. Another area where the book will have much to offer students is in its geographic scope. Many of the cinema industries discussed here will not be familiar to either anthropology or non-anthropology students. While Indian and Japanese cinemas should be at least somewhat familiar, the cinemas of Nigeria and Indonesia will likely not. In deciding which industries to include or not, some hard choices had to be made – China was left out, as were Brazil, Argentina, and European cinemas that might not be as familiar as France or Germany. The goal was to provide a range of familiarity and unfamiliarity, yet retaining some basis for comparison. For instance, India and Nigeria were both British colonies and so the influence of British policies and post-independence events could be contrasted. Indonesia is an Asian country, like India and Japan, yet does not have as successful or as internationally famous an industry. Again, this provides an opportunity to compare, contrast, and develop theories on why the various industries should be so different.

Part of my goal in writing this book was to address what I felt were gaps in two very different disciplines, film in anthropology and anthropology in film. While there are instances of each in either, overall the absence is more apparent than the instances. They both have so much to offer to one another. Film provides anthropology not only with a new venue in which to investigate the human condition, but is also an arena where so much of the unspoken (ideologies, taste and distinction, and other forms of embedded culture) come out on display, especially in terms of the culture-producing class. For film, anthropology offers new insights into arenas that film has often either overlooked or dealt with poorly: the way real people engage with the cinema and its unspoken ideological content; or the cultural embeddedness of those traits that marks French films as French or Nigerian films as Nigerian. Cinema and anthropology may never go together in people's minds like bread and butter, but neither should they be like bread and gasoline.

SUGGESTED FURTHER READING

GENERAL AND EUROPE/AMERICA

Cousins, M. (2004) *The Story of Film,* New York: Thunder's Mouth Press.

Hill, J. and Church Gibson, P. (eds) (1998) *The Oxford Guide to Film Studies,* New York: Oxford University Press.

Lewis, J. and Smoodin, E. (eds) (2007) *Looking Past the Screen: Case Studies in American Film History and Method,* Durham, NC: Duke University Press.

Nowell-Smith, G. (ed.), (1996a) *The Oxford History of World Cinema: The Definitive History of Cinema Worldwide,* New York: Oxford University Press.

INDIA

Rajadhyaksha, A. and Willemen, P. (eds) (2002) *Encyclopedia of Indian Cinema,* revised edition, London: British Film Institute Publishing.

Ganti, T. (2004) *Bollywood: A Guidebook to Popular Hindi Cinema,* New York: Routledge

INDONESIA

Salim Said (1991) *Shadows on the Silver Screen: A Social History of Indonesian Cinema,* Jakarta: The Lontar Foundation.

Sen, K. (1994) *Indonesian Cinema: Framing the New Order,* London and New Jersey: Zed Books.

JAPAN

McDonald, K. (2006) *Reading a Japanese Film: Cinema in Context,* Honolulu: University of Hawai'i Press.

Richie, D. (1990) *Japanese Cinema: An Introduction,* New York: Oxford University Press.

NIGERIA

Pfaff, F. (ed.), (2004) *Focus on African Films*, Bloomington, IN: Indiana University Press.

Ukadike, N. F. (1994) *Black African Cinemas,* Berkeley: University of California Press.

1 THE HISTORY OF CINEMA

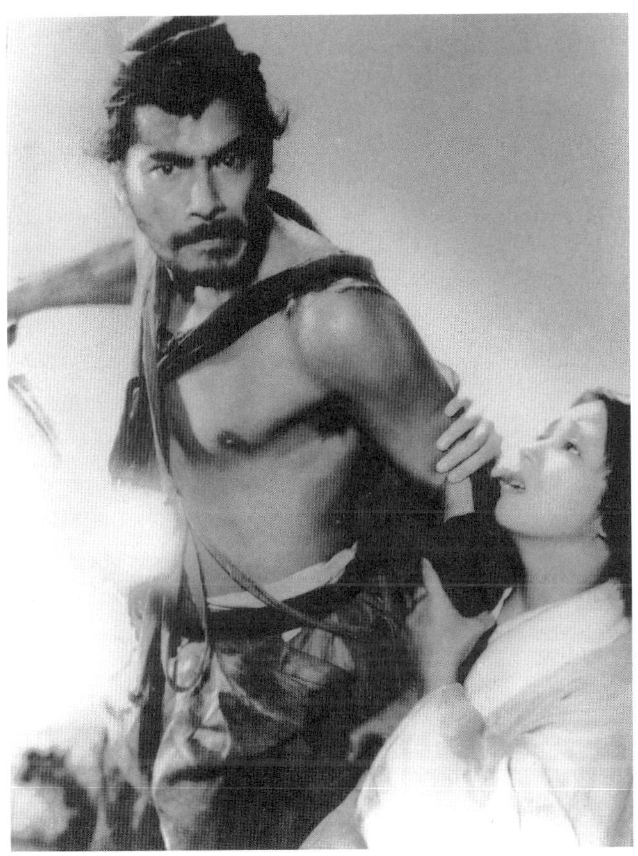

Figure 1.1   Toshiro Mifune and
Machiko Kyo in a scene from
Rashomon. (A. Kurosawa 1951)
[Credit: Daiei / The Kobal Collection]

We had gathered to watch *Fatal Attraction* on laser disc because Radhika, who was an actress, and her friends – a director, a cinematographer, a screenwriter, an assistant director, and a few actors – were thinking of remaking it into a Hindi film. Although most of them had seen the film before, they were watching it that night to decide whether to remake it.

During a particularly passionate sex scene, Radhika turned to Tarun who would be directing the potential remake, "What will you do? Will you show a song here? How are you going to show then having great sex?"

Tarun said, "I can do it."

"How can you?" pressed Radhika.

"I'll do it," assured Tarun.

"No, not like how you did in your last film, not with shadows and silhouettes and close shots. That's not going to do it."

When Tarun asserted, "Don't worry, I can do it," Radhika objected: "But wait, if you do it, I can't be seen doing that with someone I just met for the very first time! I can't do that!"

Tarun pointed out, "But you're not stable" [referring to the character, not to Radhika].

Radhika protested, "I don't want to be mentally unstable! It's quite unfashionable now; that's just not what's done!"

After the film was over, Tarun declared, "We can't make this film." Imran, who was a writer, concurred, "You're right. It doesn't work. It's really boring"

Ganti, *"And Yet My Heart is Still Indian": The Bombay Film Industry and
the (H)Indianization of Hollywood*

INTRODUCTION

The question of when cinema began has both a simple and a complex answer. The "simple" answer often given is that cinema began in 1895, with the demonstration of an invention by two French brothers, the Lumières, of a machine that could both "capture" and project moving pictures. The complex answer to the question is a lot more interesting. Parkinson describes cinema as the most modern, technologically dependent, and Western of all the arts (1995: 7), and if we agree with the simple explanation of when cinema began that is a fair assessment. However, another way of looking at cinema is that it was the convergence of several long-term processes, such as: the appeal of visual stimulation for humans; an awareness of certain peculiarities of vision; a nineteenth-century interest in technology, machinery, and spectacle; and some financial acumen by specific individuals. While some aspects of the precursors to cinema are fairly well acknowledged (for instance the relationship of photography to cinema), it is interesting also to think about what elements leading to the development of the cinema are overlooked. Generally speaking, there has been a lack of recognition of the role of the theatre in the early days of film, and that lack of recognition could be extended to other forms of entertainment. For millennia humans, more or less across the globe, have created visual stimuli – from drawings and paintings to shadow puppets to theatre and opera. The addition of technology in the form of photography and the various types of magic lantern shows expanded that repertoire of visual stimuli as much as they created new visual media. While the genealogy of photograph to cinema (the motion studies of Muybridge when combined with persistence of vision equals moving picture) is well documented (Charney and Schwartz 1995; Parkinson 1995; Usai 1996; Gunning 2000; Cousins 2004), there are other lineages that should be explored.

There are numerous books on the history of cinema, both in general and on specific countries. Most of the authors of these works note the rapid and extensive proliferation of this new media, but very few actually question why this should be, when, as noted above, there remains a general assumption that cinema is a particularly Western art form. We not only need to reassess our assumptions as to where cinema comes from, but we also need to investigate all three aspects of cinema (production, distribution, and exhibition) to make sense of its success globally. Distribution and exhibition are often overlooked in standard film histories (see, for instance, Cousins 2004), but can have a crucial role in the success, or lack thereof, of cinema in a particular context. This chapter will incorporate the standard narrative of cinema history with a more wide-ranging regard for factors influencing the paths of cinema in various countries around the world.

PRECURSORS

Cinema is one of the most successful optical illusions of all time. Film works because the human brain has a threshold for perception above which a series of still images will appear to be continuous; this phenomenon is known as persistence of vision. The 24 frames per second (fps) that cinema employs is above that threshold.[1] Persistence of vision has been known since at least the ancient Egyptians, and over time that and other optical illusions have resulted in various optical toys based on those illusions. For instance, researchers have found that the brain will tend to impose three dimensions onto a two-dimensional image, if given enough basis to do so (such as in perspective drawing), which is very handy when drafting and is indispensable for the other key technology involved in the development of cinema – photography. A particularly good example of this comes from one of the "optical toys" that have been mentioned, namely magic lantern shows. Magic lantern shows were an early form of slide show, where images were painted on pieces of glass, which were then set into "lanterns" that projected the image onto a wall or screen (Parkinson 1995). Various special effects, such as smoke and multiple images, could be added, and the effects could be quite sophisticated. Indeed, these "toys" were thrilling audiences from the 1600s to the late 1800s. Over that time, the magic lanterns became increasingly advanced. Just three years before the Lumières, Emile Reynaud was using mirrors, a projecting lens, and strips of film in his Praxinoscope to present a show that was very close to cinema (Parkinson 1995).

As with both an awareness of persistence of vision and devices to exploit the phenomenon, photography has existed for a considerable period of time. Initial experiments with the camera obscura, effectively a large dark box (like a room with no windows) with a small opening to allow light to enter, go back hundreds of years, and the gradual development of photography from those roots in the sixteenth century continues today. Among the differences between a camera obscura and a camera is one very important one, namely that a camera can *record* and a big dark room with a hole in it cannot. You could use a camera obscura to view an image of Edinburgh, for instance, but you could not take that image home to show your family. One of the most important innovations in photographic terms was some way of recording the image from these early pre-camera devices. Before this discussion becomes too technophilic though, there were other very important contributors to the development of cinema – I have already mentioned some of these, such as the theatre and even painting. While these tend to get overlooked, they reflect a deep-seated human interest in visual stimuli and as such "tapped into" a vast repertoire of existing *visual* conventions. Indeed, Cousins suggests that at least part of the reason that cinema exploded across the globe as it did was because it was *silent* – the filmmakers depended upon the visual image more than on dialogue and hence the films were more international (Cousins 2004: 18). None of this is intended to dismiss the importance of the technological advances that were indeed necessary for film to come about, but to make clear that there was an entire other level of activity beyond the mechanical.

Speaking of the mechanical, the aforementioned technologies began to converge and Muybridge's famous series of images of a moving horse was (as much as anything) the catalyst that brought that convergence together. The story, which is usually simplified in various retellings, is that to settle a bet on whether a galloping horse's hooves are all off the ground at one time or not, Muybridge developed a system of twelve cameras with trip wires along a racetrack to capture images of the horse as it was running (Parkinson 1995).[2] As Muybridge found out, thereby winning the bet, a running horse will have all of its hooves off of the ground at various times. Around the same time, Etienne Jules Marey developed a "photo-gun," the *fusil photographique,* which recorded 12 pictures per second on a revolving plate. When

Marey began using the celluloid film produced by Eastman Kodak to create strips of images, the stage for cinema, at least in hindsight, was set. The penultimate act was the invention of the Kinetograph (1890) and Kinetoscope (1891) by William Dickson, then head of Thomas Edison's West Orange laboratory.

Edison's company established the first film studio, and film "hits" such as *Fred Ott's Sneeze* (1894) and *The Rice/Irwin Kiss* (1896) began to play in Kinetoscope parlors. The Kinetoscope parlor was a row of "peep show" machines at which a single customer could for a small fee (around 5 cents) watch a few seconds of unedited film footage of activities like the sneeze or kiss mentioned above. In a rare instance of myopia in an otherwise stellar career of financial ruthlessness, Edison neglected to take out overseas patents on his technology, believing film to be a fad limited to the peep show. As Parkinson puts it, "[Edison's] avaricious misjudgment would ultimately cost him dear" (1995: 15).[3] However, it may have been just as well, as the Kinetoscope had an important limitation, which may have led to it being superseded whatever Edison's actions – it could not project the images being shown and, therefore, only one person at a time could view the moving pictures. This severely limited the audience for the films, and ultimately would not have allowed the cinema to become a global mass media, with resulting sociological and economic effects (such as those discussed throughout much of the rest of the book).

The convergence I have been discussing was almost complete, as inventors in England, France, Germany, and the USA raced to develop what was in effect "a workable method of combining the Kinetoscope with a magic lantern" (Parkinson 1995: 16). The French Lumière brothers are usually regarded as having won the race with their 1895 showing to a paying audience of a short program of their Cinématographe films, including the now famous *The Arrival of a Train at La Ciotat Station* (1895). While it is true that no one person "invented" cinema, the Lumières and their Cinématographe are important for several reasons beyond their status as progenitors. Perhaps most importantly of those is that the Cinématographe was portable and could shoot, print, *and* project film. The Lumières exploited that portability and versatility to the utmost. Within one year of the 1895 demonstration, Lumière films had been shot and screened in countries around the world, including India and Japan. By 1900, Lumière films had been seen in Senegal and Iran (Cousins 2004: 24). Perhaps as importantly, the films that the Lumières shot were engaging in their own right, with a semblance of narrative structure. Cinema had arrived.

EARLY CINEMA

Once cinema got its metaphoric "foot in the door," it soon became arguably the preeminent visual medium of the early twentieth century. Shortly after the Lumières sent their cameras out on the road, British films were being shot and shown both at home and abroad. One instance is the newsreel-style *Queen Victoria's Diamond Jubilee* (aka *Diamond Anniversary Celebrations of Queen Victoria*) shot in 1897, possibly by Richard John Appledon. The film had been screened in many of the British colonies by the following year, and, as for example in Malaya (present-day Malaysia and Singapore), was often the first film shown in that colony (Hatta Azad Khan 1997: 58). Contrary to the way early cinema was perceived in Europe and the USA, where it was often perceived as low-class entertainment for the working class or immigrants, in colonies such as Malaya and India it was the elite who were the consumers of cinema. The first films were screened to select audiences, such as colonial officers and important businessmen, rather than as entertainment for the masses. From that seemingly inauspicious beginning, films were soon being shown in venues such as hotels, traveling cinema exhibitions, and amusement parks. Following local practice for other forms of entertainment, there was a variety of ticket prices, which were both physically and racially organized, with less attractive and lower-priced seats being open to Malays (and children), whereas the more expensive seats were for Europeans and Chinese. The first purpose-built cinema in the country was the Alhambra in Singapore, built in 1907. To put that date into context, the first purpose-built cinema in the USA in Pittsburgh, Pennsylvania was also built in 1907. The Malayan example is, if anything, a conservative example of the rapid engagement of non-Western countries with cinema. And while cinema was taken up perhaps most vigorously in the USA – though the early American cinema was dominated by French productions – it was incredibly successful around the globe (Parkinson 1995; Cousins 2004).

The period between the "invention" of cinema and the development of what we would now regard as "real" movies (edited narrative cinema) has been variously referred to as "early cinema," "cinema of attractions," and transitional cinema. Whichever term is preferred, the early development of cinema was marked by several elements. Perhaps first among these, and a quality shared with the preceding era, was the innovation and creativity that the surviving works demonstrate.[4] Méliès' famous *A Trip to the Moon* (1902), with its animation and creative spirit, or Edwin Porter, who produced some of the most sophisticated early films (such as *The Life of an American Fireman*, 1902, or *The Great Train Robbery*, 1903) also demonstrated that innovative spirit in early cinema (Pearson 1996a, 1996b).

Until quite recently, Porter was credited with the first use of cross-cutting (cutting between two separate scenes) to create a sense of simultaneous action in a film. It may be that the cross-cutting that audiences saw was a fortunate accident, as some historians have speculated (a creative, or inattentive, projectionist played the wrong reel at the wrong time), or that the cross-cutting came at the suggestion of

Figure 1.2   Scene from *Le Voyage dans la Lune* [Voyage to the Moon] (G. Méliès 1902). [Credit: Méliès / The Kobal Collection]

a colleague, as other historians have suggested. Either way, it was largely thought at the time that audiences would not be able to follow such an abstraction. At the time, most films followed a strictly chronological order. If there were separate but simultaneous actions, these scenes would be shown in entirety one following the other. After *The Life of an American Fireman* and *The Great Train Robbery* (which also featured the shock ending of a bandit firing a gun straight at the camera), it was evident that audiences not only could follow cross-cut scenes, but also enjoyed the more complicated way of telling a story (Cousins 2004: 37–8). The cut, along with many of the other innovations that the cinema engendered, if not required, such as eye-line matches (where the camera pans or cuts from a character's face to what the character is looking at – from the character's perspective), are often referred to as film "grammar" (the codes and conventions for putting the different elements of the film together to create larger meaning).[5] That film "grammar," which is now more or less taken as the "natural" way of storytelling in fiction film, began to be developed during the early days of cinema. As the example from what is now Malaysia suggests, this new film "grammar" became very quickly and very successfully disseminated around the world. The person most credited with developing the mechanics of cinema as we know it today is D. W. Griffith – or perhaps more accurately

Figure 1.3   George Siegmann and Lillian Gish in a scene
from *The Birth of a Nation* (D.W. Griffith 1915). [Credit:
Epoch / The Kobal Collection]

D. W. Griffith and his cameraman Billy Bitzer. Between them, with Griffith coming
up with new ways of combining some already established cinematic techniques, such
as pans, tilts, and tracking shots, with new ideas and Bitzer coming up with ways to
make the ideas work, they arguably did more in films like *Birth of Nation* (1915) to
hasten the development of narrative cinema than any others (Parkinson 1995: 23–7;
Cousins 2004: 51–3).

While Griffith and Bitzer were establishing many of the aesthetics and codes of
cinema, filmmakers in other parts of the world were making their own marks. In
Australia, Charles Tait made the world's first feature film, *The Story of the Kelly Gang*,
in 1906. Early French cinema was notable in the attention directors paid to *mise en
scène* (literally "putting on stage" – usually referring to sets, props, lighting, etc., it
also refers to using the setting in a scene to convey information without resorting
to exposition). The very theatre-like sets and typically static camera work in films
such as *The Assassination of the Duke of Guise* (Le Bargy and Calmettes 1908) and

Case Study: D. W. Griffith

Born in Kentucky, the son of a Civil War veteran, David Wark Griffiths (1875–1948) is widely known as the father of modern cinema (Parkinson 1995: 23–7; Pearson 1996c: 30–1; Cousins 2004: 51–6). His introduction to film was in 1907, when he began working for both Biograph and Edison as a writer and actor, gaining his first directing job, with Biograph in 1908 at the age of thirty-three. Five years later he would have mastered the new media, combining techniques of several of his peers into a coherent and intelligible code of cinematic expression (Parkinson 1995: 23). During the course of directing over 400 films for Biograph, Griffith, or as mentioned in the text, perhaps more accurately Griffith and his cameraman Billy Bitzer, made several lasting contributions to the cinema industry (Parkinson 1995; Pearson 1996c).

Among these contributions was that Griffith codified Edwin Porter's use of pans, tilts, and tracking shots. This is significant, as they were to become some of the fundamental elements of film "grammar," the components of cinematic technique that help the filmmaker tell the story, as by repeated and consistent usage they are understood as meaning certain things by the audience. Griffiths was also noted for his elaborate editing techniques, especially his sophisticated cuts. Again, this was not new technique, but a more nuanced use of established techniques, and again significantly his use became standardized (Pearson 1996c). Some specific instances of this usage would be as follows. The use of cross-cutting (an editing technique that involves cutting between two disparate scenes) for narrative and geographical clarity as well as creating tensions and pace. For instance, in *Birth of a Nation* (1915), to create a feeling of anxiety and fear in the audience, Griffith cuts between a shot of a black man (actually a white actor "blacked up") and a vulnerable white woman who is unaware of being watched, Griffith then cuts back to the watching man who now has a leer on his face. Very simply but very powerfully Griffith creates tension and fear by a series of cross-cuts (this is not an eye-line match as we do not see the woman as the man sees her, but rather we are put in the place of a helpless bystander, who can see that something bad is going to happen but is helpless to do anything about it). Perhaps more than anyone, Griffith established one of the most important elements of film "grammar," the use of close-ups (Pearson 1996c: 30). Through cutting to close-ups of actors at times of fear and stress, Griffith established one of the primary ways in which filmmakers can create a subjective position for their characters. We "know" this person is important and that what they are feeling is important as they are filling the whole screen. Thus we begin to identify with that character. Perhaps not quite as crucial, but important nevertheless is that Griffith also used flashbacks, dissolves, irises, and masks in a coherent manner to create particular narrative effects (Parkinson 1995; Pearson 1996c: 30). For instance, a dissolve tells the audience that continuity of time or space is being broken, and that this often signals a fantasy or dream sequence. In more recent films, where there is a certain self-awareness about the way film is made, this can be used to set up the viewer's expectation only to have it broken for comedic effect. The different *Scary Movie* films employ this type of "in joke" humor, for instance. The point being that these codes can only be broken because we understand what they mean, and the construction of that can largely be attributed to Griffith.

Besides helping to develop the codes and conventions of modern narrative film, Griffith also helped create certain aesthetics in early American cinema as well, for instance, in his care for *mise en scène*. Griffith disposed of painted backdrops and used natural props, creating depth and allowing different camera placements and angles (Parkinson 1995: 24). His work also to a degree anticipated both Eisenstein's montage and Murnau's subjective camera, though he did not take either idea to the limits that these other filmmakers would come to do. And he also instituted rehearsals and emphasized restraint in acting techniques, leading to a more "natural" acting style in contrast to the more "theatrical" (overblown) acting style of the day (Parkinson 1995: 24–5). One of the signatures of much early cinema is that without synched sound, there were more limitations to how meaning could be conveyed. The overly dramatic facial expressions of much early cinema was partly a product of an uncertainty within the industry that the audiences could understand what the characters were feeling without the actors overemphasizing their facial expressions. As time went on, Griffith became increasingly dissatisfied with the Biograph studio's refusal to consider producing multi-reel features. As mentioned in the text, "films" were often one reel, or approximately 17 minutes, long. Griffith worked in secret on a four-reel biblical epic, *Judith of Bethulia* (1914), before he left Biograph to produce his own films. Griffith's work reached both its pinnacle and its nadir in the same film, *Birth of a Nation*.

While cinematically *Birth of a Nation* was an admirable achievement, successfully combining the elements mentioned above as well as incorporating other achievements – detailed accurate historical reconstructions, night photography, use of tint, and an exquisite control of editing techniques – the film was also an overtly racist paean to the Ku Klux Klan (Parkinson 1995; Pearson 1996c; Cousins 2004). The first part of the film depicts two families, one Northern (the Stonemans) and one Southern (the Camerons), leading up to, during, and immediately after the American Civil War. The Stonemans visit the Camerons at their South Carolina estate. When war breaks out, the young men of both families all join the army, the Stoneman sons join the Union army and the Cameron brothers the Confederate army. During the war the Cameron house is attacked by a black militia, but the women of the Cameron household are saved by the Confederate army. The older Cameron sons are killed during the war, and the youngest son, Ben, is wounded and taken to a Northern hospital to recover. The war ends and the film shifts to the postwar Reconstruction period. Congressman Stoneman and a mixed-race subordinate (Lynch) are actively working to "fraudulently" empower black voters in South Carolina. Ben, who has observed white children dressing up as ghosts to scare black children plans to overturn the "powerlessness" of Southern whites and forms the Ku Klux Klan. A former slave (Gus) who works for Stoneman and Lynch pursues a white woman, who falls to her death. Gus is caught, lynched, and his corpse left on Lynch's doorstep. Lynch orders a reprisal against the Klan. To move straight to the climax of the film – the Klan saves the day, defeating the forces of evil and dispersing the "crazed negroes" running rampant and endangering the good white citizens. The end of the film shows the next election where blacks are once again disenfranchised and disarmed by the Klan.

There was a powerful backlash (though commercially the film was a success – recouping expenses in only two months) and that criticism wounded Griffith profoundly (Parkinson 1995). To try to rectify that situation and salvage his reputation, Griffith produced *Intolerance* (1916). As with *Birth of a Nation*, *Intolerance* was cinematically masterful, however, the overt sermonizing in the film turned away audiences (Parkinson 1995: 27). Griffith never really recovered from the twin failures of *Birth of a Nation* (critical) and *Intolerance* (commercial), and his work was increasingly marginal and old-fashioned. Sadly, the man who did so much to create the codes and conventions that are still in use today is remembered for one of the most unpleasant films ever made and not for his contributions to the industry.

Queen Elizabeth (Mercanton 1912) rendered the film set critically important, and the beautiful painting-like tableaux were a notable feature of early French cinema (Parkinson 1995). In Italy, filmmakers were pushing the length of film with an outpouring of lengthy historical melodramas such as *The Last Days of Pompeii* (Maggi 1908), *Lucrezia Borgia* (Caserini 1910), and Pastrone's *The Fall of Troy* (1910). *Quo Vadis?* (Guazzoni 1913) was very successful commercially despite vast sets and more than 5,000 extras. The running time for *Quo Vadis?* was around 120 minutes (or ten reels), at a time when most films were still being produced and exhibited at one reel (approximately 17 minutes). While German cinema started somewhat more slowly than most of its European neighbors it contributed a great deal to the development of feature film, particularly between the First and Second World Wars. Produced in the interwar years, works by directors such as Wiene (*The Cabinet of Dr. Caligari* 1919), Murnau (*Nosferatu* 1922), and Lang (*Metropolis* 1926) are justifiably regarded as classics. These films and directors remain famous today for creating new cinema aesthetics through innovative use of camera angles, unusual usage of the *mise en scène* to create tension and convey or suggest non-visible information (for instance implying a character's unbalanced mental state through jarring stage sets and camera angles as in *The Cabinet of Dr. Caligari*). Murnau in particular involved the camera almost as one of the characters and to create subjective position. For

Figure 1.4   Max Schreck in a scene from *Nosferatu* (F. W. Murnau 1922). [Credit: Prana-Film / The Kobal Collection]

Case Study: F. W. Murnau

One of the silent film era's most gifted artists, F. W. Murnau (1888–1931) made only twenty-one films before his premature death in a car accident (Bergstrom 1996: 146). Unlike many within the film industry, Murnau grew up in a cultured environment and attended the University of Heidelberg, one of the most prestigious universities in Europe. At university, Murnau studied art history and literature. While directing in Germany, Murnau created some of the most visually stunning and famous films of the 1920s (Bergstrom 1996: 146; Cousins 2004: 101).

While the first *Dracula* film (Browning 1931) is difficult to watch, or at least watch as a horror rather than as a comedy, Murnau's *Nosferatu* (1921), also based on Bram Stoker's novel *Dracula*, remains spooky and chilling. Some of the effects and acting are less convincing than they might have been at the time, but other scenes in the film are wonderfully disturbing. One of the aspects of the film that remains effective is how "normal" situations become infused with the supernatural. One example is when after meeting Count Orlov, Hutter goes into his room. The doorway to the room frames him, with plenty of room between Hutter and the doorway. While Hutter is asleep, the Count enters, barely fitting through the doorway Hutter passed through so easily. This is very simple, yet highly effective, scene. Even more effective, and of lasting importance to the cinema industry was the Expressionist aesthetic running throughout (Parkinson 1995: 60). Lighting to create elongated and menacing shadows, off-center and low angle camera compositions to create senses of dislocation and unease in the viewer, and dislocated editing all contribute both to the visual style of *Nosferatu* and to the wider industry. Carol Reed's *The Third Man* (1949), justly famous for his use of shadow and camera angles to create a tense and jarring atmosphere, owes much to German Expressionist films such as *Nosferatu*.

In what some historians argue was an attempt to create a universal visual language (Bergstrom 1996: 146), in *The Last Laugh* (1924) Murnau began employing the camera in a way little seen until this point. *The Last Laugh* tells the story of Jannings, the pompous doorman for a famous hotel. The owners of the hotel come to consider Jannings too old and infirm to be the image of the hotel, and so he is demoted to washroom attendant. With his pride in tatters, Jannings tries to conceal his demotion from his friends and family, but eventually he is discovered. His friends, thinking he has lied to them all along about his prestigious job, taunt him mercilessly, while his family rejects him because of what they consider to be his shameful job. With nowhere to turn, Jannings returns to the hotel to sleep in the bathroom where he works. The only person to be kind towards him is the night watchman, who takes care of Jannings as he is sleeping. This is where the only title card of the film occurs: "Here the story should really end, for, in real life, the forlorn old man would have little to look forward to but death. The author took pity on him and has provided a quite improbable epilogue." That epilogue is that Jannings inherits a fortune, quits his job, and is able to dine at the same hotel he used to work for.

Murnau uses the camera to help tell the story rather than the standard practice at the time of relying on intertitles – as noted above, there is only one in the entire film (Parkinson 1995: 61). "Unleashing" the camera in order to use it to show the world from the doorman's point of view also led the camera to become a performer. When the camera was still it had meaning, when it moved it also had meaning. The significance of the camera taking on, or portraying, a subjective position was significant. As mentioned in the Griffith case study, this allowed filmmakers to develop a way to engage the viewer into the subjective world of the character, creating empathy and understanding (if not always liking) – key elements in a successful film. While not the first, Murnau, like Griffith turned a technique into a convention, understandable by both filmmaker and audience.

economic and political reasons, several German directors would end up in the USA helping to create Hollywood as we know it (Parkinson 1995: 58–64).

Perhaps unsurprisingly, given its far-flung colonies, Britain was producing a large number of travelogues and "information" films for consumption both at home and in the colonies. In light of this, it is probably no accident that British directors such as Grierson would be among the first to develop documentary film. The early British cinema industry was vibrant, largely because the colonial situation meant there was a large potential audience. As other cinemas began to assault that market, the British government eventually placed import duties on non-British (especially American) films (Vasey 1996; Jaikumar 2006). As we will see, this move may have been counterproductive, as those economic policies would ultimately spur the British film industry to concentrate its efforts on quantity rather than quality. In colonies such as India and Malaya, it appears that those films were not very popular, and the restrictions may have directly contributed to the development of local film industries (both of these points will be discussed in the third chapter).

The Japanese film industry also began very soon after film's introduction into the country in 1897 – by 1908 four production companies were producing films. That cinema "caught on" so quickly should come as no shock, though many works by non-specialists of Japanese cinema often seem to find it thus. Japan was, at the turn of the twentieth century, a regional power actively engaged with becoming "modern," and in doing so becoming an international power. As has been pointed out, cinema at that time was almost uniquely "modern," certainly very much marked as Western, and the most technologically dependent form of expression around. All of which may help to explain why Japanese officialdom might have readily accepted cinema; but why cinema found the same acceptance with the Japanese audience or even filmmakers is another matter. Standish makes the argument that to understand non-Hollywood cinematic traditions we need to understand the adaptation of the cinematic forms to local "markets" (Standish 2005: 14). So, to understand the attraction of cinema in the Japanese local market, we have to look at other factors, such as the influence of existing theatre forms (predominately *kabuki* and *noh*) and the *benshi* on early productions. Much like the early French cinema, the first Japanese films were in essence filmed plays that followed the characteristics of Japanese theatre traditions: men played all of the roles; traditional costumes and make-up was worn; there was no contact during fight scenes; movements were often stylized; and action would occasionally pause to highlight a particular moment. The other important aspect of Japanese theatre tradition to follow into cinema was the *benshi* (sometimes also referred to as *katsuben*). In theatre the role of the *benshi* was to act as narrator, whereas in cinema their role became more involved (McDonald 2006). Standing to the side of the screen, the *benshi* had several duties to fulfill:

before the film began, they would provide a synopsis for the audience; they would explain the action on screen (if the film was an American or European film, this would include a significant amount of interpretation); provide sound effects; and speak the lines for the silent actors on screen. Perhaps most importantly was an "invisible" role that the *benshi* served – the *benshi* acted as mediators between the Western cinematic form and local audience expectations mentioned above (Richie 2005: 19–22). This role was extremely important in what was then a very culturally conservative society. Skilled *benshi* became quite famous, and they began to exert a great deal of influence over local film production, especially over the length of scenes. It was not until the suspension of film production following the massive earthquake of 1923 that Japanese cinema began breaking away from the *benshi* and *kabuki/noh* theatre links.

While it may not be readily apparent to a contemporary view of any of the surviving examples of films from this period, this was a time of great change and where most of the codes and conventions of filmmaking (and thus watching) employed to this day were created. Cinema in 1896 took place in exhibition halls and traveling shows. Nickelodeons moved cinema into converted shops, often rundown and in seedy neighborhoods (Parkinson 1995: 28). Eventually, cinema began to be displayed in glamorous picture "palaces." Paralleling that physical shift, films went from being perceived as scientific curiosities and toys, to a cheap and tawdry entertainment for poor immigrants (particularly in the USA), to a glamorous "dream factory." The industry had gone from the technological experiments of innovators and inventors to large studio-run enterprises operating internationally and touching the lives of millions (Vasey 1996). And, while this development was uneven and influenced by different cultural factors and specific national histories, by the late 1920s, cinema had become an established entertainment medium. Throughout much of the world, cinema was about to enter its "Golden Age."

THE "GOLDEN ERA" OF FICTION FILM

By the late 1920s and early 1930s, most of the key elements of cinema were in place. Many of the codes and conventions of cinema had been developed, familiar genres of film were established, the studio and star systems were in full force, and cinema was a global phenomenon. One element still missing was sound, although this statement is slightly misleading (Marks 1996). Synchronized sound, where sound and picture capture was simultaneous during filming and playback, so that the sound audiences were hearing was both "natural" (i.e. what the sound would "really" be if the viewer were actually at the scene in real life – also referred to as "live" sound) and matched to the action, was missing (Parkinson 1995). This took longer to develop than simply having sound in, or for, films. From the earliest days of cinema there was sound, indeed one of the reasons Edison apparently worked on cinema at all was as a medium for selling his phonograph. Regardless of Edison's intentions, sound of various descriptions was heard during the "silent" film era. Scores were composed especially for early film productions, and silent feature films had cue sheets of music to be played at appropriate times during the showing. Many of the grand picture palaces had their own bands, in some cases even whole orchestras, to provide the soundtrack for the film being shown. Later, and especially in smaller venues, prerecorded music or a pianist/organist would do a similar job (Marks 1996). Sound effect machines were relatively common, at least in the USA, from 1910 onwards.

For "natural" sound to work in cinema several problems had to be overcome, not least of which was studio reluctance to invest huge amounts of capital into what they feared might turn out to be a fad. There were also technological issues that had to be resolved, such as keeping the sounds and images in sync, but most of these had largely been overcome by the 1920s. Ironically, while American studios were initially reluctant to invest in sound, it may have been sound that saved Hollywood during the Depression of the 1930s. While small towns in the USA and much of the export market remained silent, by 1931 most domestic American films were sound. The investment was huge, somewhere in the region of 300 million dollars, and created a link between the studios and corporate America that has continued to the present. The positive side is that even during a global Depression, American audiences rose by 33% and profits by 50% between 1927 (when Crosland's *The Jazz Singer* – the first Hollywood "talkie" was made) and 1930 (Parkinson 1995).[6]

The switch to sound brought with it a host of other issues. Early sound technology was limited and thus limited the filmmakers in using it. The camera which had recently been liberated by people such as Griffith and Murnau once again became static due to the problems of live sound recording during filming. As anyone who has used the on-board microphone on a video camera will be aware, sometimes at great cost, the microphone picks up *everything*, including the sound of the camera itself. Therefore, actors and sets also became more static and austere respectively so as not to interfere with the microphones. Perhaps the best known of the issues that sound introduced was the problem of voices. Many of the silent era stars had either strong European accents or voices deemed inappropriate to their film personas. Several different artistic and technological developments took place very rapidly: filmmakers began using multiple cameras simultaneously to recreate "movement" through cutting between different angles; post-recording sound (such as dubbing) was used; Roubert Mamoulian used two separate microphones recording sound separately to overlap dialogue; and perhaps most importantly was the invention of the microphone casing called "blimps," which blocked ambient sound such as the hiss from lights and freed the camera to move on cranes and dollies.

Sound is often overlooked as a component of cinema,[7] but the introduction and development of sound added layers of possibility and meaning into the medium. Indeed, it was the introduction of sound that turned movies from "a multimedia show with live performance" to "a complete show in themselves, independent of local performers, and this show would be the same in every theatre all over the world" (Dibbets 1996: 214). Dibbets further argues that the very concept of what a film was changed, becoming a complete, finished "text" – with implications for film theory (1996: 214), as we will see in the next chapter, rather than a semi-finished product mediated by local performers and exhibiters. Certain film genres gained much through sound – imagine a car chase without screeching tires and roaring engines. This was possible before, but as something added on by special effects machines, not an aspect of the film itself. Although all genres of films gained from sound, one came out of the introduction of sound – the musical (Parkinson 1995: 88). Stars such as Fred Astaire and Ginger Rogers and the choreographer Busby Berkeley became household names, as did many of their films: *42nd Street* (Bacon 1933); *The Gold Diggers of 1933* (LeRoy 1933); or *Top Hat* (Sandrich 1935). Musicals were popular throughout most of what we now refer to as the "Golden Age" of Hollywood (1927–1941) and well into the 1960s. Even today, parodies and pastiches of classic musicals such as *Oklahoma* (Zinnemann 1955) or *South Pacific* (Logan 1958) appear in popular culture. The opening credits of the television series *Family Guy* is a combination of a homage to the opening credits of the 1970s' American television show *All in the Family* with a Busby Berkeley-esque musical. While the musical lost popularity in Hollywood over time, in India it has remained a mainstay of the popular cinema (i.e. Bollywood), in films like the 2004 *Bride and Prejudice* (Chadha). Different analysts argue as to what the historical relationship between music and film is in India, how important they are relative to one another, etc., but there is no argument that the combination has been extremely productive – helping to create the largest film industry in the world.

To return to a point raised earlier, the introduction of sound to film changed the financial landscape of American (and eventually most other) cinemas forever. Much like the "blockbuster" films would do later (see below), sound raised the stakes for film production companies. Many of these companies disappeared or were assimilated into other companies. The risks of filmmaking extended into the cinema in various other ways. One way of alleviating some of this risk was the structure by which most of the studios operated. The studio system, which had been in place for decades, was becoming formalized to a previously unheard of degree (Schatz 1996). The control of studios over the careers of their "stable" of directors, writers, and

Figure 1.5   Actress Aishwarya Rai in a Bollywood song and
dance number from *Bride and Prejudice* (G. Chadha 2004).
[Credit: Pathe Pictures Ltd. / The Kobal Collection]

actors (typically under exclusive long-term contracts) became entrenched. The Coen
Brothers' 1991 film *Barton Fink* is centered upon that dynamic. The experimentation
and innovation of early cinema was largely relegated to the smaller studios, where
the risk to reward ratio was quite different. That the first horror franchises, *Dracula*
(Browning 1931), *Frankenstein* (Whale 1931), and *The Mummy* (Freund 1932),
came out of the major Hollywood studio least positioned to take risks, Universal,
was something of a surprise.[8] With exceptions such as *All Quiet on the Western Front*
(Milestone 1930), Universal had largely churned out genre films (westerns, crime
dramas, etc.), although it had success in the 1920s with two "horror" films *The
Hunchback of Notre Dame* (Worsley 1923) and *The Phantom of the Opera* (Julian
1925). However, when the studio acquired the rights to several successful Broadway
plays, including *Dracula*, capitalizing on this opportunity would have been too
good to pass up. The distinct advantage of the studio system was that Universal, or
any of the other major studios, had a number of talented individuals that could be
put on any project, whatever the inherent "value" of that project might have been.
In this way, the studio system directly contributed to the creation of many classic
films. *Casablanca* (Curtiz 1942) is a case in point. The story itself was a throwaway

Figure 1.6   Filming *Casablanca*. Humphrey Bogart
and Ingrid Bergman (M. Curtiz 1942). [Credit:
Warner Bros. / The Kobal Collection / Jack Woods]

piece of wartime melodrama with a hearty portion of propaganda mixed in. When
a studio can throw an Academy Award nominated director (*Captain Blood* 1935;
Angels with Dirty Faces 1938; and *Four Daughters* 1938), as well as international stars
such as Humphrey Bogart, Claude Rains, and Peter Lorre onto a project, even an
unpromising script could become one of the most famous films of all time.

Certainly in terms of quantity (and arguably also in terms of quality) the studio
system achieved remarkable productivity. Even auteur directors like Hitchcock
generally did very well under the system.[9] For reasons listed above, the pinnacle of
the studio system and Hollywood's Golden Age are, for the most part, the same.
However, the studio system was restrictive, both in terms of how people were

treated and the product being produced as well (Schatz 1996). The system was, in many ways, to become a victim of its own success – the stars that the system both created and relied upon soon outgrew that dependency, and the global spread of the American "dream factory" began to encounter opposition of various kinds. The anti-Hollywood agendas of movements such as *cinéma vérité* (lit. cinema "truth") in France, *neo-realism* in Italy, and national cinema in several places around the world were actively opposed to what they saw as facile and irrelevant films swamping the world's cinemas (Parkinson 1995: 125–6, 185–95; Morandini 1996a; Vincendeau 1996; Cousins 2004: 186–216). Some nation-states were also concerned with the influx of American films, and various censorship policies and financial restrictions, like import tariffs, were put in place to control the access to or markets for American films. Possibly for the above reasons, the Golden Age of Hollywood either overlapped

Figure 1.7　An example of the Golden Age "Picture Palace" – the Eros Cinema Mumbai, India. Built in 1938. Photograph by Madhav Pai 2008.

with or preceded the Golden Age for several other cinema industries, many of which also employed a variation of the Hollywood studio system. While the Golden Ages for different countries were different, the period from the 1940s to the 1960s was a vibrant period for most cinema industries. Most of the Hollywood stars and famous directors of this period are well known enough to forgo in-depth treatment here, but there were many other important filmmakers outside of the Hollywood system. Indeed, two of the most famous non-EuroAmerican filmmakers were of this era.

Case Study: Satyajit Ray and Akira Kurosawa

Akira Kurosawa and Satyajit Ray are two very different filmmakers who also share some surprising similarities. Kurosawa had seen over 100 foreign films by the time he was nineteen, in 1929 (Richie 2005: 28). Ray was born into a politically active family and initially worked as an advertising illustrator (Rajadhyaksha 1996: 682). As filmmakers, however, they both had to negotiate combining a Western developed media with their own cultural traditions and expectations. They also had to negotiate developing their artistic visions, while working under very powerful studio systems. That they both succeeded speaks highly for their abilities to make that negotiation.

Coming to the cinema later than Kurosawa, Satyajit Ray was influenced by meeting French Realist director Jean Renoir, but it was seeing the neo-realist *The Bicycle Thieves* (De Sica 1948) that convinced him to become a filmmaker (Rajadhyaksha 1996: 682). Probably his most famous work outside of India is *Pather Panchali* (1955), based on a Bengali fictional work from the early twentieth century. Set in rural Bengal of the 1920s, the film focuses on the lives of Apu and his family members, living in their ancestral home in Nischindipur. The family is impoverished – the father earns an insufficient living as a priest. Apu's mother takes care of the two children, Apu and his older sister Durga, and her elderly sister-in-law, Indir. Durga often steals fruit from a neighbor's orchard and shares it with Aunt Indir, with whom she feels affinity. Durga even steals a bead necklace, though she later denies taking it. Apu and Durga share a close relationship and an important portion of the movie relates this relationship. Apu's father travels to nearby cities to search for better employment, promising his wife that he will return with money. Unfortunately, the family's economic situation gets even worse in his absence. Durga, Apu's sister, catches a cold while playing in the rain, develops a fever, and dies. Apu's father eventually returns home to discover that his daughter has died. The family decides to leave the village. The film ends with Apu and his parents leaving their home in an ox-cart. Ray's commitment to shooting in a neo-realist style was not always welcomed by the Indian studio system he operated within and led to a series of problems (Rajadhyaksha 1996: 682). However, *Pather*

Panchali was a major success and led to two sequels (possibly at Nehru's suggestion), called the Apu Trilogy. Ray's Realist cinema worked well in the early days of post-Independence India – indeed his films corresponded well with the goals and agendas of post-Independence Indian governments, who in turn promoted the development of an Indian art cinema. However, by the 1960s the changing political and social landscapes in India were no longer a good fit for this style of representation. During the late 1950s and into the 1960s Ray's films became more stylized, focusing more on psychological interactional set pieces. The upheavals of the 1970s were reflected in Ray's films of the period as melodramas about the collapse of traditional Indian social values and the failure of the elite to deal with the problem (Rajadhyaksha 1996: 683). Ironically, the Indira Gandhi government was simultaneously promoting Ray's Realist films as what authentic Indian cinema should be (as opposed to Bollywood escapism). Ray began making commercially successful children's films, and though some did satirize the failures of the Indian state, for the most part Ray removed himself from the political sphere.

Akira Kurosawa grew up watching film while the *benshi* were still a powerful presence in Japanese cinemas. At the same time Kurosawa is perhaps the most "Western" of any Japanese filmmaker of that era – he is certainly often depicted thus by many Japanese and Western film scholars (Richie 2005: 176). Kurosawa's films, while firmly sited in Japan are nevertheless told in Western idioms, for instance, in *Rashomon* (1950), which ushered Japanese cinema into the Western art cinema world, is the tale of the murderous attack on a samurai. The film contains four different versions of the murder, expressing what some commentators view as a uniquely Western concept, that truth is relative. The director of the studio that made *Rashomon* and many Japanese commentators as well as the Japanese cinema audience were skeptical of the film and it was not commercially or critically successful in Japan. Kurosawa believed that Japanese audiences and critics distrusted a film that was successful with Western audiences. This may be where some of the claims of Kurosawa's "Western-ness" come from. Further, Kurosawa's films are often also read as being about the shift from a feudal to a more modern or democratic society – something that Kurosawa himself denied. As with Satyajit Ray, Kurosawa worked largely within the Realist tradition, his films often dealt with social problems and human nature (Komatsu 1996: 716; Cousins 2004: 212). Kurosawa's early and prolific exposure to Western cinema paid off in his ability to combine and refine techniques and ideas from both Hollywood and European cinemas effectively. Kurosawa often adapted Western literary classics and yet was also openly admiring of Hollywood studio era filmmakers like John Ford. Ford's westerns were the inspiration behind Kurosawa's films *The Seven Samurai* (1954) and *Yojimbo* (1961). These films in turn inspired American filmmakers like Sturges who remade *The Seven Samurai* as *The Magnificent Seven* (1960), and European filmmakers like Leone (*A Fist Full of Dollars* 1964) who would influence Hollywood filmmakers in the late 1960s and 1970s (Komatsu 1996: 716). The themes of Kurosawa's films, especially their focus on humanity, came to be seen as old-fashioned and irrelevant to the politically and socially volatile 1960s. Unlike Ray, Kurosawa overcame his artistic and personal problems (such as his attempted suicide in 1971), directing two classic epics, *Kagemusha* (1980) and *Ran* (1985), and more human scale dramas in the 1990s (Komatsu 1996: 716).

Both Ray and Kurosawa were successful both at home as well as in foreign markets. There are several reasons for this, but an important issue here is a characteristic that the two share, which is their ability to combine the "grammar" of Western with culturally relevant and specific aesthetics, ideologies, and narratives. Ray combined neo-Realist filmmaking techniques with an Indian narrative, synthesizing the two to produce a masterpiece of cinema. Kurosawa combined the Realist tradition with specifically Japanese stories, though as with *Rashomon*, he was not averse to experimenting with different ways to tell that story. That both directors worked within a readily understood Western film tradition both helped and hindered their careers. As too did the fact that both operated within relatively powerful studio systems, which provided them both with resources and personnel, but also were generally financially and artistically conservative. As long as both directors were making successful films, the system helped them, but until they established their ability to produce hits and when they did not produce a hit, the converse of the benefits of the studio system was that they could also constrain the directors. When Ray and Kurosawa were able to successfully blend Western cinematic codes and conventions, with Indian or Japanese culturally relevant elements, they produced films that served to translate the former to a Western audience without alienating the local audience. When they were not successful, as with *Rashomon*, both also faced criticism and artistic crises. Predominately, however, both Ray and Kurosawa successfully navigated the two sets of expectations and assumptions, providing cinema with two of its most eloquent champions.

As noted, numerous forces were operating in opposition to the Hollywood studio system, and they began to chip into the edifice in different ways. American demographic changes, such as the growth of suburbs, led to a decline in audiences. In 1948, the government put in place laws to break up studio ownership of theatre chains and bring an end to unfair trade practices such as "block booking" (forcing independent theatres to accept "blocks" of films in order to get premier movies). Government action on issues such as block booking will be discussed in more detail in Chapter 3. Further, the increasing disquiet of the very stars and big-name directors the studios depended upon began to come to a head. The more "artistic" resistance to Hollywood also began to filter back into the system after the Second World War.

Neo-realism especially began to influence American filmmakers – not always for artistic reasons, however; a "cinema of real life" was much cheaper for the studios to produce (Morandini 1996a). One of the genres most influenced by neo-realism, and particularly suited to the immediate post-Second World War era was *film noir*. As Parkinson states, *film noir* is "[e]ssentially a 'cinema of moral anxiety'" and that moral anxiety combined with cinematic innovations, and indeed exiled filmmakers from Europe, into (usually) crime and detective stories was a heady brew – and commercially very successful. The pessimistic and cynical portrayal of American society that *noir* portrayed so clearly did not sit well with everyone, however. The very success of *film noir* may have contributed to the McCarthy witch-hunt for communists and communist sympathizers in Hollywood during the late 1940s and early 1950s (Parkinson 1995: 158–9). For a sense of the fear and paranoia of the period, see Clooney's 2005 *Good Night, and Good Luck*.

While in itself the McCarthy period did not kill off the studio system, it did severely damage Hollywood at a time it could ill afford it. Political, aesthetic, technological, and social changes were coming too quickly for a dazed and safety-first Hollywood to cope with. Increasingly, studios had to bargain for the services of actors and directors, and budgets once again became an important issue. New technologies were introduced to try to win audiences back, widescreen and color in particular, which made budgets even tighter. As when sound was introduced, Hollywood's reaction was to try to limit damage by producing commercially "safe" films. While American cinema was struggling with change, European cinemas were flourishing (Vincendeau 1996) – art cinema in France in particular built on ideas of auteurism, *cinéma vérité*, and intentionality and led to the French New Wave filmmakers (e.g. Truffaut, Godard, Chabrol). In Britain, a form of social commentary cinema was developing, often sited in the industrial north of England, featuring disenfranchised youths and their milieu, these "kitchen sink" dramas were in response to both Hollywood and the legacy of banal "quota quickies" in Britain (Parkinson 1995: 185–95; Cousins 2004: 186–216).[10] Both *cinéma vérité* and the British kitchen sink dramas shared a distaste for the romanticism of Hollywood and Hollywood-esque film and for the escapism and conformity of many of the films being made at the time. The work of Godard (such as *Breathless* 1959) and Truffaut (*Jules et Jim* 1961), for example, was artful and experimental, possibly even disingenuous at times in playing with the codes and conventions of cinema as known at the time. In Godard's *Breathless*, for instance, the director subverts one of the oldest codes in film editing, that when you have a *jump cut* (a direct transition from one scene to another) it is to show something else. Godard makes nine jump cuts to the same scene, of the back of actress Jean Seberg's head, with the only changes being of background and the way the light is falling on her head (Cousins 2004: 269). This may seem a fairly trivial difference, but it is almost like a friend asking how you are doing and then walking away without waiting for you to reply. Godard was purposefully *mis*communicating with his audience – by breaking with an expected and established "grammar" of that shot he draws attention to the film and to the created-ness of his film. In *Week End* (1967), he actively provokes, challenges, and even alienates his viewer by his uncompromising use of long takes, like a 10-minute tracking shot of a traffic jam and the irredeemable unpleasantness of the main characters.

The social realist films being produced in Britain were also challenging the status quo, but as the name suggests through a more-or-less direct social commentary rather than through artistic license. Films like *Look Back in Anger* (Richardson 1959) or *This Sporting Life* (Anderson 1963) were intense commentaries on life in Britain and British society. Focused almost exclusively on male protagonists and typically depicting working-class life, frequently in the north of England, these films were in many ways as distant from the French New Wave as they could possibly be, yet there was a shared dissatisfaction and provocative rebelliousness that was mutually nourishing these disparate filmic endeavors (Petrie 1996; Cousins 2004: 298–300). The films from this era of British filmmaking were unrepentantly social statements from leftist perspectives. The "warts and all" portrayals meant that it was easy to sympathize with the characters even as it was difficult to like them. An example of this is *Billy Liar* (Schlesinger 1963), the story of a young man, Billy Fisher (Tom Courtney) in the north of England who, dissatisfied with his life, makes up a fantasy world of lies and exaggerations by which to escape reality. Having stretched the truth too many times with his friends and family, they nevertheless stick by him, even if (as with his parents) they do not entirely understand him or what motivates his lies and fantasies. Just as his lies begin to have serious consequences, he meets free spirit Liz (Julie Christie), who offers him the opportunity to really escape his humdrum life. While the moralizing can be a little thick at times, as a portrait of life in the north of England in the late 1950s and early 1960s, the film is very good social history. It also captures England on the brink of the Swinging Sixties, and the creation of London as *the* music and fashion capital – at least of Europe. This is brought home at the end of the film where Liz (the perfect representation of what is to come) is leaving for London on the train, expecting Billy to come with her. The doubts and realities are too much for Billy, and for all of his bluster and pontificating, he stays behind. Ironically, the Swinging Sixties hinted at in *Billy Liar* would replace the "kitchen sink" dramas with frothy lightweight fare (Petrie 1996: 605; Cousins 2004: 299–300), leaving those dramas behind with as much finality as Liz leaves Billy.

Europe was changing as least as much as the USA, and both the French New Wave and British social realist films gave way to new cinema trends. In America as well times had changed, the cracks in the edifice were too deep, and by 1960 the Hollywood studio system had broken down. The collapse of the studio system forced American cinema to retrench. Independent studios and filmmakers began experimenting with new visual and narrative styles as well as more "adult" content (Cousins 2004: 333–6). Grittier, edgier films began to replace some of the genre films. Spaghetti westerns (so called because the directors and much of the cast were Italian) such as *A Fistful of Dollars* (Leone 1964), which was based on the screenplay for Kurosawa's *Yojimbo* (1961), and *Once Upon a Time in the West* (Leone 1968) replaced the white hat-wearing good guys of the American western, like Roy Rogers or Tom Mix, with violent and morally ambiguous anti-heroes such as Clint Eastwood or Lee Van Cleef (Parkinson 1995: 202; Morandini 1996b: 592–4; Cousins 2004: 286–8). Independent studios as well as the major studios began to target youth audiences with low budget films and different varieties of exploitation films, such as blaxploitation and sexploitation. These two genres are exactly what they sound like: films that exploit particular groups such as black culture or women (respectively). Blaxploitation films in particular have a controversial place in cinema history as they presented very stereotyped aspects of urban American culture (pimps, gangs, drugs, and violence). However, they were almost the only opportunity for black actors and directors to have leading roles in American films (Pines 1996). Sexploitation films on the other hand were less ambiguous – they did not open opportunities for either the actresses or female directors.[11] However, they were often made by some of the mavericks of the immediate post-studio system era, such as Roger Corman and Russ Meyers (Newman 1996), who provided some of the biggest names of the following decade (and beyond) their opportunity in the industry: Francis Ford Coppola, Martin Scorsese, Peter Bogdanovich, James Cameron, Jonathan Demme – not to mention Jack Nicholson, Peter Hopper, and Sylvester Stallone (Newman 1996: 513). Directly and indirectly, their role in the development of post-studio system Hollywood was significant (Newman 1996: 513–14). A further development that would have long-term effects was the arrival of a new generation of "cine-literate" filmmakers, like the aforementioned Coppola and Scorsese, as well as directors such as Allen and Spielberg. With films like *Taxi Driver* (Scorsese 1976), the 1970s ushered in the age of the Hollywood auteur, and these cinephile directors would lead the charge (Parkinson 1995: 248). For the reasons mentioned above, the 1970s and early 1980s would come to be seen as a period of experimentation, of pushing boundaries, and of director-focused film projects. Sometimes referred to as *New Hollywood*, the films of this period were influenced by European art cinema and Japanese films, especially those of Akira Kurosawa, and probably most importantly for the studios could connect with the youth audience (Parkinson 1995: 245–7; Gomery 1996). Realism and countercultural themes were the order of the day. When I show films from the 1970s to students in their twenties, they are often surprised – even shocked – by the

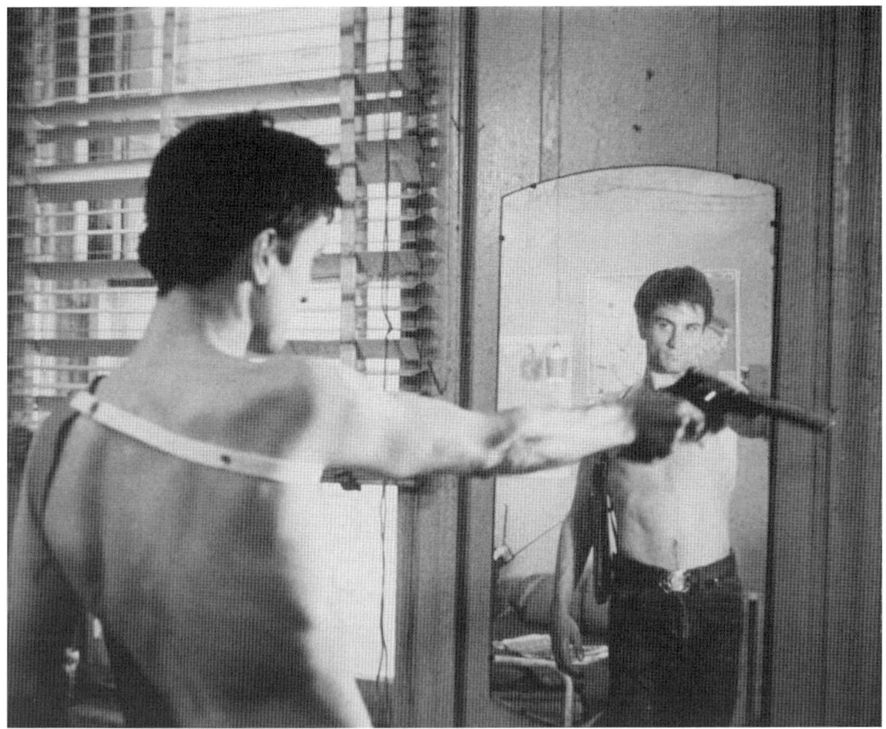

Figure 1.8   Robert De Niro in *Taxi Driver* (M. Scorsese 1976).
[Credit: Columbia / The Kobal Collection]

graphic, sometimes gratuitous, portrayals of sex and violence, as well as the moral and intellectual challenge some of the films made of the audience. To be fair though, they also commented on what passed for "special effects," the slow pace, and the relatively poor production values. As the Hollywood studios struggled to keep in touch with their audience, many of these directors would have a large role in events to come – though not always for the good.

One of the demands that most of these directors made of the studios was that to make successful films the directors had to have creative and budgetary control over the pictures. Successes by the New Hollywood directors led each of them in turn to make more and more extravagant demands. There began to be a public perception that Hollywood was out of control (Cousins 2004: 385–6). The career of Michael Cimino is a case in point. After a minor hit with his directing debut, *Thunderbolt and Lightfoot* (1974), and huge critical and commercial success with *The Deer Hunter* (1978), Cimino's career seemed set. Then came *Heaven's Gate* (1980). Given absolute control over the project by United Artists, *Heaven's Gate* ran several times over budget due to Cimino's extravagant demands, becoming a financial disaster. The film came to symbolize everything wrong with Hollywood, and Cimino's career never recovered. The results were just as devastating for United Artists as the studio was nearly bankrupted by the film and this ultimately led to the sale of the studio. Between the disasters of *Heaven's Gate* and Coppola's *One from the Heart* (1982) New Hollywood had come to an end, but a new paradigm was already pushing Hollywood into a new phase. In 1975, a film about a shark (Spielberg's *Jaws*) changed the cinema industry in ways felt to the present day (Gomery 1996: 479; Cousins 2004: 381–3).

AUTEURS, INDEPENDENTS, AND GLOBAL BLOCKBUSTERS

A film about a shark, no matter how good, is not going to change the history of cinema by itself, but *Jaws* did come at a very particular juncture, establishing (along with Lucas's 1977 *Star Wars*) a new agenda for Hollywood (Gomery 1996: 479–82; Cousins 2004: 381–5). As noted above, the collapse of the studio system was at least partially attributable to a new alignment of stars, directors, and studios. Blockbusters like *Jaws* and *Star Wars* also created a new alignment of finances. Major corporations, realizing the potential profits of the blockbuster were immense, began buying up studios. Budgets once again, as with the coming of sound and color, became large enough to force studios to maximize profits and avoid loss. The studios would be trying to do this anyway, but the stakes had become much higher. It was clear the public would flock to big budget, special effects-laden, star-filled extravaganzas created by famous (or sometimes infamous) directors (Parkinson 1995: 245–52). The studios began to shift away from previous models for produc-tion, namely churning out numerous B movies for every A list feature, to attempting to consolidate resources into select "can't miss" features. This is not to say that the studios stopped making B movies, straight to video productions flourished as small-scale money earners, but the number and variety both diminished.

The changes during the blockbuster era were not limited to the financial sphere however. The focus upon special effects and story-driven narratives combined with new aesthetics for editing film to change the way films looked. Beginning in the 1980s, music video inspired fast cut, quick tempo editing and exaggerated camera angles began to become standard within television shows like *Miami Vice* and the short-lived *Stingray*. Often termed "MTV style" after the music channel where that style of editing/camera work became popularized, this aesthetic also began spreading into feature film (Cousins 2004: 398–400). In terms of blockbusters, although even seriously intended films employ this aesthetic, the MTV style is now ubiquitous. The 2006 film *Smokin' Aces* (Carnahan) epitomizes this style. The expectation of fast-paced film combined with the elements mentioned above, often at the expense of building strong characterization, has had a negative consequence on contemporary feature film according to many film historians and critics. As an example, Guillermo del Toro's *Hellboy* (2004) was largely regarded as being underwhelming by both critics and audiences. Some of the comments, by both viewers and critics, were that there was little characterization, that the viewer was left disengaged from the main characters and felt little empathy. If you have the chance to listen to the DVD commentary by del Toro, he makes clear that in any circumstance where there was an editing decision between action and characterization, action won every time.

The potential payback from the blockbusters was seen to outweigh the risks of limiting the range, style, and number of films being produced. As the case of *Heaven's Gate* warns though, if things did not go well the penalty was steep for all concerned. The huge revenues produced by *successful* blockbuster movies maximized that potential and, importantly, not just in the USA. While foreign revenues have always played a role in Hollywood, the new stakes made overseas box office very important for the long term. The globalization of Hollywood, dating back to the silent era, went into overdrive (Gomery 1996: 482). Both at home and overseas, Hollywood studios increasingly worked under the dictum of low risk and high return. The corporatization of Hollywood has had a serious consequence on filmmaking. Even the most profit-driven studio era producer still wanted to make films, whereas the new focus had become: high-concept – with greater concentration on tie-in merchandise such as toys;[12] spin-offs into other media (such as soundtracks); mass-audience; and wide-release films. The Hollywood star system is such that paying an A list actor to headline a film is critical. Other strategies for maximizing profits and limiting risk include: advertising and building hype for the release of blockbusters; controlling the distribution and exhibition of new releases – again, not just in the USA, but globally; producing a film that will appeal to the widest possible market; and, perhaps most obvious, the tendency to play it safe by producing sequels and remakes (Gomery 1996) – such as the commercially successful *Terminator* franchise. That is not to say that Hollywood will not experiment, but that experimentation is almost always regarding something that has already been proved successful. For instance, in the 1970s noting the popularity of martial arts films, Warner Brothers co-produced a film with Golden Harvest, a Hong Kong production company that had been producing the films of an American-born martial arts star named Bruce Lee. The film was called *Enter the Dragon* (Clouse 1973). *Enter the Dragon* was a sensation, making Lee a global star and leading to a kung fu "craze" in the USA.

Hollywood would mine Hong Kong for profit again in the 1980s with Jackie Chan combining slapstick comedy with martial arts (again, Chan's films were already a staple within the Hong Kong film industry and audience) and then in the 1990s with the director John Woo. Perhaps the most influential of all (though Lee is by far the most iconic of the three), Woo's highly stylized action scenes, violence, and use of slow motion in fight scenes has had a dramatic and lasting effect in Hollywood, with countless films adopting elements of Woo's aesthetics: *Blade* (Norrington 1998), *The Matrix* (Wachowski and Wachowski 1999), *Shoot 'Em Up* (Davis 2007), and *Wanted* (Bekmambatov 2008) all incorporating some of the elements of Woo's signature directing style. More recently, producing content for the massive DVD market (and increasingly Blu-Ray) enables studios to sell two or even three versions of a film. These strategies have all come to be at least as important as producing a quality product. That is, unless it is "Oscar season," which in itself has become at least as important for marketing purposes as it has been for rewarding excellence in filmmaking. The picture is not all bleak, however. The increased budgets and reliance on computer effects (Belton 1996: 484–5) have had some positive results – Tolkien's classic fantasy *The Lord of the Rings* for instance was widely regarded as unfilmable until recent advances in both budget and technology. All of this has had ripples across the globe. Some of those ripples have been positive, others not necessarily so. French filmmaking had a brief return to prominence with a group of talented young filmmakers, who produced artistic and provocative films (Cousins 2004: 407–8). Sometimes termed the New New Wave or *cinéma du look*, these filmmakers produced some classics of the 1980s and 1990s, films such as Beineix's *Diva* (1981) and *Betty Blue* (1986), or Besson's *Subway* (1985), *Nikita* (1990), and *Leon* (1994). In France as well as the rest of Europe, international co-productions became the norm, sometimes with five or six nations involved. In Britain, the television station Channel 4 became a leading source of funding for independent movies through Channel Four Films (Petrie 1996: 612), renamed FilmFour in 1998. Some of the successful films Channel 4 has funded include *The Crying Game* (Jordan 1992), *Trainspotting* (Boyle 1996), and *Buena Vista Social Club* (Wenders 1999). Channel Four's role in funding filmmaking was scaled back in 2002 for financial reasons, but they have still been involved in projects such as *The Last King of Scotland* (Macdonald 2006). China had its own "New Wave" of cinema (referred to as the Fifth Generation); films such as Chen Kaige's *Yellow Earth* (1984) and *Farewell My Concubine* (1993), or Yimou Zhang's *Red Sorghum* (1987), *Ju Dou* (1990), and *Raise the Red Lantern* (1991) brought critical and commercial attention to Chinese cinema (Cousins 2004: 419–20). With all of the above, and with the case study on globalization, the secret of their successes (or not), as with Hollywood, was being able to crack markets outside of the country of origin.

Figure 1.9   Movie poster for *Terminator 2: Judgment Day*
(J. Cameron 1991). [Credit: Carolco / The Kobal Collection]

As I was writing this chapter in the summer of 2007, the "big" summer block-busters included multiple sequels, for instance, the *Fantastic Four: Rise of the Silver Surfer* (Story 2007), *Pirates of the Caribbean: At World's End* (Verbinski 2007), *Spider-Man 3* (Raimi 2007), *Harry Potter: The Order of the Phoenix* (Yates 2007), and *The Bourne Ultimatum* (Greengrass 2007);[13] several "safe" genre pictures such as *I Now Pronounce you Chuck and Larry* (Dugan 2007), *Surf's Up* (Brannon and Buck 2007), *Knocked Up* (Apatow 2007), and *1408* (Håfström 2007); and remakes of past successes such as *Halloween* (Zombie 2007) and *Hairspray* (Shankman 2007); not to mention film versions of successful television shows including *The Simpsons Movie* (Silverman 2007), *Transformers* (Bay 2007), and *Underdog* (Du Chau 2007). All of these films spent time on the USA box-office top ten. It is fairly safe to say that the Hollywood status quo continues to hold, at least for now.

Increasingly, filmmakers outside the mainstream have turned to alternative fora and media through which to put their films out into the world, bypassing official distribution and exhibition circuits. Sometimes that is for financial and artistic reasons, the conservatism of studios works against "risky" investments in new artists or challenging storylines; sometimes that circumvention is for political and legal reasons, in countries that have strict censorship codes for instance. The proliferation of film festivals worldwide is one alternative venue to the normal theatre–video–television path. While not a panacea for the problems of the Hollywood, one of the first major independent film festivals – Sundance – is now so commercial and difficult to "crack" as to be almost indistinguishable from the mainstream system, for each Sundance there are literally dozens of smaller venues that welcome new and/or alternative filmmakers. Another important venue is the Internet. The development of sites such as YouTube and Google or Yahoo Video, along with streaming technologies and faster Internet connection have made the uploading and distribution of short films or trailers/previews for longer films readily accessible throughout much of the world.

Hollywood has not overlooked the opportunities that the Internet has provided either – the films *Snakes on a Plane* (Ellis 2006) and *Cloverfield* (Reeves 2008) both exploited viral video strategies for advertising their wares. Viral video refers to the process of sharing video clips over the Internet – through email, blogs, and other media sharing websites, usually of humorous examples of either self-produced or "found" video (the in/famous "Obama Girl" video for instance). In the case of the films mentioned above, this was not a spontaneous phenomenon, but one that was very intentionally directed. Viral video has been merged with advertising to create viral marketing – advertising techniques that use preexisting social networks and networking sites to spread news of opinions about certain products. These campaigns may also be covert (as with *Snakes on a Plane*, but unlike the very overt *Cloverfield*) giving the impression that they are actually spontaneous displays of enthusiasm (sometimes this is referred to as *astroturfing*), for instance many user reviews on Internet Movie Database (www.imdb.com) are accused of being planted by studios to increase interest in the relevant film. To date the results of viral marketing have been mixed, but the role of the Internet, social networking, and video or other forms of sharing sites looks to be a factor in the future developments of the cinema.

SUGGESTED FURTHER READING[14]

GENERAL

Cousins, M. (2004) *The Story of Film,* New York: Thunder's Mouth Press.
Nowell-Smith, G. ed. (1996a) *The Oxford History of World Cinema: The Definitive History of Cinema Worldwide,* New York: Oxford University Press.
Parkinson, D. (1995) *The History of Film,* New York: Thames and Hudson.

INDIA

Rajadhyaksha, A. and Willemen, P. (eds) (2002) *Encyclopedia of Indian Cinema,* revised edition, London: British Film Institute Publishing.
Vasudevan, R. (2000) *Making Meaning in Indian Cinema,* Oxford: Oxford University Press.

JAPAN

Richie, D. (2005) *A Hundred Years of Japanese Film: A Concise History, with a Selective Guide to DVDs and Videos,* New York: Kodansha International.
Standish, I. (2005) *A New History of Japanese Cinema; A Century of Narrative Film,* New York: The Continuum International Publishing Group Inc.

2 FILM THEORY

Figure 2.1   An art-house cinema in Nagoya, Japan.
Photograph by Ryuhei Okada 2008.

There are many reasons why these genres [horror, thrillers, pornography, comedy, melodrama, and the musical], which have been – and in France still are – numerically important, are critically virgin territory. One is the art cinema bias. Popular European genres (unless personalized by an auteur, such as Sergio Leone's "spaghetti" westerns and the comedies of Claude Chabrol and Jacques Tati) simply do not correspond to the international ideas of European cinema. In addition, national agencies promote art cinema and are somehow embarrassed by their popular films. Ironically, perhaps, popular genres require more complex decoding than art cinema, because of their closeness (through language, character's gestures, topical references) to popular culture.

Vincendeau, *Issues in European Cinema*

INTRODUCTION

Given the antipathy that frequently exists between theory and practice in the study of film, it is ironic that the development of fiction film and the development of film theory are inextricably intertwined. From the "Kino-eye" of Vertov to the Dogmes of the 1990s, theory and practice have influenced one other a great deal. This reason alone makes understanding that latter development an important goal, but there are several other reasons why film theory is important for non-film students. At a most fundamental level, film theory provides a set of conceptual tools for students to engage the study of film with, beyond "I enjoyed *Blade Runner*" or "*Hellboy* was boring." The different theories provide students with different types of tools or concepts through which to make sense of, but perhaps even more importantly to discuss and articulate, ideas about film. The earliest theories, such as formalism, still provide us with the terms used in film criticism that we read in the newspaper or watch on TV today. They also provide students with the foundational concepts, such as *mise en scène*, composition and framing, or lighting, from which to push our analyses further and deeper into the meanings and motives that the later theories would go on to concentrate upon, as I put it elsewhere, "how film works." Social science approaches generally focus their analyses and attentions on the factors and phenomena that underlying surface appearances. This is also a feature of many of the theoretical perspectives in this chapter. However, while some of them share an overarching goal – and in several cases these theories were or are also employed in the social sciences – there are differences in the application of these theories. Marxism, for instance, has a different relationship with and application to the study of cinema than it does to studying subsistence strategies cross-culturally or analyzing urban housing patterns. Understanding these differences also gives us insight into the different approaches and epistemologies of the disciplines. Further, for both film and non-film students understanding the history of theory and the developments within film theory is crucial to understanding contemporary film theory and, in an age of very cine-literate and film school-trained directors, contemporary films themselves.

The format of this chapter will be somewhat different from the others as the different theories will be discussed quite discretely in a somewhat abstract fashion. There are a couple of reasons for this, not least being that this is how it was easiest for me as a student to grasp these diverse ideas about the cinema. Setting the ideas out in this manner also meant that it became possible both to concentrate on particular theories and to forgo discussing the antagonistic relationship that existed between many of the theorists promoting these various ideas that presenting them in, for instance, a more chronological format might necessitate. As such, this chapter will summarize some of the important film theories from the 1920s onwards. The ideas of Eisenstein, Kracauer, or Benjamin, developed in the 1920s and 1930s, remain important for film theorists today. Other theoretical developments, such as Marxist approaches, structuralism, semiotics, and psychoanalysis-derived theories will also be summarized.[1] The turn to literary theory in the latter part of the twentieth century will also be addressed. As we will see, within this chapter the main foci of most of the above mentioned theories are upon the *content* of the cinema. Theories and approaches that investigate the *context* of cinema, such as third cinema or national cinema, which have a larger role in later sections of the book, will be noted.

EARLY FILM THEORY

As noted in the previous chapter, in the very early days of the cinema, particularly in the USA and Europe, film was seen as a somewhat seedy entertainment for the "lower" classes and immigrants. Likewise, there was an initial reluctance among cultural commentators/theorists to take this new medium seriously – or to only comment negatively when they did. So, from the very earliest discussions of cinema, the question of what it is has been important and the answers have continued to be debated.

FORMALISM AND CINÉ-ART

There were, however, those who did take cinema seriously. One of the first tasks of these early film theorists was to legitimize film. This was done in two ways: by distinguishing film from its predecessors – a somewhat difficult task given how intertwined film was with those other media at that stage – and by analyzing film as an art form. Before going into more specifics regarding some of the ideas promoted by various film-as-art theorists, it should be noted that these early theorists were exceptionally successful in achieving their goals vis-à-vis legitimizing cinema. By the advent of sound, the idea of cinema as an art form was more or less universal. One of the earliest and most successful of the film-as-art theories was formalism (Andrew 1976: 11–101). Promoted especially by Béla Balázs (Balázs 1979: 288–98; Andrew 1976: 76–101), Hugo Munsterberg (Munsterberg 1979: 349–58; Andrew 1976: 14–26), and Rudolf Arnheim (Arnheim 1979: 28–32; Andrew 1976: 27–41), what this set of theories did was concentrate analyses on the formal elements of the cinema – lighting, editing, and aspects of camera work such as composition. While it might seem "quaint" to a contemporary reader that formalism could be a film theory in itself, this set of ideas remains a crucial part of the theoretical "toolbox" for many people writing about film to this day. Indeed, until the 1960s some version of formalism was the predominant paradigm for any critical discussion of cinema. For these early film theorists then, the question of definition was an important one, and for them cinema was an expressive visual art form, much as painting or theatre (see esp. Munsterberg 1979). Cinema was defined purely in terms of its content.

Formalism aside, much of the early film theory came out of the French avant-garde. While it may be stretching the definition of "theory" to apply it to many of the positions taken by these early writers on the cinema – the arguments are more emotive and lyric than rigorous or critical – they were very influential. One of the most important of these early film theorists, Louis Delluc (1890–1924) was initially antagonistic to cinema, but went on to become one of the medium's most crucial proponents in France. Foreshadowing a later major film theory (national cinema), Delluc tried to fashion a truly French cinema within the commercial industry. The films of Delluc, and others influenced by his theory that cinematography has "the unique ability to transform objects into symbols for thought and emotion" (Parkinson 1995: 64), are intentionally ambiguous and thought provoking. Besides making a compelling argument for the legitimacy of cinema, this early group of French filmmaker/theorists also established much of the visual style that marks French cinema even today. The attention to the *mise en scène* and the use of symbolic elements to create mood and atmosphere are as much elements of early French cinema as either the New Wave (Goddard, Truffaut, etc.) or New New Wave (Besson, Beineix, etc.). An example might be of a shot of a car traveling through the countryside. For many filmmakers, though by no means all, that scene would be used to "set the stage" and to locate the action and/or actors. In films such as Beineux's *Roselyn and the Lions* (1989), that same shot is held much longer, forcing the viewer to "read" the scene for deeper meaning – of the elemental beauty and force of the vista in which the actions are taking place, and the transience and alienation of the characters. Again, for the early French theorists, cinema was important for the visual artistry possible to this art form. They also, however, acknowledged the ideological aspect of the medium, and to an extent also the industry involved. While they were more interested in the content of cinema, they did relate that to the context, if only in the broadest of terms.

EXPRESSIONISM

In Germany, the expressionist movement had no spokesperson like Delluc, but the filmmakers themselves may have been the most eloquent theorists anyway. Though never a distinctive movement in itself, expressionism is an art form where the artist forgoes objective portrayals of "reality" for a subjective depiction of a state of mind or emotional effect – usually angst.[2] Arguably, the only true expressionist film was

The Cabinet of Dr Caligari (Weine 1920). However, the works of Murnau, Lang, and others embodied the ideas of expressionism, as did others less directly connected to the theory. In *The Cabinet of Dr Caligari* sets were highly stylized and distorted to convey the insanity of the narrator (Parkinson 1995: 58–9).

One of the true gifts of the expressionists to cinema was to conceive of the camera as a subjective force, to free it from a distanced observational role to an active agency in the filmmaking process (Parkinson 1995: 60–2). While the use of the camera itself in telling the story would have likely developed independently of Murnau et al., the impact of the subjective camera was profound and without it much of contemporary film grammar would not exist. Imagine *Psycho* (Hitchcock 1960) or *Halloween* (Carpenter 1978) without the first-person shots from the perspective of the murderers and how much less powerful those scenes would be. Beyond the subjective camera, expressionist filmmakers also used lighting and camera angles to convey emotion and, as with Delluc and company, strategic use of the *mise en scène*. Many of the German expressionist directors went to Hollywood in the 1920s as part of an agreement with the German state film company, Ufa (Parkinson 1995: 63–4). However, under the studio system, their success was mixed; some such as Robert Siodmak and Billy Wilder did quite well, but most returned to Germany. With the rise of the Nazi Party, many of the expressionist directors would again return to the USA a short time later. Expressionism left an indelible mark on many aspects of what would become classic Hollywood aesthetic, particularly in lighting and cinematography – as exemplified in films by Hitchcock (see the Hitchcock case study) or Carol Reed's *The Third Man* (1949). As they are discussed in the same terms as an art movement, it would come as little surprise to suggest that as with the earlier theorists and movements, cinema for expressionists was predominately understood as its content. Developing concurrently with expressionism was a theoretical perspective that took a very different approach to the cinema

KRACAUER AND THE FRANKFURT SCHOOL

Almost simultaneous with the move of expressionist filmmakers to the USA was the development of another set of ideas, more in tune with the dismissive conceptions of film that formalism and Ciné-Art had fought so hard against (Kracauer 1979: 21–2; Andrew 1976: 106–28). Siegfried Kracauer writing in the early 1920s, initially for the *Frankfurter Zeitung* (a leading German newspaper), was a leading cultural critic and theorist of modern everyday life, such as film, literature, tourism, photography, even city planning (Andrew 1976: 106–7). Over the 1920s and 1930s he developed a critical perspective on what he increasingly saw as the new middle class's indulgence in shallow unenlightening entertainments (Andrew 1976: 125).

Figure 2.2   Orson Welles in a seminal
scene from the expressionist influenced
The Third Man (C. Reed 1949). [Credit:
London Films / The Kobal Collection]

Critical of capitalism and "low-brow" media, Kracauer's ideas, along with those of his *Frankfurter Zeitung* colleague Walter Benjamin, were influential for one of the most important of the theoretical schools that dealt with media – the Frankfurt School. These theorists were more concerned with the reception of cinema, the apparatuses of cinema production, exhibition, and distribution, and with the social and political economic ideologies embedded within the cinema industry. While these various theorists and commentators did not march in intellectual lock-step, roughly speaking, the position of the Frankfurt School was that mass or popular culture are tools of dominance that subjugate the masses through alienating them from meaningful experiences and ideas, in effect "dumbing down," and leading the masses to expect and demand exactly that same sort of trivial entertainment. Kracauer saw a particular problem with the Weimar-era German cinema, rather than an issue with cinema per se (Mast and Cohen 1979: 3).

A major difference in the way Benjamin and Adorno (one of the leading lights of the Frankfurt School) understood this situation was that while both understood that mass culture had taken away the "aura" of art, Adorno saw this as meaning mass culture was thereby alienated from having a positive educational or revolutionary political role. Benjamin saw this separation more ambiguously and that mass art could be used for political purposes (as for instance Russian social realist art) or for negative political purposes (as the Nazi Party would do – using mass culture for social control). Something of an irony is that the film that summarizes many of the Kracauer/Frankfurt School ideas concerning the issues of 1920s' German society and culture is *Metropolis* (Lang 1927), which is the very sort of film Kracauer was so critical of. Kracauer, one of the first non-filmmaker theorists, is arguably also the founder of modern film criticism. In 1947, he published *From Caligari to Hitler: A Psychological History of the German Film* (where he traces the rise of Nazism to the aforementioned shallow entertainments of Weimar Republic film), which with his 1960 *Theory of Film: The Redemption of Physical Reality*, in which he argues that realism is the most important role of cinema, are his most famous and influential works. Realism has meant different things to different theorists at different times, but, in short, it is the idea that a piece of fiction (novel, film, etc.) should be as "realistic" as possible. For instance, people in a film scene should act as they would if this were happening in everyday life. Characters and storylines should also display an internal coherence to that reality as well, even if that reality is not as we might know it – as for instance in fantasy or science fiction films like *Stardust* (Vaughn 2007) or *Star Wars IV: A New Hope* (Lucas 1977) respectively. Realism for Kracauer meant a realism that was a mechanical reproduction of what exists in the world, done nevertheless in the manner appropriate to the medium of film. Realism will be discussed in more detail later in this chapter, and, as will be shown, Kracauer's is a different definition of realism than others would employ. One of the problems, as well as one of the strengths of this idea is that ultimately what is "proper" realism comes down to the intent of the filmmaker. One method by which to understand the intent of the filmmaker is to analyze the product, and this is where other elements of Kracauer's approach impact. As the earlier mentioned critique of expressionist cinema argues, cinema that promotes artistry over a realistic expression of the world we live in is a cinema that fails its purpose – and serves to distract rather than to enlighten (Andrew 1976: 113–14). In analyzing the product and effect of

Weimar expressionist film, Kracauer based his analysis on the then state of German society. For the theorists discussed here, cinema began to take on a wider definition, one that went beyond the content of the medium to incorporate the contexts of the medium as well.

MONTAGE AND EDITING

Roughly concurrent with the shift of expressionists to Hollywood and the demise of Ciné-Art, a new locus of film theory/practice arose – Moscow. Sergei Eisenstein and Dziga Vertov are probably the best known of the Soviet filmmakers of this period, but there were others who created an influential set of ideas around techniques and theories of editing. After the 1917 Revolution, many Russian filmmakers saw film as more than just entertainment. Dziga Vertov, for instance, shot and exhibited newsreel-style film around the country as a form of agitating propaganda (agit-prop). His *The Man with the Movie Camera* (1929) was a culmination of his ideas about the use of film as part of the Revolution. Vertov and his co-editor Elizaveta Svilova employed numerous editing techniques such as superimposed images, split screens, and dissolves among others to create what Parkinson refers to as ciné-poetry (1995: 72). Lev Kuleshov and Sergei Eisenstein also developed theories on editing; Kuleshov was, for the most part, unable to put those theories into practice due to a lack of resources, but Eisenstein created some of the most famous early Russian cinema, as well as some of the most famous writing on cinema (Eisenstein 1979: 85–122; Andrew 1976: 42–75; Parkinson 1995: 73–8).

Both Kuleshov and Eisenstein worked with the idea of *montage*. Montage literally translates as "putting together," which in the context of film refers to the editing together of short, separate sequences of film footage, often to condense time, space, etc. to advance the narrative. Training sequences in sports films such as *Rocky* (Avildsen 1976) or *Million Dollar Baby* (Eastwood 2004) are examples of this use of montage. Eisenstein, Vertov, and Kuleshov were trying to develop the use of montage into a sophisticated technique of storytelling, in this case the juxtaposing of not necessarily related shots into a sequence in order to evoke new associations in the minds of the viewers (Eisenstein 1979: 104–22; Andrew 1976: 48–9). Eisenstein

Case Study: Eisenstein

Sergei Eisenstein (1898–1948) began his career in the theater. By the age of twenty-five, he was noted for creating highly unorthodox experimental theater productions

(Bordwell 1996: 168). He was invited to make a film for Proletkult, an agit-prop theatre and art movement. *Stachka* [Strike] (1925) set Eisenstein on his way to becoming one of the most famous Soviet filmmakers and theorists. *Strike* was a taste of what was to come from Eisenstein, containing as it did many of the thematic interests he would pursue in later films: it does not focus on particular characters portrayed by actors but uses people chosen to depict "types" of characters, and in his use of montage. Eisenstein's theatrical background comes across in many ways: attention to and choices of lighting, costuming, and set design; facial and bodily expression that often went beyond the realistic to create a reaction in the viewer; and a proclivity for the dramatic (sometimes to a fault). The film itself takes place during the 1912 Factory Strike in Russia, and depicts the struggle of the working class against the Tsar. *Strike* contains many stunning and innovative visual images, and uses what even today are regarded as creative edits to create feeling and emotional connection, and remains watchable and engaging.

The film begins with the implication, through titling, that while things are at present quiet, this is imminently to change. After scenes of machinery in motion, the administration of the factory is shown to be spying on the workers, reviewing a list of agents. Conditions are tense, with agitators and Bolsheviks planning a strike prior to the catalytic event. That event is the theft of a machine (a micrometer), which is valued at about three weeks' pay. A factory worker is accused of the theft and subsequently hangs himself. Fighting ensues and work stops. The strikers throw rocks and loose metal through the foundry windows, and then confront the administrators. They seize one of the managers, carting him off in a wheelbarrow and then dumping them both into the water before dispersing. The shareholders discuss the workers' demands. As the strike continues, Eisenstein juxtaposes the family life of the strikers with the "fat cat" mentality of the shareholders and factory owner. Then, presumably on the orders of the shareholders, the police raid the workers. As the strike draws out, scenes are shown of the lines forming at a closed store, a baby needing food, and other depictions of the human cost of the strike. Events begin to escalate, with the factory spies involved with the beating of a striking worker, and the provocation of the workers by agents of the administrators, leading to fire hoses being turned on a crowd. Finally, the army is sent in and it is soon made clear that the strike will not end well. A rioting crowd is chased off through a series of gates and barriers, eventually ending up being whipped on the balconies of apartments. A policeman raises and drops a child from the balcony, killing it. The workers are driven into a field by the army and shot – the shooting is shown with alternating footage of the slaughtering of a cow. Like many of Eisenstein's films, *Strike* at times feels more like a contemporary avant-garde film than something almost a century old.

For Eisenstein, film was the synthesis of all preceding art forms, and montage was the acme of that synthesis (Bordwell 1996: 168). Through editing distinct images together, new and unique ideas could be created, emotions could be elicited in the audience, and ideological statements transmitted. In both his filmmaking and in his writing on film, montage was to be a principal concern and focus. Examples would include cutting between the killing of workers in *Strike* with images of cattle being slaughtered, inter-cutting between shots of crowd mayhem and the slow methodical march of the soldier down the Odessa Steps in *Battleship Potemkin* (1925), or the bridge scene in *October* (1928). Montage was not just visual, the arrival of sound allowed Eisenstein to create new layers of montage, with sound/music adding new drama to the scenes. Always, though, the use of montage, or any of the other tools of the filmmaker's trade, was subordinated to the ideological message (Bordwell 1996: 168). This is the one area that a contemporary viewer may struggle with, and some of this comes across as heavy-handed if not actually naïve (especially in light of what was to happen under Stalin). Certainly throughout the silent era, Eisenstein felt that as with the *Proletkult* movement, art and propaganda could happily coincide. Works such as all of those already mentioned, as well as films like *The Old and the New* (1929), serve almost as Soviet mythology or folk tales as much as works of art. Indeed, aside from a brief stint in Hollywood and Mexico (1930–32) all of his films were aimed at serving some ideological goal. Even outside of Russia, the strength of his filmmaking meant that his films gained the Soviet state a fair amount of support. The overt ideological overtures in his filmmaking ultimately proved to be a double-edged sword, as ideologies changed – particularly under Stalin. While *Ivan the Terrible Part I* (1944) was about a czar, and theoretically not someone the Soviet government would want portrayed sympathetically, Stalin at the time was supporting a form of Russian nationalism and encouraging the recovering of some former Russian leaders. However, *Ivan the Terrible Part II* (1958) fell foul of the Soviet Central Committee and was banned (Bordwell 1996: 169). Originally made in 1946, due to censorship the film was not released until after the death of the Stalin. These two films are sometimes read as being critical of the way the Soviet government had evolved, which may also have led to the latter at least being banned.

Eisenstein did not recover from the effects of the criticism of *Ivan the Terrible Part II* either artistically or personally. He became isolated and died in 1948 still under suspicion and official disapproval. It would take ten years after his death for his legacy to be reevaluated within the USSR, although he remained famous outside of Russia. Eisenstein remains the most famous Soviet filmmaker, and is one of the most influential and respected filmmakers anywhere (Bordwell 1996: 169). Eisenstein's skills as a director and especially as an editor, as demonstrated in any of the films mentioned here, remain examples that film students can learn from. And while his theories of montage have been somewhat overtaken by time, they too remain important contributions to the development of the cinema.

went on to develop the idea of montage further, stating that there were five types of montage, the most important being intellectual montage, where the images are juxtaposed to make ideological statements. This form of montage is actually quite common. Michael Moore uses this often in his films – juxtaposing images of rich corporate America with poverty in places such as Flint, Michigan (in *Roger & Me* 1989). The "Odessa Steps" segment of Eisenstein's *Battleship Potemkin* (1925) is arguably the acme of his ideas of montage and definitely among the most powerful – forcing viewers to both witness *and* identify with the victims of the brutal advance of the Tsarist soldiers (Parkinson 1995: 77). While Eisenstein's films were admired outside of Russia, the films of V. I. Pudovkin were more popular within Russia itself. Pudovkin used many of Kuleshov and Eisenstein's ideas of montage, but to link images rather than juxtapose them (Pudovkin 1979: 77–84). He also focused on more identifiable (and identifiable with) main characters than Eisenstein's "mass man" (workers as heroes, etc.).

It is interesting to speculate why theorists from Russia should have played such an important role in the development of early film theory. At least one answer reflects a point that will be made in different ways in different parts of this book – Lenin regarded *silent* film as an incredibly important tool in a country where more than 100 different languages were spoken (Parkinson 1995: 72). For that reason, film in the Soviet Union was incorporated into the Soviet propaganda machine and promoted as an important art form in the early Soviet Union. This is not to say that Vertov or Eisenstein would not or could not have promoted their ideas in pre-Soviet Russia, the rest of Europe, or the USA, but that there was a wider context that they operated within, and which facilitated their work. In other words, while the montage and editing theorists and filmmakers would likely define cinema primarily in terms of content, the context in which they were writing and working was of conspicuous importance. The introduction of sound affected the "universality" of Russian silent film as much as anywhere, and the theories also changed. As mentioned in the previous chapter, the advent of sound (initially at least) led to a "play it safe" mentality within the Hollywood studio system and the experimentation and debate of the silent era was at an end. That very stifling of creativity, however, led in turn to new theories and practices.

CRITICAL FILM THEORIES

There were two interlinked developments occurring mostly just after the Second World War. One was the aforementioned backlash against Hollywood and/or the Hollywood studio system, arising initially in France and Italy. The other was the academicization of film theory. While there were, as mentioned, links between the two developments (auteur theory for instance), the two were also quite distinct as the former was more like the earlier situation of film theory from a filmmaker, the latter was more like Kracauer and Benjamin, theory from non-filmmakers. This period is significant as it is also where the shift of film theory discourses from largely one of film-as-art (formalism, Ciné-Art, montage) to one of film-as-medium (ideology, political economy, "meaning") took place. This also marks a change in the definition of cinema, while the majority of the theoretical work in either of these approaches to cinema was in terms of content, there was a growth in the acknowledgment of the context, and that understanding cinema needed to incorporate more than the formal mechanisms of filmmaking (Lapsley and Westlake 1988: vii). The importance of that context was not always agreed upon however. The most prominent European cinema movements of the post-Second World War era were Italian neo-realism and the French New Wave.

NEO-REALISM AND THE FRENCH NEW WAVE

While neo-realism was arguably more of a moment in Italian film, rather than a "school" of cinema, its impact has been enormous on movies throughout the world (as we saw with the case study on Satyajit Ray in the previous chapter). With its beginnings in the latter years of the Second World War, but predominately taking place in immediate postwar Italy, neo-realism was characterized by stories set among the poor or working class, filmed in long takes, usually shot outdoors on location, and frequently used nonprofessional actors (Parkinson 1995: 150–4). To a degree the neo-realist aesthetic was an ideological move – away from the fantasy of Fascist-era escapist cinema and the artifice of Hollywood cinema – and partly a pragmatic reflection of the wide-scale destruction that postwar Italy was dealing with. In terms of their content and subject matter, Italian neo-realist films predominately dealt with the desperate economic and moral conditions of postwar Italy.

Although neo-realism began with the ideological declarations of theorist Cesare Zavattini and critic Umberto Barbaro (Parkinson 1995: 150), specifically that there must be an emphasis on the values of ordinary people, a refusal to make easy moral judgments, and a focus on emotional veracity rather than the articulation of abstract ideas, few of the actual filmmakers could live up to these lofty ideals (Cousins 2004: 189–92). As mentioned above, the shared aesthetics of neo-realist cinema were location shooting, the use of amateur actors, and dubbing dialogue (inserting dialogue during postproduction). The dubbing freed filmmakers from the studios, which were either destroyed or serving other purposes, and allowed for a more open *mise en scène* (Nowell-Smith 1996b: 435). The dialogue itself was also different from earlier Italian cinema as neo-realist filmmakers made use of conversational speech rather than formal, more literary language. While trained actors would often portray principal characters, the supporting cast was usually nonprofessional. Indeed, the cast of one of the most famous neo-realist films, *Ladri di biciclette* [Bicycle Thieves] (de Sica 1948), was entirely amateur. The use of ordinary people rather than professional actors was intended to create a greater sense of realism and thus give the scenes more authentic power. There was also a general avoidance of trickery in editing, camerawork, and lighting in favor of a more immediate "documentary" style. Some of the most famous Italian directors, such as Roberto Rossellini, came out of the neo-realist movement.

Cinematic development in France after the Second World War overlaps the anti-escapism movement of the neo-realists and also was one of the main influences in the academicization of film theory. The film magazine *Cahiers du cinéma* founded by André Bazin, Jacques Doniol-Valcroze and Lo Duca in 1951 (Andrew 1976: 135), was one of the most important arenas for film criticism and theory in France, and was directly responsible of the French New Wave filmmakers of the 1950s and 1960s. Bazin, in particular, became a powerful force in film studies. In addition to editing *Cahiers*, two volumes of Bazin's four-volume *Qu'est-ce que le cinéma?* [*What is Cinema?*] were translated into English and became foundations of film courses in the USA and United Kingdom. Bazin promoted deep focus, wide shots, long takes, and the *mise en scène*, much like the Ciné-Art movement. However, Bazin also championed realism (Andrew 1976: 137), which was not something that the Ciné-Art movement focused on. Bazin's idea of realism is quite specific as he is attempting to explain how film works. For Bazin, realism helps to explain film's appeal to an audience (Andrew 1976: 140). Cinema is appealing as in it we see the link to the reality that is being expressed, and these links are understandable. I will come back to this argument later in this chapter, as it foreshadows a couple of important later theories (semiotics, Peircian symbolism, and Bakhtin's literary theories). This is crucial, as it frees the idea of realism from a mechanical reproduction of reality, as Kracauer would have argued for, or as documentary film would strive to achieve, but creates the space for the form of realism mentioned above, one that is not in a one-to-one relationship to "reality."

In many ways Bazin was the antithesis of Eisenstein and Vertov, as all of the ideas just mentioned were the opposite of montage and ideological lecturing. Indeed, Bazin wanted the director to be "invisible" to the viewer, rather than foregrounding him/herself. That is not to say that the director should not leave their mark on the film – in fact the *Cahier* theorists ardently argued that the director's personal vision should be reflected in their films. Orson Welles's *Citizen Kane* (1941) is an example of this vision. These ideas became formalized, as for instance the latter argument became auteur theory, and helped to establish the groundwork for film studies as we know it today. Finally, Bazin also understood the "institutional" aspect of cinema (à la Kracauer and the Frankfurt School), and the sociological role of cinema, its ties with popular culture for instance, was also of extreme importance. At its purest, Bazin's ideas sought to incorporate the outer realism of the world being addressed with the inner realism of the individual director's vision (Andrew 1976: 170–8). As

Figure 2.3　Director Orson Welles and cinematographer Gregg Toland filming *Citizen Kane* (O. Welles 1941). [Credit: RKO / The Kobal Collection / Gaston Longet]

such, the most direct influence of Bazin and other *Cahier* theorists' ideas was upon the French New Wave (*nouvelle vague*). As the French New Wave was discussed in the previous chapter, the following is a more general overview of the ideological positioning of the filmmakers.

As neo-realism gave Italian cinema some of its most famous directors, so too did the New Wave give France some if its greatest directors – Claude Chabrol, Jean-Luc Goddard, François Truffaut, and Alain Resnais. Encouraged both by the *Cahier* critics and by the commercial successes of some early New Wave-esque films (notably Vadim's 1956 *And God Created Woman*), more than a hundred filmmakers produced New Wave influenced films between 1959 and 1962 (Parkinson 1995: 186). New Wave cinema aesthetics followed Bazin's prescriptions to some extent, but they also struck out on their own in several ways – especially concerning the "filmness" of their cinematic productions. While Bazin had argued for an "invisible" director – New Wave directors championed some stylistic elements that extended Bazin's ideas. For instance, New Wave filmmakers used some very specific cinematic techniques to draw attention to the constructed-ness of cinema: unmotivated camera movements, irising,[3] jump cuts, and other attention-drawing mechanisms. These devices created an intentional disconnect between viewer and film – one that foregrounded the role of the auteur both in the creation of the film and in the viewer's relationship to the film (as was illustrated in the previous chapter by the examples from Truffaut and Godard). Along with the devices, New Wave filmmakers incorporated spontaneity, cinematic homages, and in-jokes alongside ideas from neo-realism and Bazin, such as locations shooting, hand-held cameras, and natural light. The experimentation even extended into the very "stuff" of cinema since its earliest days – realism – "with loose causal connections, disconcerting shifts in tone, digressions, [and] ill-defined character motivations" (Parkinson 1995: 186). If all of the above sounds like it would be hard to sustain, it was. The success of New Wave was as much because of the personal and very individualistic success of its members than a coherent program, aside from a desire to replace the conventions of narrative film with new models of artistic self-expression. Nevertheless, the French New Wave was hugely influential. British social realist dramas of the 1950s and 1960s (the "kitchen sink" dramas discussed in the previous chapter) as well as more commercially oriented filmmakers working in Britain, like Richard Lester (*A Hard Day's Night* 1964), and American filmmakers such as Stanley Kubrick, Sidney Lumet, and Frank Peckinpah were all influenced by the French New Wave. Further, documentary filmmakers looking for something beyond the classic British "Voice of God" documentary style found much of interest in both French New Wave and Italian neo-realism. Possibly as important, along with the ideas of neo-realism, the aesthetic concerns of the French New Wave formed the basis of film theory during the 1950s and 1960s.

MARXISM

For various reasons, such as the political activism in universities in France, theory in the late 1960s and early 1970s built upon the theories of the Frankfurt School, *Cahiers du cinéma*, and neo-realists, and took a turn away from film-as-art. It is also in this era that film theory truly turns into an academic subject (Freiberg 2000: 181), and some of the division between filmmaking and film theory takes place. With this turn to issues of *ideology*, the need to understand how film worked as an ideological tool became foregrounded. Structuralism, semiotics, psychoanalysis, and Marxism provided answers to this set of questions. Marxism in particular enjoyed a renaissance in the 1970s, to such an extent that Marxist-influenced theories are among the most significant, as well as ubiquitous, theories within academe. Indeed, it would not be much of an exaggeration to suggest that it would be harder to find theories without any engagement with Marxism (or at least engagement to the level of arguing against Marxism). Figures such as Adorno and Horkheimer (of the Frankfurt School), and Althusser are important in the history of film theory, as their positing of the media as purveyors of ideology and apparatuses of the state somewhat paradoxically lent credibility to the cinema, and by extension to the work of film theorists.

Louis Althusser had a significant impact upon the expansion of Marxism in post-1960s film theory (Lapsley and Westlake 1988: 2–8). Briefly put, Marxism, the political and philosophical theories of Karl Marx, argues that human history is marked by certain progressions (from feudalism to capitalism, for instance). Capitalism brought with it and is distinguished by certain characteristics based upon economic relations. Indeed, economics is the base upon which the superstructure (kinship, politics, religion, etc.) of society rests. In capitalist society, this leads to particular orderings of society, such as the way in which capitalists rely upon the exploitation of a dormant and acquiescent working class, whose value is purely in terms of the labor they perform, to maximize profits. To keep the working class dormant, the ruling class takes steps to ensure that the working class remains disjointed and passive (controlling the modes and means of production, and controlling access to and content of information and other sources of intellectual growth, etc.). When these steps are effective, the working class will eventually begin to contribute to their own exploitation by incorporating the ideologies of the ruling class as their own. To rectify this situation, what is necessary is a revolution in which the workers become the owners and in control of the modes and means of production. Only then can a fair and equitable economic system (socialism/communism) develop.[4] Until Althusser, there seemed to be some intractable problems with Marxist theory: whether it was itself merely another form of ideology; how determinant economics truly were in relation to other aspects of society; and finally, just what "ideology" meant. Without going into detail as to how Althusser solved these issues, his

Figure 2.4 Palace Talkies theatre Mumbai India. Built for millworkers. Photograph by Madhav Pai 2008.

reconciliation of some of these problems was incredibly influential throughout academia (Lapsley and Westlake 1988: 8). In short, what Althusser achieved was establishing Marxism as offering scientific knowledge and a non-reductive analysis of how social formation takes place and works, and contributing a term, "ideology," which is both based in the real world and has power in that real world. All of which were to be important for the use of Marxist ideas to understand the cinema (Lapsley and Westlake 1988: 8). Analysts more interested in issues of how film operates regarded much of the film criticism pre-1960s as trapped in dominant ideologies, and based upon impressions and feelings rather than from a firm (scientific) base of criticism. In trying to make sense of the relationship between economics and society, Althusser developed the idea of *interpellation* – an individual's identity is forged by society, but that same individual is also complicit in that creation (Lapsley and Westlake 1988: 7–8). Ideology comes into play throughout this process, as it is via state ideological structures such as the media or educational institutions that the subject is created, but the subject by acknowledging and accepting that creation affirms, reaffirms, and eventually replicates and passes on the ideology. The cinema, long understood as an ideological apparatus, could now be interrogated in terms of just how it did so, i.e. how it "works" (Lapsley and Westlake 1988: 8). Furthermore, film "works" via its form as much as its content, meaning that the nuts and bolts of the cinema needed to come under as much (if not more) scrutiny as the narratives had done. Indeed, once raised, the issue of how film functions (in the Marxist sense in terms of ideology) has remained foundational to film theory and critical analysis.

Marxist approaches to film were perhaps the ones that went farthest away from an understanding of film via its content, and certainly of its content alone. Content was important as particular examples of the forms of interpellation, but not as important in itself as it was in earlier theoretical models. Further, it is relatively rare to find a purely Marxist analysis of a particular film, as opposed to Marxist structuralist (such as in the French journals *Cahiers du cinéma* and *Cinéthique*, or the British *Screen Magazine*) or Marxist feminist analyses of film that include examples from particular films. An example of the former is the analysis of *Young Mr. Lincoln* (Ford 1939) by the editors of *Cahiers du cinéma* (1979).[5] In their analysis, the editors go to lengths to make clear that while an artistic product (film in this case) cannot be linked to its socio-historical context in some form of linear and direct causal relationship, that same film while an independent and individual text, nevertheless, *is* part of a larger historically and socio-politically determined text, within which the individual texts are created and given meaning. To understand *Young Mr. Lincoln* it is necessary to understand its relationship to the general text ("classic" Hollywood cinema) and specific historical events (late 1930s' American political economy). The analysis of *Young Mr. Lincoln* therefore rests in a nested set of analyses of late 1930s' Hollywood, late 1930s' USA, the studio (20th Century Fox) and its manager (Zanuck), the director (Ford) and the subject matter, and then the various constituent elements of the film. The first two analyses are crucial in understanding the film as they provide a context for making sense of the ideology underlying and expressed through *Young Mr. Lincoln* (1979: 783–4) That wider context was firstly that of late-Depression-era Hollywood, which found itself under the control of Big Business, in this case the banks. This control had already been expressed through various economic and ideological occurrences, such as the creation of the Hays Code. At the same time national box office figures were decreasing. This was a reflection of the second context, that of late-Depression-era USA, which was under the control of Roosevelt's Democratic Party, which had put in place political and economic policies antithetical to Big Business. These policies (the New Deal) had arguably run their course, as major economic indicators, such as unemployment figures, worsened. In short, the situation was thus:

> Federal centralism, isolationism, economic reorganisation (including Holly-
> wood), strengthening of the Democrat-Republican opposition, new threats

of internal and international crisis, crisis and restrictions in Hollywood itself;
such is the fairly gloomy context of the *Young Mr. Lincoln* (1939) undertaking
(Editors of *Cahiers du cinéma* 1979: 785).

In this case, 20th Century Fox supported the Republican Party and through Zanuck
put into production a film that linked Lincoln and the Republican Party with being
the epitome of Law and Truth. The mechanisms by which this was done are layered
throughout the film, such as the electoral speech, where, in a few short words, the
film simultaneously creates Lincoln as an eternal champion of Republican values
and as being above "normal" politics, indeed an American hero. Another example
is later in the film during the trial scene where Lincoln, through "common sense"
(using an almanac) wins the case and thereby guarantees Truth and Justice – by
extension the Republican Party also guarantees Truth and Justice (Editors of *Cahiers
du cinéma* 1979: 820–2). In the year before a presidential election, the motivation
and ideological purposes of *Young Mr. Lincoln* were clear, to help defeat the enemy
of Big Business and the Republican Party. In the end, in their analysis the editors of
Cahiers du cinema do not really manage to avoid the causal relationship they refer to
(Lapsley and Westlake 1988: 116).

As is the case with many of the theories mentioned here, which came into film
theory from other fields, the way Marxism is used in film theory is both similar to
and yet different from the way it is employed in other disciplines, such as the social
sciences. Part of that is due to the symbolic level of abstraction that is involved in
studying film (as we saw in the case study above), rather than kinship or market
forces on job creation. What Marxist film theory is forced to do is study the
ideological forces through the medium rather than first hand and, because of that,
the effects and the targets of the ideological forces are more hypothetically derived
than empirically determined. What this means is that often the context of cinema
is assumed rather than researched. As we will see later in the book, this approach to
how film works has some problems. Marxism was not the only theory attempting to
establish how film works though.

STRUCTURALISM

Building on the linguistic work of Saussure, structuralists (and, as we shall see later
in this chapter, semioticians) set about establishing the fundamental units of filmic
meaning (Lapsley and Westlake 1988: 10–12). Structuralism is simultaneously complex and simple. The basic preposition of structuralism is that humans engage with,
make sense of, and function in the world through sets of binary oppositions – good/
bad, left/right, earth/sky, land/water, etc. For instance, in *Star Wars*, Luke Skywalker
is "good" and Darth Vader is "bad." I could have chosen any of a thousand films for

this comparison, but as we will see there are reasons for using *Star Wars*. Structuralists argue that much of how we understand the world we live in is achieved through comparing and contrasting those aforementioned structural oppositions. Indeed, it could be said that humans are made up of predetermined structures (Lapsley and Westlake 1988: 11). So far, this is the simple part of structuralism. Where it gets more complex is that humans (or the world for that matter) rarely stay the same, and may have aspects of both good and bad. People, places, and things may change from one set to another, or may take on elements of the other. To understand this, structuralists suggest that what happens is that certain things, stages of life, times, etc. are mediations or transitions between those two sets. Many, if not most of, human rituals and myths are either to explain or rectify these transitional zones and periods. Indeed, it is the transitional zone where most fictional narrative takes place.

The person who did the earliest work on understanding structural elements in terms of fiction was Vladimir Propp, who analyzed Russian folk/fairy tales by breaking them down into their smallest narrative units. By distinguishing types of characters and kinds of action, Propp concluded that there were thirty-one basic narrative units and eight character types (Propp 1968). The eight types include the hero, the villain, the princess, the donor (who prepares the hero or gives the hero some magical object), the (magical) helper, and the dispatcher (who sends the hero off on their quest). These roles are sometimes distributed among various characters, and sometimes one character plays more than one role. In terms of the action, Propp found that while not all thirty-one elements are necessarily present in any one tale, in all the tales he analyzed the units that did occur, occurred in the same sequence. So, in fairy tales, after the initial setting of the scene is depicted, the tale takes the following sequence (for reasons of brevity, I will not list all of them): a member of a family leaves home (this is usually the hero's introduction); an interdiction is placed on the hero (he/she is told "don't go there/do that"); the interdiction is violated (this is typically also where the villain enters the tale); the villain attempts to deceive the victim to take possession of the victim or the victim's belongings; the victim is taken in by deception and unwittingly helps the enemy; the villain causes harm/injury to the family; the misfortune or lack is made known and the hero is sent on their quest; the hero leaves home (Propp 1968). If any of that sounds familiar, take that list and watch *Star Wars IV–VI*. One of the reasons for the massive international success of those particular Star Wars movies (as opposed to *Star Wars I–III*) is that Lucas followed (fairly closely) what Propp might call a universal script.

In his analyses, Propp was not seeking out any deeper meaning, and as such most structuralists would not consider Propp a structuralist. However, his attempt to find the elemental building blocks of narrative were influential on famous structuralists and, particularly in terms of character types, on media and film studies to this day. What structuralists did was take these preexisting structures and give them new roles – principally in helping constitute the way that people hearing those tales, or watching those films understand themselves and their role or roles in society (which is related to interpellation). The very processes of successful cinema, eliciting empathy in viewers and the suspension of disbelief, were seen as aiding in constituting the viewers as subjects of the ruling orthodoxy. A critic of structuralism might be tempted to argue that a structuralist approach to cinema is very similar to a structuralist approach to kinship or economics, as it exists in the researcher's head either way, and there is indeed a level of abstraction inherent to the structuralist approach that is hard to overlook. That same level of abstraction is useful in dealing with symbolic media such as cinema, where the content is already abstracted from the "real" world. As such, a structuralist analysis of *Blade Runner* (Scott 1982) would have many similarities with Lévi-Strauss's structuralist analysis of a more "anthropological" matter, such as masks (Lévi-Strauss 1982). An example would be Peter Wollen's analyses of the works of directors such as Ford, Hitchcock, and Hawks (Lapsley and Westlake 1996: 109–10). For each of these auteurs, Wollen argues that there is a "master antimony" (or fundamental opposition) in their work. In the films of Ford, for instance, this master antimony is between nature and culture, which in turn manifests in a series of binary oppositions: "settler/nomad, European/Indian, civilised/savage, book/gun" (Lapsley and Westlake 1996: 110). The exact relationship between these oppositions will depend on the actual film, as European may align with civilized in one film and savage in another, but the overall system fits into a "Fordian" structure or system based on the underlying opposition. This brief example shows some of the abstractness of the approach, as well as the attraction, in that it allows the theorist to build a persuasive case for the coherence of a director's body of work and for a more theorized approach to film study – especially in Wollen's case for the auteur. It is perhaps for similar reasons that a structuralist approach to cinema would be integrated into other theoretical models, such as Marxism, as we have seen, or semiotics, as we will turn to next.

SEMIOTICS

Another set of theories that attempted to establish how film works was semiotics. Like structuralism, semiotics is simultaneously simple and complex. Simply put, semiotics is the study of the "language" of signs or symbols. However, things are rarely left so simple. From a relatively benign attempt to understand the systems of usage and understanding of signs, semioticians began to push a much more aggressive agenda. This aggressive agenda threatened many other theorists and critics and, unsurprisingly, met with considerable resistance.

As with the Marxists, semioticians sought to make film analysis/criticism scientific and to get away from the "impressionistic" style of criticism (i.e. one based on impressions and "feelings" rather than a scientific basis). The work of French theorist Christian Metz is one example of this project. Metz was attempting to move film theory away from what he felt was a necessary initial stage, one that was general and philosophical rather than specific and scientific (Lapsley and Westlake 1988: 32–3). In that vein, Metz's goal was to create an exact description of *signification* in the cinema employing structural linguistics as a starting point. Signification is crucial to this and many of the following theories, the basic idea is that different elements in a film *mean* things – they signify something, e.g. a zoom shot or a close-up means something specific (unless they are unmotivated, in which case that is a good example of bad filmmaking). To do this it was necessary to set some guidelines. First of all, Metz distinguished two fields of problems – filmic and cinematic (Andrew 1976: 216). Filmic problems incorporate elements outside of the film itself, or film's relations to other activities (what is being referred to in this book as the context of production). Cinematic problems involve only the films themselves. Metz's semiotics is not interested in filmic issues, only cinematic problems. Once those distinctions were made, much of Metz's work was devoted to setting out the "science" of the cinema. Initially, this project consisted of a highly structured and formalized hierarchy of elements of cinematic narrative, beginning with what he considered the smallest unit of meaning – the shot. Shots were then put together in a system to create sequences, like words are put together in a sentence using grammar and syntax, and thus to create meaning. While interesting, this system has not been very useful in practice, and Metz turned to a more productive project – outlining the codes of the cinematic text. In this later project, Metz attempted to set out a wider set of laws of signification, those which make understanding a film possible, both cinematic and non-cinematic, which are incorporated in the signifying process (Lapsley and Westlake 1988: 40–1). So, cinematic elements such as lighting, particular shots, blocking, and framing all have codes through which filmmakers and audiences understand meaning/significance (a close-up shows a character's emotion, so for both filmmakers and audiences a close-up means that the emotion of the character, and by extension the character, is important, and is one that audiences are to identify with). Codes from outside the cinema would include matters like gesture, costume, facial or dialogic expressions (Lapsley and Westlake 1988: 42–3). These codes can then be demonstrated at work in a particular film or genre of film, for example the use of close-up shots in Hitchcock's *Vertigo* (1958) or 1940s' American *film noir*.

Metz's attempt to create a scientific semiotics for the language of film may now appear misguided, and indeed, as we saw, his projects changed over time. However,

Figure 2.5 Some Bollywood codes on display – hand-
drawn movie posters on a wall in Bangalore, India.
Photograph by Paul Keller 2008.

the work of Metz initiated a set of intellectual arguments, both between himself and others, and between others. Eco and Heath, for example, attempted to introduce cultural and social ingredients to Metz's more sterile undertaking. Eco employed a Peircian form of symbolism (more about this below) and Heath was interested in the relationship between audience and cinema. Willemen and McCabe, writing against one another, attempted to problematize the relations between text, ideology/signifier, and subject (Lapsley and Westlake 1988: 32–62). These and other battles during the 1970s helped to ensure that attention on *meaning* became one of the main trends in film theory, even as these battles became increasingly insular – focused more upon addressing one another's ideas and arguments as opposed to analyzing films. Semiotics also helped to open up the theoretical discourse to ideas of the signifier, which was also of importance to psychoanalysis-derived theories. As we will see later, though the semiotic approach to the symbolic within cinema fell out of favor, other symbolic approaches (particularly Peircian-influenced approaches) have come back into vogue.

PSYCHOANALYSIS

Freud and Lacan are two more key figures for the development of film theory in the 1970s. Overlapping with Marxism and semiotics, and in fact employed by both as well as by feminist theorists, psychoanalysis-derived theories were critically influential. The application of psychoanalysis to cinema by no means began in the 1970s. The productions of Hollywood in particular – and it is no accident that Hollywood is referred to as the "dream factory" – displayed a range of familiar/clichéd Freudian motifs, such as trains going into tunnels to represent sex (Lapsley and Westlake 1988: 67). Hitchcock, for one, enjoyed playing with Freudian ideas or symbolism in films such as *Rear Window* (1954) and *North by Northwest* (1959). However, the use of "old school" Freudianism over time became clichéd and eventually resulted in reductionist readings of all films as Oedipal/voyeuristic/castration anxiety fantasies.[6] These reductionist analyses led to the discrediting of Freudian psychoanalysis as a productive or meaningful tool for film theory (Lapsley and Westlake 1988: 67).

Psychoanalysis was reintroduced to film theory in the 1970s via Lacan's more nuanced reading of Freudian psychoanalysis, especially in regards to the subject. It is in terms of the subject that psychoanalysis has arguably had both the most impact and the most utility within film theory. Lacan's ideas of the subject are very complex and controversial, but bear going into in some detail as they have been very influential for later theories. One of Lacan's foundational ideas is that a baby is not initially aware of itself separate from its mother and so feels complete and whole. Once the baby becomes aware that it is in fact separate from its mother it begins to become aware of itself as a self (this is the beginning of the development of subjectivity). This awareness comes at a price, as with the separation comes a feeling of lack (of unity with the mother). The child (and eventually adolescent and adult) seeks to overcome that lack and regain completeness, but this project is doomed to failure (Lapsley and Westlake 1988: 67–8). The awareness of lack and the desire to overcome that lack leads the child to seek other solutions to that feeling of lack. Some of these solutions are socially sanctioned (love, marriage) others are not (unhealthy fixations or fetishes). For Lacan, there are three defining moment in the development of subjectivity: self-awareness (the mirror phase), acquiring language, and socialization (Lapsley and Westlake 1988: 68–74). Each of these moments grants the child/subject new vistas on its world, but also comes at a price. Self-awareness grants the child an awareness of self as self and an awareness of the Other, but comes at the price of the awareness of lack and of alienation. Language brings the subject into the sphere of the symbolic and signification as well as Objects, but also of desire (unfulfilled) and furthering of the sense of lack (Lapsley and Westlake 1988: 73). Language is also necessary for socialization, which provides many of the ways in which the child will attempt to rectify its lack and is crucial in forming the child's identity (at least its social identity – see interpellation); however, it also places laws and limitations on the child, and learning these is often a painful process. Lacan's reworking of Freud and in particular his ideas on the development of the subject are important to film theory as they take the search for how film works to a very different level – that of the individual. Lacan's ideas help film theorists to understand why a person enjoys either particular films or films in general, rather than how films work in abstract terms. To give an example of this, Lacan's ideas were central to Laura Mulvey's classic work on "the gaze" in mainstream cinema (Mulvey 1975).

Mulvey's work investigates the idea of pleasure, and how mainstream cinema provides pleasure. Pleasure comes via the exploiting of or tapping into preexisting psychological structures within the viewer. This pleasure is part and parcel of cinema's role in communicating dominant ideologies, in this case sex/gender ideologies (Lapsley and Westlake 1988: 77–9, 98). Male pleasure is created in mainstream cinema in three ways: identification, voyeurism, and fetishism. Cinema-goers identify with the glamorized male heroes onscreen, projecting one's self onto that character to feel good about one's self. The very act of cinema-going is voyeuristic, and by looking the subject (the male viewer) gains power and control over the object of their gaze – usually a woman, or perhaps more precisely a woman's body. This last point takes us into fetishism, as the separation of a woman's body into aspects of that woman – breasts, legs, etc. – turns them solely into objects of desire and frees the male spectator from anxiety over alienation or lack. Through satisfying, to some degree, the alienation and lack, even if temporarily, the cinema "works"; on an individual level – it provides pleasure. Mulvey's argument was extraordinarily persuasive, and by the late 1970s it had become taken as read in much feminist and other forms of ideological film criticism that mainstream cinema was ordered for the power and pleasure of a single (male) spectator-subject whose voyeuristic gaze became the principal tool of visual domination. Over time, Mulvey's ideas were brought into question, for instance the role for female spectators in this model or the possibility of male identification with female characters (Lapsley and Westlake 1988: 98–104). However, the issues raised by this arena of criticism highlighted the audience, the subject, and "identification." As such it has contributed a great deal to broadening the scope of film theory. The use of psychoanalysis-derived theories in studying the cinema are somewhat controversial outside of film theory itself, as the ideas are (from an outsider's perspective) used somewhat uncritically and in a broader manner than Lacan may have envisioned. This is a stone that is often cast when one discipline uses the ideas of another, but it is hard to ignore the criticism when reading the umpteenth paper on voyeurism that mentions no other film than something by Hitchcock (as will be discussed in the case study on Hitchcock). This is less of a criticism of the theory than its usage, however, and as with structuralism and symbolic approaches to film theory, psychoanalysis-derived theories are well suited to the task of understanding film even if they are used differently than in other disciplines.

Case Study: Hitchcock – Auteur and Psychoanalysis

Alfred Hitchcock (1899–1980) is one of cinema's most famous directors (O'Neill 1996: 310). Hitchcock worked in Britain, Germany (where he was able to observe first hand Murnau's filmmaking, and his early films were clearly influenced by expressionism), and America. With his career lasting over fifty years, his work spans the transition from silent to sound films, from the height of the studio system to the beginning of the blockbuster era – his final film *Family Plot* (1976) was released one year after Spielberg's *Jaws*). He directed films that encompassed genres from romantic comedy, *Mr. & Mrs. Smith* (1941), to a prototype "slasher" horror film, *Psycho* (1960). While a large number of his films were produced under Hollywood's studio system, he is also one of the first directors to be referred to as an *auteur*, and that understanding of his work was vastly important to the *Cahiers du cinéma* and ultimately to the academicization of film studies. Even though Hitchcock's films were unique products that manifested his personal interests and agendas, he nevertheless was a commercially successful mass-market director as well. A prominent and successful Hollywood director, Hitchcock also had the respect of the French New Wave filmmakers. This highly influential director is one of the most written about filmmakers, and his legacy has been dissected in a multitude of ways – for instance through structuralist, feminist, and psychoanalysis approaches – not to mention in formalist "cinema as art" interpretations as well (O'Neill 1996: 311). While some of the work Hitchcock produced towards the end of his career places a blot on his accomplishments (from the mid 1960s onwards his films became increasingly misogynist), his premier place in both the history and theory of film is firmly established. As Cousins states: "From the start of his career, this precisely-spoken, rotund son of a London fruit and poultry dealer was exceptionally talented. Few, however, would have guessed that by the 1960s he would be a visual artist to rank with the painter Pablo Picasso" (Cousins 2004: 155). Due to the array of influences upon his work and Hitchcock's own intelligent filmmaking, while simultaneously evincing a unity of technique and aesthetics, his films have been a treasure trove for film theorists. Two of the most prominent ways of understanding Hitchcock's role in cinema history have been regarding his status as auteur and analyzing his films through the theories of psychoanalysis. This case study will focus on these two aspects of Hitchcock's legacy, and in so doing demonstrate some the benefits and shortcomings of these approaches.

While Hitchcock's films cover a vast range of time, space, and even genre, they also share many characteristics that can only be called *Hitchcockian* (O'Neill 1996: 310). His films are famous for their pace and suspense – he compared suspense with surprise by using the analogy of a scene with a couple sitting at a table with a bomb underneath: if the bomb goes off that is surprise, but if it doesn't that is suspense – bleak humor and plots that often turned on ordinary people caught in extraordinary situations. His films, perhaps more than any of his contemporaries', push the boundaries of narrative cinema; he used the codes and conventions developed by earlier filmmakers exquisitely. And his films demonstrated that unique vision that was so important to the *Cahier du cinéma* theory of the auteur. Among the traits of a "Hitchcock" film are: (as we have seen) suspense; voyeurism and especially suggestions that the audience is the voyeur; the wrong man or wrong woman at the wrong place at the wrong time – *North by Northwest* (1959) is a perfect example of this; likeable criminals; the use of staircases to express and heighten tension and danger; domineering mothers (do I need to even mention *Psycho*?); sexuality – along with narrative conventions, Hitchcock also pushed boundaries in term of the depiction of sexuality – sometimes playfully as with the train going into a tunnel (also discussed in terms of psychoanalysis) to express consummation of the marriage in *North by Northwest*; blonde women (*Vertigo* 1958 takes this to the extreme); and scenes that convey information visually rather than through dialogue; and perhaps most famous are Hitchcock's cameos in many of his films (O'Neill 1996: 310–11). There are others, but these are some of the key features of Hitchcock's films. All of which would seem to indicate that Hitchcock was an auteur, and I certainly would not argue that point; however, he was also a commercially successful director who flourished under the selfsame studio system that auteur theory decried. The other issue is that films are not produced in vacuums nor are they the work of a single person, a point that more contemporary film studies and film historians are acknowledging. As an instance, Hitchcock married his assistant director, Alma Reville, in 1926. Alma worked with him on all of his films and wrote some of his screenplays. Further, because of the studio system, Hitchcock could reliably make films with some of the most talented people in Hollywood: Cary Grant in *Suspicion* (1941), *Notorious* (1946), *To Catch a Thief* (1955), and *North by Northwest* (1959); James Stewart in *Rope* (1948), *Rear Window* (1954), *The Man Who Knew Too Much* (1956), and *Vertigo* (1958); Ingrid Bergman in *Spellbound* (1945), *Notorious* (1946), and *Under Capricorn* (1947); and Grace Kelly in *Dial M for Murder* (1954), *Rear Window* (1954), and *To Catch a Thief* (1955) among others. While this in no way means that Hitchcock was not a talented director, the sole focus on his role in these films perhaps bears some examination.

Even more worthy of examination is the often facile use of psychoanalysis approaches to understand Hitchcock's films. As Lapsley and Westlake state "a cliché of Hitchcockian studies is that his narratives play out an Oedipal scenario in which the desire embodied or aroused by the woman is experienced as transgressive and punished by an act of aggression – all deriving, of course, from Hitchcock's unresolved Oedipal problems" (Lapsley and Westlake 1988: 153). Discussions of Hitchcock often refer back to certain instances in his early life, such as his father taking him to the police as punishment (leading to part of the Oedipal issue) and his mother making him stand for prolonged periods at the foot of her bed as punishment (certainly the image of the domineering mother frequently in Hitchcock's films). As mentioned in the main text, one of the problems with Freudian psychoanalysis approaches in particular is that they become banal – in this case even more so, as many of the examples in Hitchcock's movies were put there quite purposefully (*Spellbound* 1945), even playfully, as in the case of the train going into the tunnel to symbolize sex in *North by Northwest* (O'Neill 1996: 311). These readings become even harder to defend when one is reminded that sex/eroticism was not allowed to be overtly depicted and thus had to be represented in roundabout ways – i.e. symbolically. It sometimes got to the point that psychoanalysis approaches were analyzing elements that Hitchcock had put into his films to purposefully express ideas from psychoanalysis (look for ad nauseam analyses of voyeurism in *Vertigo* for instance). The more sophisticated Lacanian forms of psychoanalysis fare better. Analyses of *The Birds* (1963), *Vertigo*, or *Rear Window*, for instance, are intriguing and useful paths to understanding issues of voyeurism and cinema, audience identification, and fetishization. Hitchcock's use of the camera to create audience identification with certain characters is masterful – restricting the information that the audience receives, careful use of close-ups, and other point of view techniques were all means to create the empathy and identification that makes film successful. In films like *Psycho* that identification was not always pleasant, as we realize that we have been identifying with a psychotic killer. In *The Birds* (1963), Hitchcock takes some of these techniques further, and many psychoanalysis analyses of this and other later Hitchcock films comment on both the overt violence to the female characters, the camera's fixation on aspects of female bodies, and the subjectification of women to the gaze of men (O'Neill 1996: 310). Other analyses argue that rather than a cut-and-dried misogyny, what is going on is that identification is being shifted between characters and that there is a complex problematization of those same issues – that viewers become viewed and vice versa, and the creation of an external "Other" viewing position, and that it is this third position that dwells, that fetishizes (Lapsley and Westlake 1988: 98–104). This latter form of analysis suggests Hitchcock is deconstructing "easy" readings of male viewer and female subject, while simultaneously reminding the audiences that these are the expected roles and points of identification and that they, the audience, are complicit. Perhaps not easy viewing, but also a more nuanced reading of the films of one of the media's most celebrated directors.

LITERARY THEORIES

Since the 1980s, one of the most important influences on film studies has been literary theory. Literary theory is not so much one theory (as for instance structuralism) as it is a set of interrelated theories with some shared foci and themes (Collier and Geyer-Ryan 1992). Cinema and literary theory have a large area of intellectual overlap and share many of the same theoretical concerns. Marxism and structuralism, for example, were important within literary theory as they were in film studies. One of those areas of thematic overlap has to do with issues surrounding the narrative conventions relating to the formation of subjectivities, those of the individual and of the state (Willemen 1995: 101–3).

While film theory, as a body of knowledge, has several theoretical roots and sources of inspiration, many of which have already been outlined above, it is the literary theory-informed approach that has provided much of the current terminology and rhetoric intrinsic to film studies. An important debate within literary theory has surrounded the formation of a modern subjectivity (a self-conscious individual awareness of the self), and that formation's relationship to modern narrative form and how the story is told. While the seemingly simple split between pre-modern and modern is not really so simple, as a rough and ready guideline it has been useful in attempting to delineate a similar shift ("pre-modern" to "modern") in both literature and the cinema (McKeon 1987; Fujii 1993).

In literary theory the move towards the modern narrative – the novel – has been placed at various places and times, but the manifestation of this shift centered on narrative structures. One argument is that the shift from a "pre-modern" (sagas, oral traditions, etc.) to "modern" literary form hinged on a re-categorization of literary genres in combination with the development of a new literary format – the novel (McKeon 1987). The development of the latter was in response to massive changes in the wider society at the time. The re-categorization of literary forms may have been one example of those wider social changes playing out in a particular sphere – literature. The argument, in brief, is that at the time of the development of the novel in Europe, Europe itself was undergoing massive changes in terms of how Europeans understood the world (McKeon 1987). Europe was in the midst of changing from what was a religious and alchemic understanding of how the world worked to a scientific model. New concepts, such as the nation, were forcing people to reconsider who they were and how they fit into the wider world. In literature, these social changes surrounded questions of "truth," particularly in terms of narrative depiction and representations of "the truth," and questions of "virtue," the relations between social order and its members. Issues of authority, who tells the story, who sets the agenda link these two questions and the establishment of how these issues are to be depicted stylistically. The changes in belief, thought, and society (feudal to democratic, religious to secular) led to new forms of legitimization (Cascardi 1992: 43). The feudal/religious model of legitimacy was that there were certain "natural" voices of authority – the king and God respectively. What those voices said was by the very nature of who said it the truth. The shift to a democratic/secular model required new models of authority. One way of establishing authority/truth was through reason and the claim to be able to theorize or articulate the world from a purely objective, third person point of view (a scientific perspective). In terms of literature, new narrative forms resulted from this shift, marked by a new way of establishing the authority of the text, and thereby that of the author, with the reader (McKeon 1987; Bracht Branham 1995). What happened is that the author, in order to establish authority, became involved in the structuring of the story by choosing whose point of view to promote and at what point in time, a kind of Eye-of-God third person narrative. The author had to become, at least to some extent in the act of writing, a character or internal lecturer/narrator in his or her own work.

Film theorists have also attempted to pin down the window of time where "premodern" and "modern" cinema parted ways (e.g. Gunning 1991, 1995; or Abel 1996, 1999, 2006). To an extent paralleling the debates within literary theory aforementioned, one view is that the "modern" cinema began with the privileging the narrative function. The "classic" period of Hollywood (and the director D. W. Griffith in particular) was when cinema began in earnest telling stories and when filmic elements became subordinate to the narrative (see Parkinson 1995 for examples of this argument). There are problems with this idea, the move from "early" (pre-modern) to "modern" cinema was much more processual and was, as we saw in Chapter 2 and as will be discussed in more detail in the following chapter, inherently bound up with the economics of film distribution and exhibition (see, for instance, Abel 1999). Further, the increasing sophistication of cinematic equipment and techniques contributed to, if not enabled, the switch from the often static-tableaux-like "spectacle," and to the development of the internalized lecturer (as we saw with the novel) so necessary to narrative cinema. Very important for the success of this development was the introduction of various cinematic conventions, such as point of view (POV) shots, eye-line matches, the 180° rule,[7] and close-ups. In other words, conventions were established eliciting, constructing, and manifesting subjectivity, notably in terms of positioning the narrator. However, these developments also positioned an audience differently, engaging the viewer in actively stitching together the elements of the film into a coherent whole. Through the subjective portrayal of characters, actions, and events, the audience both gained understanding of these elements and became involved in the *diegesis* (the world within the film, including elements not necessarily seen on screen) itself.

The above may seem to be a very esoteric argument, but it is actually quite important for understanding how film works. The claim that literature or the cinema are not value-free entities, that they articulate ideological positions, has been made by several other theoretical positions (Marxism, structuralism, actually almost any of the theories interested in how film works), but aside from psychoanalysis-derived theories, they do not *explain* how authors or filmmakers establish the ability to serve as the transmitters of ideology. They do not explain the mechanics by which audiences/readers are persuaded to believe what they are being told. These ideas also make the relatively simple ideas of interpellation and "the subject" (and that relationship vis-à-vis the cinema) a lot more complex. In this regard, the work of Bakhtin is particularly interesting.

Mikhail Bakhtin (1895–1975) was a Russian philosopher and literary critic. His works have inspired theoretical perspectives as diverse as those of neo-Marxists, structuralists, and semioticians (Lodge 1990; Bracht Branham 1995). Although he arrived somewhat late on the scene (many of his works were only published after

Figure 2.6   Stall selling Nigerian VCDs at the multicultural Kwakoe festival in the Bijlmermeer district of Amsterdam, the Netherlands. Photograph by Paul Keller 2006.

Case Study: Globalized Cinemas – Bollywood, Anime, and Nigerian Video Films

As an illustration of the kinds of *dialogism* and *context* that Bakhtin proposes, the global nature of film acts as an intriguing example. When discussing globalization, the perception tends to be that the flow is one way, i.e. from the West to the "Rest." As the case study of Kurosawa in particular illustrates, that perception is not accurate. In this case study, three globalized cinemas of very different scale and impact demonstrate in more detail the interconnection of both the world in general and the film industry in particular.

Bollywood – popular Hindu language Indian cinema is, depending on the definition used, the largest cinema industry in the world. In 2002, Bollywood outsold Hollywood by over a billion cinema tickets worldwide – though Hollywood's total revenue was almost $50 billion more. The term Bollywood is often used to refer to the whole of Indian cinema, but Bollywood is only a part of the Indian film industry. Bollywood films are usually musicals, containing song-and-dance numbers woven into the script (Gokulsing and Dissanayake 2004: 31). Something notable to a Western viewer is that the song-and-dance routines in Indian films often shift location unrealistically, and costume changes can occur between verses of a song. The close relationship between music and cinema can extend into the public sphere, as the success of a particular film often depends on its musical numbers, and a film's music is often released before the movie to help create a "buzz" and increase the audience. Bollywood plots are typically melodramatic and feature formulaic ingredients such as star-crossed lovers, angry parents, conniving villains, and family ties. Indeed, one of the reasons for the global success of Bollywood-style films is that they are so readily understood cross-culturally (Gokulsing and Dissanayake 2004: 28–31). It does not take much exposure to "get" a Bollywood film. The "bad" guys look and act in a particular way, for instance, and the storylines focus on almost formulaic components (much like Propp's analysis of folktales discussed earlier in this chapter). By Hollywood standards, the films are long, often being three hours or more. A large Indian diaspora (especially in English-speaking countries) throughout the world, combined with the previously mentioned formulaic almost universally intelligible storylines, has meant a global market for Bollywood films. Bollywood films have become multi-million dollar productions, with the most expensive productions costing up to $10 million. Sequences shot overseas have proved a real box office draw, so Bollywood films are increasingly shot in the United States, the United Kingdom, continental Europe, and elsewhere. Bollywood is not only a fundamental part of the popular culture of India, but also of the rest of South Asia, the Middle East, parts of Africa, parts of Southeast Asia, and among the South Asian diaspora worldwide (Gokulsing and Dissanayake 2004: 2–6). Bollywood cinema has been influential in the development of the Nigerian and Ghanaian video film industries discussed later in this case study. Bollywood has also spoken back to the West in a dialogic move, at the very least through making the Western film industries aware of the power of Indian popular cinema. More directly, the Oscar-winning *Slumdog Millionaire* (Boyle and Tandan 2008) perhaps speaks most eloquently of the impact that Bollywood has begun to have on other cinema industries, including Hollywood. The one-way traffic of Hollywood blockbusters moving out to colonize movie theatres across the globe is still happening, but there is a movement back, a dialogue rather than the monologue that has come to be expected.

Anime is by far the best-known form of Japanese cinema for non-specialist film-goers in the West. People who have never heard of Ozu, Mizoguchi, or Kurosawa have heard of *Akira* (Otomo 1988). Indeed, the phenomenal commercial and critical success of *Akira* in Western markets (McDonald 2006: 176) is sometimes credited with reinvigorating *manga* (Japanese comics) and *anime* outside of Japan, and setting the tone for the more sophisticated *anime* that was produced in the 1990s and 2000s. *Anime* is a Japanese abbreviation for animation, though in the West it refers to Japanese animation. With roots as far back as the 1920s, for financial and other reasons animation in Japan was regarded as more of a legitimate alternative to live-action cinema than in the West (see, for instance, Richie 2005: 251–8). Japanese animation developed some very specific aesthetic features that largely remain to this day. The person who is credited with having the most input on that aesthetic is the "father" of *anime*, Osamu Tezuka (Richie 2005: 254). Influenced by the widely available and successful Disney animations, such as *Snow White* (director uncredited 1937), and animated series like *Betty Boop*, Tezuka created much of the look and many of the genres of contemporary anime. For instance, the exaggerated eyes of anime characters, one of the most noticeable aesthetic differences, were drawn from characters like Betty Boop and Bambi. Tezuka realized that overly large eyes allow much more expression to be shown by characters than "normal" sized eyes do. Aside from some other stylistic conventions such as exaggerated facial expressions and sweat beads, the *mise en scène* in *anime* is much more important than in much Western animation, where it can be quite static – more like a theatre stage. Anime has had a Western market since the 1960s, the *Astro Boy* television series was shown on NBC in the USA, for instance. However, it grew as a major cultural export during the 1980s and 1990s. The anime market for the United States is over $4 billion. Anime has been even more of a commercial success in Asia, Europe, and Latin America, where anime has become even more popular. That success of anime has also led to a cultural impact, with anime-inspired aesthetics and other conventions entering into not only Western animation, but live action cinema as well. An instance of this borrowing is the use of an anime staple – fly-around shots (where during an action scene the camera completely circles the actor or actors) – as used several times in *The Matrix* (Cousins 2004: 459–60). The 2008 Wachowski and Wachowski film *Speed Racer* –based on the classic anime of the same name, which was shown on American television in 1967–1968 – most clearly shows the influence of the anime aesthetic, though other animated cartoons and feature films (Tarantino's *Kill Bill* films from 2003 and 2004 spring immediately to mind) have also adopted some elements of that aesthetic. Arguably the most influential and best-known anime film was *Akira* (Otomo 1988), which was a commercial success in Western markets and pushed awareness of anime outside of its traditional young male market. *Akira* also influenced a generation of anime that was to follow by employing high quality production values, such as lip-syncing dialogue to the movements of the character's mouths and its themes of cyberpunk, social awareness, juvenile delinquency, and alienation and corruption struck a nerve with viewers around the world (McDonald 2006: 176). Aspects and aesthetic elements from *Akira* show up in many, sometimes unexpected, American films and television productions. An episode of *South Park* "Trapper Keeper" employs a *Terminator* (Cameron 1984) storyline, where Eric is absorbed by a computer to create a monster similar to the one in *Akira*. The animated television series *Batman Beyond* employs many aesthetics from *Akira*, notably the motorcycles that feature heavily in the series. We have already seen with the discussion of Kurosawa, that Japanese cinema has had a significant impact on global cinema. Perhaps even more pervasively anime has become a global cinema in its own right as well as influencing other cinemas.

A global cinema of another order entirely is the *Nigerian video film*. As will be discussed in Chapter 3, for various reasons film production took much longer to come about in the former British colonies in Africa than in other British colonies (Diawara 1992: 2–11). Newsreels and documentary films were being produced, principally as a legacy of the colonial period (i.e. propaganda films), but next to nothing in the way of a feature film industry, though there were (until recently) unsuccessful attempts in Ghana and Nigeria (Diawara 1992: 5–8). When local production did get underway, there was a severe lack of resources at all levels. There was little in the way of funding, and equipment was unavailable, financially unattainable, or obsolete. Film developing, for instance, was usually done in the UK at an unsustainable cost. Attempts at producing feature film typically came about as part of an intellectual nationalist agenda to limit cultural domination from the USA and Europe, as well as Bollywood, while promoting local cultural values, mores, and art forms. For instance, in Nigeria there is a history of producing films based upon Yoruba (one of the largest ethnic groups in the country) theatre. These films seldom found a wide public audience outside of the targeted ethnic group, but ensured that film production remained operating at some level (Diawara 1992: 116–27). In the early 1990s a new method of making films came into being. Foregoing the expensive celluloid film route, filmmakers began exploiting a cheaper medium – videocassettes (Adesanya 2000: 41). The video filmmakers trimmed budgets in other ways as well: sets, lighting, and other aspects of production were kept to shoestring level; the same actors would appear over and over in the titles; special effects were rudimentary; and the video films were very, very long, maximizing the costs of filming for each video film. The stories are usually local myths or legends, or at the very least incorporated local myths and legends, melodramas, morality and cultural value plays, or some combination of all of them (Haynes and Okome 2000). The video films make few concessions to viewers who are not knowledgeable about the stories or with local storytelling conventions. In fact, to the uninitiated watching one of these films can feel like you have begun watching an intricate soap opera without anyone to explain who any of the characters are. I would struggle to provide a synopsis of a film like *Wedlock of the Gods* (Arase 2007). The back cover provides the following road map for the 175-minute film: "Kofi the wrestler saved his Kingdom and the Prince from a disgrace that was about to befall them. The king asked him to make any request of his choice and the Prince made friends with him for his bravery. On one of Kofi's visit to the Prince he was attacked and Sarpoma the girl with the hunched back who was banished from the village with her mother years ago saved him. Now he must save her in return for the first time he must make his request known to the King. Will the King fulfill his promise and what happens after that?" (*Wedlock of the Gods* DVD back cover 2007) What happens after that is about 140 minutes of the story. Initially, Nigerian video films were produced on miniscule budgets with outdated or insufficient equipment and the video films are typically of poor quality, though more recent films like *Wedlock of the Gods* have comparatively high production values. They are also extremely popular with wide distribution (not always legal) in Nigeria and elsewhere. Within three years, video filmmakers had produced over 450 official titles, not to mention unknown quantities of unofficial video films (Adesanya 2000: 41). The format has spread to Ghana (*Wedlock of the Gods* is actually a Ghanaian film) and by the time you read this may have spread to other parts of Africa, as the commercial success of this type of filmmaking has been noted elsewhere, and even established directors are questioning whether this model of filmmaking is better suited to the African context. While the low costs at both ends of the cinema chain, making and buying, no doubt play a large role in the international success of these video films, the large numbers of Nigerians living in the UK and the USA have provided a ready market. Cheaply and readily accessible (they are sold by street vendors in New York for instance), these video films provide expatriate Nigerians (and to an extent other West Africans) with familiar and/or nostalgic glimpses of home. By accessing new (at the time) media technologies Nigerian video filmmakers have been able to sidestep state interference, socio-political expectations for and of "Third World" cinema, and produce culturally consistent films for an increasingly global audience (Haynes 2000b: 4–9). Indeed, the Nigerian video film industry has become successful enough that is being referred to as *Nollywood*. To date, this globalized cinema has not made much impact upon Western cinemas, but is engaged dialogically with other non-Western cinemas such as Francophone African cinemas (discussed in a later case study) and Bollywood. To return to the other element of Bakhtin's theories, understanding the *context* of the Nigerian video film also aids us in comprehending the success and influence of this particular, *seemingly unlikely*, cinema industry. We will also return to this point in a later case study.

his death) the influence of Bakhtin on literature studies cannot be overestimated. Bakhtin's ideas of *dialogism* – that literature is not a one-way monologue by the author, but exists in a dialogue with other works of literature, other authors, and with the audience (Holquist 1990; Lodge 1990), and of the value of understanding the spatial and temporal specifics (i.e. contexts) of the literary "act," or as we shall see – the film "act," have been extremely productive analytic tools. In particular two aspects of Bakhtin's theories have proven useful. First, is that he allows space for those aspects outside of what is normally considered as germane to analyzing a novel (context in other words). The second is that for Bakhtin literature is not a straightforward imposition of ideology, but is actually a site of communication and contest between dominant and dominated subject positions. Keeping these thoughts in mind, in the next chapter the discussion will turn to theories of the cinema that focus upon these two points, namely national cinema and third cinema, as well as looking at the issue of context.

FILM THEORY

There are many other film theories not mentioned so far. Since the 1970s, feminist (in which Mulvey's work discussed above is normally located) and queer theories (see, for instance, Ruby Rich 1998) have put the *politics of representation* front and center. Recent work in both of these arenas has pushed our understandings of how different groups of people are represented in cinema, make sense of those representations, and how that intersects with the "viewing pleasure" of audiences, including by those who are neither female nor gay. Other theoretical models foreground the roles, both pro and con, played by the cinema apparatus. Apparatus theory posits that the very tools of the cinema affect how we understand the cinema (Baudry 1985, 1986; Comolli 1985). The mechanical implements of the cinema thus become ideologically "loaded." This latter idea had been influential in discussions of non-Western cinemas – that not only the "grammar" (the codes and conventions) of filmmaking is inherently Western, but so too are the actual machines (Lapsley and Westlake 1988: 79–81). The implication is that there may always be a question of how "Western" non-Western cinema will be, a point that will also be returned to in the next chapter. Cognitive and phenomenological approaches attempt to understand how film works in terms of actual brain processes and as a bodily mediated and understood experience respectively. Most of these theoretical standpoints overlap with other theoretical approaches, for instance feminist and apparatus film theories have been combined with psychoanalytic theories, as is the case with Mulvey's work. Today, it is much more usual that film theorists use more than one theoretical model to attempt to make sense of the cinema. Part of the

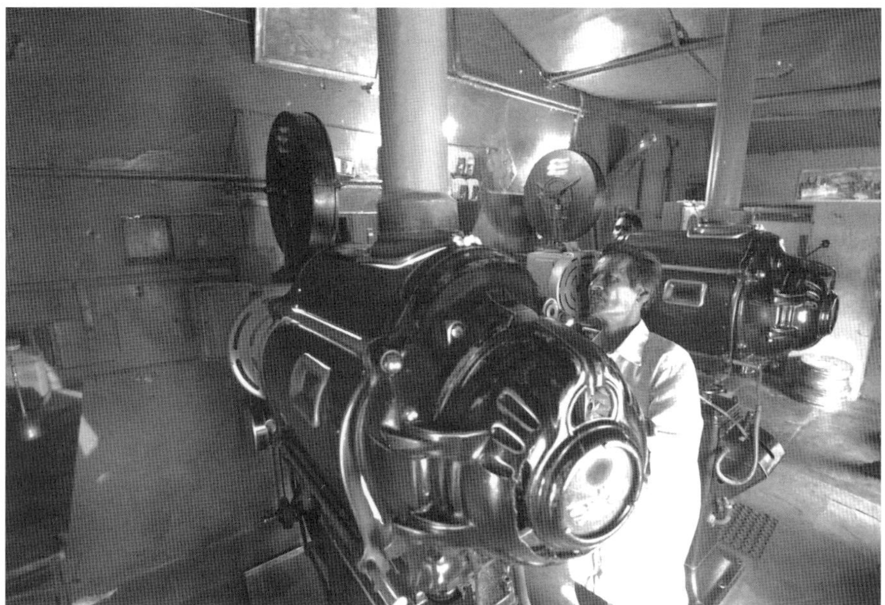

Figure 2.7   Projectionist checking the equipment at the Elgin
Talkies movie theatre (built in 1896) Bangalore, India. The
equipment is from the 1930s. Photograph by Paul Keller 2008.

reason for that, and one of the main problems with several of the theories presented above, such as psychoanalysis, semiotics, structuralism, and Marxism, is that they tended to be totalizing quests for universal truths. These "Grand Theories," having been questioned from both within and outside the discipline (Nichols 2000), have begun to be employed in more nuanced forms. The tendency mentioned above of the proponents of these theories to engage more in incestuous debates than with the products of cinema itself may have exacerbated both the split between theory and practice and for these theories to be challenged by newer, less abstract, theories.

The employment of theoretical models from outside film itself, such as with literary theory, has made valuable contributions to film theory. The semiotics of Peirce, which is different from Metz's semiotics, has been turned to by many studying various symbolic media such as the cinema, in particular his idea of indexical – the level of real connection between a symbol (or sign) and the viewer – has led to some interesting work that adds to our understanding of how film works (Erhat 2005). Not mentioned above, but part of the literary theory tradition as well as film studies, the ideas of Foucault on power and agency (1972, 1974), Barthes on the role of the author/auteur (1977), and Derrida on deconstructing the text for meaning (1976) have added new levels of analysis. Voices such as those of Gunning (2000), Crary (1990), or Willemen (1995) have refined the way we conceive of issues such as spectatorship and subjectivity. Adding Gramsci's (1973) theories on *hegemony* (the use of various intellectual and moral means by the ruling class to create consent within the subordinate classes regarding their place in society etc., rather than the use of force per se to control people) to classic Marxism by British cultural studies scholars in particular, has created a more sophisticated way of understanding the political economy of the cinema, the national and social contests that cinema is produced and viewed in, and how this is used and understood by both the rulers and the ruled. As such, the historic focus of film theory upon the content of the cinema is at once enlightening and limiting. In terms of the latter, this is most clearly the case when film theory is employed outside of the Western milieu. Investigations of non-Hollywood and non-European cinema, most especially by non-Western film theorists, have raised serious questions about the applicability of supposedly "universal" theories, which are in fact Western based and oriented, to non-Western cinemas (Ukadike 1994; Bakari 2000). Particularly in the case of the latter, there have been appeals for, and attempts at, a more sophisticated knowledge of the contexts of production, be that national, economic, or social/cultural. More recent work on American cinema has demonstrated how important understanding the wider context in which a film is made and viewed is (Ukadike 1994; Vasudevan 2000; Bakari 2000). Finally, an issue with classic film theory is that for the most part it fails to truly engage with one the most important elements of the cinema – the audience (Vasudevan 2000; Gokulsing and Dissanayake 2004). While the audience shows up in many different ways in the above-mentioned models, rarely are real people being discussed. For many scholars that situation is insufficient (as we will see in Chapter 4), and they have taken steps to rectify that problem and find out what real people make of cinema. In the next chapters we will look more closely at national and third cinema, and audience studies, respectively.

SUGGESTED FURTHER READING

GENERAL AND EUROPE/AMERICA

Andrew, J. D. (1976) *The Major Film Theories: An Introduction*, New York: Oxford University Press.

Giannetti, L. (1990) *Understanding Movies,* Englewood Cliffs, NJ: Prentice Hall.

Lapsley, R. and Westlake, M. (1988) *Film Theory: An Introduction*, Manchester: Manchester University Press.

Mast, G and Cohen, M. (1979) *Film Theory and Criticism: Introductory Readings*, New York and Oxford: Oxford University Press.

INDIA[8]

Dwyer, R. and Patal, D. (2002) *Cinema India: The Visual Culture of Hindi Film,* New Brunswick, NJ: Rutgers University Press.

Gokulsing K. M. and Dissanayake, W. (2004) *Indian Popular Cinema: A Narrative of Cultural Change (Revised Edition)*, Sterling, VA: Trentham Books.

Vasudevan, R. (ed.), (2000) *Making Meaning in Indian Cinema,* New York: Oxford University Press.

JAPAN

McDonald, K. (2006) *Reading a Japanese Film: Cinema in Context,* Honolulu: University of Hawai'i Press.

Burch, N. (1979) *To the Distant Observer: Form and Meaning in Japanese Cinema,* Berkeley: University of California Press.

Richie, D. (2005) *A Hundred Years of Japanese Film: A Concise History, with a Selective Guide to DVDs and Videos,* New York: Kodansha International.

3 CONTEXT OF PRODUCTION, DISTRIBUTION, AND EXHIBITION

Figure 3.1   Cinema in Marrakesh, Morocco. Photograph by Mathias Klang 2008.

On December 12, 1995, two days before I received the Samburu entourage at the airport, I was summoned to a meeting with Michael Douglas at his rented house near the set. The meeting involved some initial Swahili coaching for Scene 98, as well as a discussion of his artistic vision for the Remington/Maasai arrival scene [...] Michael wanted to insert a call-and-response sequence, wherein he would call out something to the hidden warriors who would then doubly shock the audience with their sudden appearance and an audible response "something like a battle cry." So he asked me to propose a phrase in Swahili for him to call out and something for the warriors to call back in response. I asked him for time to consult with the Samburu once they arrived in the country. The invention of tradition does not come easy to an anthropologist.

Askew, *Striking Samburu and a Mad Cow: Adventures in Anthropollywood*

INTRODUCTION

In this chapter we turn from approaches that focus on content – particular films and filmmakers – to approaches that try to put those films/makers into wider contexts. As we will see in this chapter, this was sometimes taken to the extent of excluding the content of the films. Although less numerous than studies of the context of viewing (though this is changing within film studies), which will be discussed in the following chapter, studies that analyze the context of fiction film production, distribution, and exhibition exist and provide useful and original insight into understanding the cinema. Although the idea of understanding the context in which films are produced goes back at least to Kracauer and the Frankfurt School, the two main approaches within film theory to analyzing and understanding that wider context are those of national cinema and third cinema. All of these approaches share an interest in the ideological aspect of the cinema.

Often overlooked in the analyses of production is the role that distribution and exhibition have played within the cinema. This arena brings in political economies of cinema industries and in many cases also involves nationalist agendas (for instance, detrimental duties placed upon the import of films from other countries in order to protect national film production). Of current interest is that independent and amateur filmmakers have, with varying degrees of success, circumvented the politics and economics of film distribution and exhibition through non-official channels such as the Internet and independent film festivals. As we shall see, for most within these paradigms, the definition of cinema would tend to be more related to the cinema as an industry – the whole sphere of production rather than, and sometimes directly opposed to, particular films (content).

There have been attempts to understand the cultural or social context of fiction film production more specifically, for instance Powdermaker (2002), Jarvie (1987), Babb (1981) and Ukadike (1994) have all made this claim for both cinema in general as well as non-Western cinemas more specifically. Chow (1995) and Shohat and Stam (1994) in particular have made appeals for a more sophisticated knowledge of the socio-cultural contexts of film production. Indeed, Chow specifically calls for an anthropology of the cinema (1995). This chapter will delve into just what an anthropology of the cinema might entail and what it would have to offer, particularly but not only in relation to non-Western cinemas.

CONTEXT OF PRODUCTION

As has been mentioned, many traditional approaches to cinema do not pay much attention to the context in which the cinema is produced, much less the contexts of exhibition or distribution. While this is changing with several intriguing books published recently, such as Grieveson (2004), King (2008), or Whissel (2008), Abel (1999), for instance, writes on the only time, from 1900 to 1910, when films from a foreign country, France, dominated the American market. During the early cinema period, Pathé-Frère film productions in particular so dominated the American market that concerted efforts were taken by various agencies to "unforeignize" American cinemas. While, on one hand, these French imports were making the cinema attendance popular, there were also fears, linked to contemporary unease over immigration, that American audiences were in danger of assimilating to a foreign culture. Abel argues that one of the ways that the French influence was countered was by the expansion of a particularly American film genre – the western. Approaches like those mentioned notwithstanding, some of the historical neglect of context within film studies may be due to the history of looking at films as art and the links between auteur theory and the academicization of film theory. However, even the more ideologically oriented approaches often overlook these crucial factors in understanding the cinema. Of the perspectives that do seek to analyze the contexts in which film is made, the Frankfurt School, communication studies, and, within film studies itself, national cinema and third cinema have historically been the main approaches.

THE FRANKFURT SCHOOL

As the Frankfurt School was discussed in more depth in Chapter 2, this section will be more in the way of a review. The Frankfurt School refers both literally to a particular group of Marxist-influenced theorists, such as Adorno and Horkheimer, operating out of the University of Frankfurt, and to those theorists influenced by the actual school of theorists (O'Sullivan et al. 1994: 123). While the scholars of the Frankfurt School were not themselves film theorists per se, their ideas have been very influential in different forms of film studies. Perhaps the most important of these is that media, such as film, are not "value free" – that film, television, etc. are not created in a political vacuum. Indeed, from the 1920s through to contemporary

Figure 3.2 Partially hand drawn poster advertising Jean-Claude Van Damme in JCVD (El Mechri 2008) – Nagoya. Japan. Photograph by Ryuhei Okada 2009.

communications or media studies and cultural studies approaches, the argument that media are not only not value free, but are deeply implicated in promoting the agendas of the ruling groups to the wider public has been an enduring thread (O'Sullivan et al. 1994: 124; Barker 2000: 44–5). As was mentioned in Chapter 2, and will be returned to again in more detail in Chapter 4, this understanding of cinema's ideological role vis-à-vis a "mass audience," who were understood as passive receptors of this ideological message, set up an opposition that was to develop with approaches that argued for a more active role for audiences. For many theorists who fall within a Marxist or Frankfurt School orientation, only oppositional art, such as avant-garde movements, are outside of the ideology apparatus. These ideas, and in particular the latter, were crucial to the development of the *Cahiers du cinéma* and neo-realist movements as well as to film theories that analyze the contexts in which cinema takes place, perhaps most especially third cinema.

COMMUNICATION STUDIES

Communication studies (media or media and communication studies in the UK) is another of the approaches influenced by the ideas of the Frankfurt School. While film is a medium of communication, generally film studies is regarded as separate from communication studies. Although there are certainly overlaps between the two disciplines, communication studies have typically been more closely linked with fields such as journalism. Communication studies was one of the first academic disciplines that took the context in which media were being produced as important, as opposed to analyzing particular content of that medium (although that is also an important aspect of what communications scholars study). Historically, there have been some differences between various national varieties of communication studies, with a more strictly Frankfurt School approach in continental European countries, a focus on media specifically and an overlap with cultural studies (discussed in the next chapter) in the UK, and a "sociological" approach in the USA. At present there are as many similarities in these three approaches as there are differences, with certain key themes appearing in all three traditions: media content analysis, mass communication and journalism, political economy, and audience studies (which we will look at in the next chapter) being among the most important of these shared interests.

Although I have noted national traditions within communication studies, there have also been some historical similarities in how "communication" was understood and studied across those traditions. The earliest model of communication was the *Transmission Model* (sometimes also referred to as the *Hypodermic Needle Model*), which understood communication to be a mechanical process in which transmission directly leads to reception (O'Sullivan et al. 1994: 137). The relative importance of the three components of media and communication (producer/message, medium, audience) also follows, with the most important role being the producer/content, and audience having the least important role. The early *propaganda* and *media effects* studies (which were exactly what the terms suggest) in the USA, and Frankfurt School and other Marxist-influenced theories of communication/media shared this model (O'Sullivan et al. 1994: 100–1, 137). Within the Transmission Model, the content and the producers of that content are of primary importance. So, for instance, to study the media effects of violence using the Transmission Model, it would be

Figure 3.3   Inside the Elgin Talkies cinema hall (built in
1896) Shivaji Road in Shivaji Nagar district of Bangalore,
India. Photograph by Paul Keller 2008.

examples of violence in either a particular medium or across various media, as well
as rates of depictions and levels of severity of depiction, that would be studied. These
analyses would normally be compared to rates of violence in wider society at some
stage. There are advantages and disadvantages to this model – and it is still employed
and influential. Indian film critics and scholars who promote artistic cinema versus
popular cinema often fall into this model, arguing that the mass Indian audience
has a pre-modern and irrational outlook, which is easily swayed by the ideological
messages embedded in Indian popular cinema. Artistic cinema on the other hand
will lead to a more rational and enlightened audience (see, for instance, Das Gupta
1991). The main advantage is that in certain usages it foregrounds the role of media
producers, who can easily go unexamined in other forms of analyses. One of the
main disadvantages is that users of this model can overlook or diminish the roles of
both the particular media in question and the audience.

Marshall McLuhan's famous "the medium is the message" argument was at
least partially in response to the Transmission Model – highlighting the role that

technology and the particular media forms have beyond or apart from the content they carry. While McLuhan was not the only theorist working in this arena, he is probably the most famous. The argument that proponents of the *Technology Model* (for want of a better term) of communications put forth is that the medium actually has *more* impact upon people's perceptions than does the message itself (O'Sullivan et al. 1994: 176–7). As an example, McLuhan argues that the print medium (along with earlier media such as the alphabet) was one of the finishing touches in turning humans from primarily sound-oriented beings to primarily visually oriented beings. Print media changed humans' perceptions and in turn changed our societies – we begin to get more information through visual means, so our society begins to privilege visual media, which leads to more visual media in the society, and hence we get even more information through visual means, and so on in a mutually reinforcing cycle. The message itself can only be understood if the message, the medium, and the environment in which the message is being consumed are analyzed together. To use the previous example of violence, the actual incidences of violence, the rate of violence, etc. are immaterial without understanding the actual media the depictions are happening on and the context in which they are occurring. Violence in cinema is not going to affect viewers, but cinema viewing – *no matter the content* – will. The argument for understanding the role and/or effects of the specific medium on wider society is another that has been very influential not only in communication studies, but in other disciplines as well. For instance, the model has been used to try to understand the rise of the modern nation-state via new media of communication such as printing (Anderson 1991).

Another model within communication studies that was at least partially a response to the Transmission Model was to look at how audiences actually make sense of media. Sometimes referred to as the *Use and Gratification Model* (O'Sullivan et al. 1994: 325–7), this model made connections between actual audiences and how they combine the messages of the programs they watch into their social experiences in ways that inform their understandings of both – each influence and validate the other. As the Uses and Gratification Model is a forerunner of reception/audience studies, I will discuss it in more depth in the next chapter. For our purposes here, in the framework of these models, the particular approaches of communication and media studies developed.

From quite early, communications and media studies have been closely related to politics (propaganda theory) and political economy (the Frankfurt School). Particularly in the last quarter century, political economy has played a major role in media studies literature, particularly looking at how the corporate ownership of media production and distribution affects society. Linked to this are various types of *policy studies* that focus on government policy and their effects on the various media (e.g. Grenfell 1979). This arena of communication studies also puts much emphasis on understanding the effects of government policy on exhibition and distribution as well as production – so we will return to this facet later in the chapter. It is also this arena of communication studies that tends to focus upon non-Western media. John Lent, for instance, has written on many aspects of mass media in Asia, and especially on the development of cinema industries throughout Asia (Lent 1990). His work tends to fit well within the policy studies paradigm, which has been outlined already, and the national cinema approach that follows. Again, something that is soon apparent is that this approach pays less attention to particular films or filmmakers and more to matters such as the role of government agencies in film distribution and censorship. For instance, in discussing the development of cinema in Indonesia, Lent stresses some of the problems that the industry faced, such as the use of cinema for propaganda purposes by the Japanese Occupation government and by the Sukarno regime in the 1950s and 1960s (Lent 1990: 202). Lent does indeed mention historically important films such as *Pareh* (Balink and Franken 1936) and *Moonlight* (Balink 1938),[1] but does not analyze the films beyond their historical importance or financial success. As an example of this type of approach:

Figure 3.4   Cinema in Gunung Sitoli, Nias Island, Indonesia.
Photograph by Frank van den Berge/World Picture Service
2006.

> [w]ith borrowed money and very basic knowledge of film gleaned from books, Albert Balink, a journalist of Dutch-Indonesian descent collaborated with the Wongs [Chinese-Indonesian businessmen important to early Indonesian film production] to make *Pareh*. With the help of the Dutch documentary maker, Mannus Franken, Balink produced a meticulously detailed and costly movie which attracted a large audience but sent Balink and the Wongs into bankruptcy. *Pareh* attempted to do more than make money; it hoped to show Indonesian culture (Lent 1990: 203).

The Indonesian case study is representative of this approach.

Case Study: Indonesia Film/Government Ties

While some Southeast Asian governments chose not to overtly employ the cinema as a propaganda tool (see, for instance, Grenfell 1979), successive Indonesian governments were intensely implicated in various aspects of the Indonesian film industry.[2] This involvement took different forms at different points in history, but the upshot of most of them was that Indonesian films in the 1950s through to the 1970s were much more than "just" entertainment.

Shortly after the end of the Second World War, Sukarno declared Indonesia's independence and was appointed president. A bitter armed and diplomatic struggle with their colonizer, The Netherlands, ended in December 1949, when the Dutch formally recognized Indonesian independence. However, the regime became increasingly authoritarian, promoting what Sukarno termed *Guided Democracy* (Sen 1994: 27–9). Importantly, Sukarno maintained power by balancing the military, Islamic groups, and the Communist Party of Indonesia (PKI). As the military became more powerful, the Communist Party and Sukarno became increasingly closer. The army countered an attempted coup by some junior military officers in 1965. PKI was blamed for the coup attempt and violent anti-Communist suppressions took place, and PKI was effectively destroyed (Sen 1994: 48–9). Somewhere between 500,000 and one million people were killed during this period. Sukarno had lost his main political allies, and the head of the military, General Suharto, was appointed president in March 1968 (Sen and Hill 2007: 2–5). Suharto's *New Order* was supported by the US government, largely as Suharto was anti-Communist and encouraged foreign investment. As with Sukarno's Guided Democracy, the New Order began to be accused of corruption and suppression of political opposition. This continued up until Suharto's resignation in 1998. These events in themselves would likely have had significant effects upon the Indonesian cinema industry, but the national and political context for Indonesian cinema is even more complex. The cinema was used by both governments for ideological purposes (Lent 1990; Sen 1994; Sen and Hill 2007). The effect of that usage on the industry has been more than significant.

In the 1950s and early 1960s the largest market for films produced in Malaya (what is now Malaysia and Singapore) was in Indonesia. A combination of similar language and culture, a true superstar in the Malay actor P. Ramlee, a relatively unrestricted film trade, and restrictive censorship laws in Indonesia meant that Malay films were very successful in Indonesia, to the detriment of the Indonesian film industry (Lent 1990: 205–6; Raja Ahmad Alauddin 1992). Much as the British colonial government had done earlier with American films, the Indonesian government began restricting the importation of foreign films in the late 1960s through tariffs and censorship (Lent 1990: 206–7; Raja Ahmad Alauddin 1992; Sen 1994: 21–5, 58–9). This move had the intended effect in that it preserved a massive market for the Indonesian film industry. It also, along with some other historical events such as the post-Independence separation of Malaysia and Singapore, led to the decline in the Malay film industry. This was not the extent of the Indonesian governments' involvement in the film industry, however.

Sukarno's regime had promoted an anti-imperialist and especially an anti-American discourse. Part of this discourse was that Indonesian society must actively fight against these evils (Lent 1990: 202), something that Sukarno claimed that the filmmakers of the period were not doing. When in 1957 a cinema promotion organization (PPFI), formed by two of the most prominent film producers in Indonesia (Usmar Ismail and Djamaluddin Malik), announced that its members would have to cease film production, the Communist Party used the opportunity to take action against the industry in general. The actions included labeling Usmar an American agent and a "prostitute" for making light entertainment films (Lent 1990: 202). Djamaluddin was imprisoned for two years and lost his production company. In the 1960s, the links between nationalism, anti-Americanism, and a fracturing of the coalition comprising Sukarno's government along ideological lines became a dangerous mix that cinema found itself right in the middle of (Lent 1990: 202–3). The political polarization that took place in Indonesia during the 1960s meant that almost any activity would take on political significance – and that had both risks and benefits. As an instance of this, something that domestic filmmakers had long sought was some form of protectionist policy towards foreign films in order to bolster their market. During the 1960s this came to mesh with the government's anti-American stance. As anti-Americanism increased, American films became a particular target (Sen 1990: 24–5, 32–6). Organizations such as PAPFIAS (the Committee for Action to Boycott the Imperialist Films of the United States of America) were formed and gained national prominence. PAPFIAS comprised several groups with links to PKI (the Communist Party), but others were film industry groups that were not officially affiliated with any political party. In a political climate where theatres showing American films led to violence (Sen 1994: 34), it may have seemed a good idea to be at the fore. However, months after the Sukarno government officially recognized PAPFIAS, the coup attempt changed the political landscape dramatically and within a couple of years most of those with any links to leftist organizations were dead, in prison, or had fled/were in hiding. In 1967, the new government's Department of Information issued a list of people in the cinema industry who were suspected of being involved in the coup. Several of these names were of industry members whose only connection to the left was through PAPFIAS (Sen 1994: 34).

This connection was only one of the ways in which the film landscape changed with the New Order. While the Sukarno era employed cinema in what was a fairly straightforward way to promote its own political ideologies, the New Order relationship to the cinema was less obvious, though no less powerful. The New Order used a powerful combination of institutions and regulations to promote their own agenda – to create as Sen and Hill put it a "national fiction" (2007: 137–8) of order. As mentioned above, the reprisals against the PKI were brutal and included in these reprisals were leftist cultural groups and organizations, several of which were involved in the cinema industry. While the physical reprisals were taking place, the new government was also fighting an ideological battle, and it was not just the people being replaced, but the thoughts and ideals as well. Once the physical purge had been successful, new policies and institutions were put in place to effect Suharto's national fiction (Sen and Hill 2007: 138–51). Cinema has at one and the same time one of the broadest potential appeals of any media and is also one of the more readily regulated (as many examples from this case study and in the main text illustrate). And while that control (or that appeal) is not limitless, it is still powerful when employed in conjunction with other coercive forces (such as literally rewriting history). The New Order government readily employed all of these sets of ideological tools. Regarding the cinema, these included new sets of protectionist policies (including tariffs and restrictions on foreign films, and the obligatory screening of at least two domestic films a month), censorship (including of unedited material during the shoot), an active state role in cinema production (government associated organizations such as PFN – the State Film Corporation, which in the 1980s began to produce big budget feature films that glorified the state), and the positioning of cinema under the control of the Ministry of Information (Sen 1994: 50–71; Sen and Hill 2007: 138–51). While the latter of these may seem fairly innocuous, it is arguably the most important of all. Although cinema was placed under the Ministry of Information during the last days of the Sukarno regime, it was the Suharto government that exploited that placement to the utmost. The placing of cinema under the Ministry of Information meant that it was treated as "mass media" rather than as an art form, and implicated the industry in state ideological and propaganda pursuits (Sen 1994: 50–1). Between these various institutions, Indonesian cinema during the 1970s and 1980s took on and replicated aspects of the New Order national fiction – particularly the recovery of order after the disorder of the Sukarno regime.

FILM STUDIES

National cinema, which is not a theory as such as much as it is a set of approaches investigating the relationship between the cinema product or filmmaker of a particular country and that country, as used within film studies has a couple of different meanings, one that is "soft" and the other "hard." The "soft" meaning is in reference to films of a particular country, often depending on a number of factors, such as the source of funding, the language/s spoken, or specific ethnic or cultural representations within the film, as in the Lent article on Indonesian cinema (1990).[3] The "soft" meaning is the one we will look at more closely first. The "hard" meaning refers to a set of theories that deal with and even promote the formation of cinematic traditions that seek to establish films with local/national form and content different to or even opposed to those of Hollywood. French New Wave and Italian neo-realism are discussed within this paradigm, but most of the more usual examples are from "Third World" countries. Latin American and African cinemas in particular are frequently discussed in terms of national cinema; however, as this usage overlaps with some definitions of third cinema, I will combine them in the discussion of third cinema.

The "soft" definition of national cinema encompasses many of the issues I wish to raise in this chapter – namely that cinema does not develop out of nowhere, but that it occurs in contexts. Issues of production, distribution, and exhibition are not the most frequently analyzed aspects of cinema – indeed Cousins (2004) states he will not deal with these issues in a 500+ page book. However, it is exactly in these arenas that national agendas and political economies become the most apparent. Various governments place controls on their respective cinema industries as well as on the products of other industries. Sometimes, this is done very overtly via rigid censorship codes, placing financial tariffs on films from other countries, and sponsoring local film production. The UK took this approach in the early twentieth century, both at home and in its colonies. For instance, American films were often censored or even banned, particularly by colonial officials. Censorship was also used to control nationalist sentiments in films produced in the colonies (Lent 1990: 236). The justification for banning the foreign films was that these films depicted whites, especially white women, in less than glorious manner. That in the 1920s American films dominated the cinemas both in the UK and in the British colonies (Jaikumar 2006: 5), combined with the point that it was typically American film being censored, suggests that there were indeed other rationales, as it would be British productions that replaced the banned American films. In 1927 the British government put in place The Cinematograph Films Act, or Quota Act (Vasey 1996). Initially aimed at protecting the domestic cinema industry, British film producers pushed for that protection to be extended to the rest of the empire in order to extend their market.

Figure 3.5   Facade of the colonial-era Elgin Talkies cinema
hall building (built in 1896) in Bangalore, India. Photograph
by Paul Keller 2008.

The British film producers got their way and the quota system was extended to
incorporate British Empire films. This seemed to aid Indian cinema interests, which
were in the process of becoming well established (the first Indian feature film was
Phalke's 1913 *Raja Harischandra*). However, to ensure that British film production
was not threatened by its own colonies, other measures were employed, for instance
raw film stock carried large tariffs. At home, these moves had the effect of promoting
the production of "quota quickies" (low budget and low quality films produced to
fulfill government regulations) rather than promoting the development of a British
film industry that could directly compete with Hollywood. Ironically, those measures
did create a film industry more successful than Hollywood; it just happened to be in
India (Jaikumar 2006). Much of the catalyst for the development of what we now
refer to as Bollywood lay in British colonial policies. However, these same policies
had less effect in creating a healthy film industry in other colonies (such as Malaysia)
and arguably the very opposite effect in yet other colonies (such as Nigeria). We will
return to this latter point later and in more detail in the case studies.

One of the problems with the national cinema approach is that it runs the risk of essentializing the films and filmmakers in question and omitting the international influences that most films and filmmakers were, and are, affected by. One of the classic examples is the mutual admiration of Akira Kurosawa and several makers of Hollywood westerns. Kurosawa was a fan of the westerns of John Ford in particular, and many of his films – such as *The Seven Samurai* (1954) – demonstrate elements of that appreciation. In turn, Kurosawa's films heavily influenced later westerns such as *The Magnificent Seven* (Sturges 1960), which was a remake of *The Seven Samurai* in a different milieu. Another problem that follows from this is that national cinema fails to address issues such as the formation of cinema industries under colonialism (Indian, Nigerian) or more contemporaneously, cinemas that transgress national boundaries (Palestinian, Kurdish). One form of cinema that has not been mentioned so far is that of *diasporic cinema* – cinema produced by diasporic filmmakers and predominately for diasporic audiences. Depending on the circumstances of the filmmaker, this form of cinema may also be known as *exile cinema* (Naficy 1993, 2001). The former category would include Indian émigré filmmakers such as Mira Nair (*Monsoon Wedding*, 2001) or Deepa Mehta (*Fire*, 1996); the latter would include films made by Iranian exiles in the USA. The situation of Indian-born Canadian film director and screenwriter Deepa Mehta exemplifies why films defined as exile or diasporic cinema in reality do not easily fit into neat categories. Her body of work focuses on the Indian community and the Indian diaspora, but her film *Fire* was met with hostility in India, including attacks on cinemas that exhibited the film.[4] *Fire* is set in contemporary Delhi, India, in the household of a family that runs a fast food and video business. The main characters are two daughters-in-law, Sita and Radha, who both joined the family through arranged marriages. Both couples are unhappy and the two women turn to each other, eventually becoming lovers. Radha's husband Ashok discovers them in bed together. Sita leaves, while Radha, who wishes to explain matters to Ashok stays behind. In the confrontation that follows, Radha's *sari* catches fire from the kitchen stove and Ashok abandons her in flames. In the final scene, the two women are reunited. *Fire* was the first "Indian" film to show homosexual relations explicitly. After its release in India, right-wing Hindu groups staged several violent protests, setting off a flurry of public dialogue around issues such as homosexuality and freedom of speech.

THIRD CINEMA

Taking the ideas of the context of production and national cinema much further than anything before it was *third cinema*. The term "third cinema" comes from the manifesto "Towards a Third Cinema," by Argentine filmmakers Fernando Solanas and Octavio Getino, published in 1969 (Solanas and Getino 1976). Third cinema was a film movement – a set of ideals, films, and filmmakers – of the 1960s and 1970s. Briefly, what third cinema proponents argued was that the state of play for cinema, throughout the world, was thus:

> [u]ntil recently, film had been synonymous with spectacle or entertainment: in a word, it was one more consumer good. At best, films succeeded in bearing witness to the decay of bourgeois values and testifying to social injustice. As a rule, films only dealt with effect, never with cause; it was cinema of mystification or anti-historicism. It was surplus value cinema. Caught up in these conditions, films, the most valuable tool of communication of our times, were destined to satisfy only the ideological and economic interests of the owners of the film industry, the lords of the world film market, the great majority of whom were from the United States. (Solanas and Getino 1976: 44)

For the proponents of third cinema, the Hollywood, or "First Cinema," model of cinema (including the technology, the formal qualities of filmmaking, and even the spaces and places of exhibition) had become the universal (often unconscious) standard throughout the world. European art film, or "Second Cinema," which to greater or lesser degrees rejected Hollywood conventions, still centered on individual expression – the auteur. While a step away from Hollywood, second cinema was at best "testifying to social injustice" (Solanas and Getino 1976: 44). What was at stake for third cinema was to attempt to change this state of play, to actually create an oppositional cinema – one that contributed to or even led the beyond liberation and cultural revolution movements that were taking place both in the "Third World" and in Western countries as well.

To accomplish their goals, third cinema had to make films that mainstream society could not assimilate and explicitly create films to resist the status quo. Working from the documentary film model, third cinema films had not only to depict a reality, but also serve to transform that reality. Third cinema had to move beyond what its proponents argued were imperialist tools – national or regional boundaries – to create international, class-based, politicized films. Third cinema had to be a collective effort, rather than an individualist expression. The entire collective needed to be able to be skilled in all aspects of filmmaking in order to get beyond the specialization of skills and labor, which was and is such a feature of both capitalist labor in general and the Hollywood studio system in particular. For instance, people who did only sound or editing were rewarded relative to the "worth" of their specialization (Solanas and Getino 1976). Further, by controlling the means of distribution and exhibition, by only distributing to like-minded revolutionary groups and exhibiting in a clandestine manner, spectators could be transformed into active participants – an active protagonist in the struggle that the films were documenting.

Analyzing the legacy of third cinema is quite difficult. In many ways the theory was a part of the times – the widespread cultural, social, and even political ferment that was occurring in much of the world. Western nations such as France, USA, and Italy were experiencing student and labor unrest over a myriad of issues, as were some "Third World" countries like Mexico. Many European colonies were becoming independent – sometimes only through violent means. To that extent, third cinema was the right idea at the right time. However, third cinema's legacy in terms of its own ideology (transforming society) is debatable, and the third cinema discourse often took a derisive attitude to any Third World film industry or filmmaker that did not live up to its expectations of oppositional cinema (as, for instance, Bollywood). Indeed, as Guneratne states in *Rethinking Third Cinema*, third cinema "made overarching, even messianic, claims and purported to speak for a vast socio-geographical regions that even then (in the early 1960s) already produced the majority of the world's films" (Guneratne 2003: 1). However, the cinemas of non-Western and especially non-industrialized non-Western nations to that point had been (as was pointed out in earlier chapters) neglected within film studies, and it has only been relatively recently that this has been (to some extent) rectified. And while the corpus of films that came out of third cinema may be fewer in number than those produced by First World cinemas, the ones that did come out of this theory are some of the most provocative ever made – see, for instance, Rocha's 1967 *Terra em transe* [Earth Entranced], Nelson Pereira dos Santos's 1963 *Vidas secas* [Barren Lives], or Tomás Gutiérrez Alea's 1968 *Memorias del subdesarrollo* [Memories of Underdevelopment]. *Memorias del subdesarrollo* is the memoir of a morally ambiguous bourgeois intellectual (Sergio) living in Havana in the period between the Bay of Pigs Invasion and the Cuban Missile Crisis, Sergio decides to stay in Cuba even though his wife and friends flee to Miami, yet despises the country around him. Sergio reflects on the changes in Cuba, the effect of living in an underdeveloped country, and his relations with his girlfriends Elena and Hanna. His life eventually fades into nothingness, becoming a personality that has no use in this new Cuba. *Memorias del subdesarrollo* is an eloquent depiction of alienation during the turmoil of social changes, effectively told using a mélange of techniques, styles, and materials, from documentary techniques and footage to still photographs and montage sequences. While not as politically critical as many within the third cinema genre, the film was certainly artistically or cinematically in direct contrast to the aesthetics of Hollywood. Arguably, the areas of the world most affected by the ideas of third cinema were Latin America and Africa. In the case of the latter, the ideas of third cinema combined with the ideas of pan-Africanism (a movement that attempts

Figure 3.6   Sign outside the abandoned Cine Oriente in
the center of Santiago de Cuba, Cuba. Photograph by
Paul Keller 2008.

to unify all sub-Saharan Africans and those of the African diaspora in order to make
social and political gains) to produce numerous vibrant and provocative films. More
recently, African filmmakers are also questioning the rationale of "African" cinema,
in the third cinema sense (Ukadike 2002).

Distinct from the highly oppositional agenda of third cinema, but sharing
the drive within third cinema to find alternative voices for their communities is
the development of indigenous feature films, such as *Atanarjuat* (Kunuk 2001).[5]
Atanarjuat in set far in the past, around the turn of the first millennium, in the
eastern Arctic. The film retells an Inuit legend about a community split by rivalry.
An evil shaman enters a camp of Inuit and upsets its already fragile bonds. The
shaman curses the band with envy, avarice, and lust for power. After the camp leader
is murdered, the new leader Sauri belittles his old rival Tulimaq. However, over time,
power within the camp begins to change when Tulimaq has two sons – Amaqjuaq,
the Strong One, and Atanarjuat, the Fast Runner. Their rival, Oki, the leader's son,
envies their success. This is exacerbated when Atanarjuat wins away Oki's promised
wife-to-be, Atuat. Encouraged by his father, Oki and his friends attempt to murder
both brothers while they sleep. Amaqjuaq is killed, but Atanarjuat miraculously

Case Study: "African" Cinema as Third Cinema

The development of film industries throughout the African continent occurred both later and to a more limited degree than in many parts of world – as in Asia for instance. Even within Africa there are crucial differences between the development of cinema industries in former French colonies (Francophone Africa) and former British colonies (Anglophone Africa). While Francophone African cinemas have produced some of the continent's most famous and critically successful directors (such as Senegal's Sembène Ousmane, Mali's Souleymane Cissé, or Gaston Kaboré and Idrissa Ouedraogo of Burkina Faso), that critical success has not always extended to commercial success or to the growth of a more vibrant industry in the respective countries (Diawara 1992). One of the pronounced features of the work of many of the Francophone African filmmakers is the political nature of their work – with a prominent role played by ideas of pan-Africanism and third cinema precepts (Diawara 1992: 35–50; Pfaff 2004: 1–6; Roof 2004). The Anglophone African cinema has not led to the same critical acclaim, but with the growth of the Nigerian and Ghanaian video film industries – particularly into markets outside of Africa – it has had more commercial success. This case study will focus on the former model of filmmaking, through investigating differences in the colonial and postcolonial histories, with particular attention to the issues of the role (or otherwise) that a politicized third cinema trajectory may have had in development of Francophone cinema.

Prior to independence in various countries, from at latest the 1920s onwards colonies under the control of the French and British saw the training of new "native" elites: certain, usually higher class, portions of the respective society were educated in Western universities and expected to oversee the transition from European rule to self-determination and eventually independence. Instead, these elites often became the leaders of independence movements, especially in Anglophone Africa. For the most part, decolonization in both Anglophone and Francophone sub-Saharan (Black) Africa was relatively peaceful, though the white settlers in what is now Zimbabwe would control the country and fight black rule until 1980. Francophone North Africa was a different story, with a brutal war of independence fought in Algeria. Even after independence in many sub-Saharan countries, French and British experts stayed for some time to oversee certain institutions. One of these areas involved film (Diawara 1992). It might seem paradoxical, but one of the major differences in the development of post-independence cinemas in Africa is that in Francophone countries there was little if any scope for African involvement in filmmaking, whereas in many of the British colonies Colonial Film Units were established. These units trained and employed Africans in filmmaking (Diawara 1992: 1–5). However, the main products of these units were propaganda films that were aimed at promoting the quality of life under British rule and to foster African aid in fighting the Second World War. Because of this link to British interests, a focus on producing Hollywood-style films, and the economic realities post-independence, these units were largely closed down and the already limited possibilities for African filmmaking in Anglophone countries became even more limited, at least until recently and the development of a very different model for cinema – the Nigerian and Ghanaian video film. As I have already noted, paradoxically, in Francophone African countries where pre-independence African involvement in filmmaking was actively discouraged, the opposite was to occur (Diawara 1992: 21–34).

What makes this seeming paradox less of an actual paradox is that it was in some ways the very colonial actions of control that led to the growth of post-independence cinemas in Francophone African countries – as filmmaking was out of reach, and without the history linking film with propaganda (in fact the very opposite – film was almost inherently an act of rebellion) it was understood very differently than in Anglophone African countries. Further, film was understood, again in a context where it was not linked to colonial propaganda, as a powerful tool of nation-building and political consciousness raising (Diawara 1992). As such, in Francophone countries, cinema was understood very much in the third cinema vein, or in a way similar to how Vertov understood the cinema – not, emphatically not, as escapist fantasy but as a medium for expressing anti-colonial and pro-African sentiments (Roof 2004). There is another factor here, however, and that is that those elite independence leaders were acutely aware of the use of film as nation-building and for expressing political sentiments. So, the early post-independence political leaders were more than happy for a generation of politically savvy filmmakers to espouse the values that they, the leaders, were trying to inculcate in their new nation-states – in this case Pan-Africanism and leftist politics. Pan-Africanism was, as the name suggests, a political platform which argued that African peoples and countries were more similar than different, and at least partially because of that African interests were better served by cooperation between African nations rather than competition, where other more powerful nations could play Africans off against each other for those outsiders' own benefit (Diawara 1992: 39–45; Shaka 2004: *passim*). Further, post-independence, France no longer held out against African participation in filmmaking and even began aiding African filmmaking through the establishment of various Paris-based organizations to provide support for African filmmakers.

Films from this period, by directors such Sembene, Hondo, or Cissé, have a number of things in common, even as they are also very different. There is an overarching agreement that cinema is not for entertainment, but for reappropriating African history and culture, and for producing a social cinema rather than a commercial cinema (Diawara 1992: 140–66). This is not to say that these filmmakers did not or could not produce entertaining films, but that the entertainment came as a by-product of the story and way of telling, it was not an end in itself. The filmmakers mentioned above all combined classic film "grammar" with cultural conventions of their peoples (oral traditions or the use of music and dance interspersed with the narrative) to create intriguing syntheses. Something that is interesting in terms of the films from this period in particular is how different Western and African (or Africanist) film scholars analyze these syntheses – with Western scholars calling the work of Hondo, for instance, avant-garde, whereas the Africanist scholars foreground the links to "traditional" oral culture (Ukadike 2000: 187). This is a point that I wish to return to later in the book, as it is a variation of an argument made by many scholars of non-Western cinemas, that there are inherent difficulties in unproblematically applying Euro-American derived theory wholesale onto non-Western cinema. For now I wish simply to point out the issue, but it is an important argument within this book.

As time went by, the easy relationship between African filmmakers, their governments, and the French bureaus assisting the filmmakers began to break down (Diawara 1992: 104–15). The early optimism of independent Africa fairly soon led to disillusionment and disappointment. The post-independence African economies were in disarray, as they had been based since colonial times on cash crops, like cocoa, and natural resources, like copper. In the 1970s world markets for these commodities began to falter and there was no infrastructure to shift the economic bases. Political goals had been set aside for personal gain or simply the realpolitik of the Cold War, where once again Africa became one of the playgrounds of outsiders – in this case the USA and USSR. Pan-Africanism became second fiddle to nationalist economic and political interests. The same filmmakers, and those they trained, who had been so welcomed by the early leadership, were now sometimes seen as troublemakers for their criticism of the failures of post-independence Africa (Diawara 1992: 80–1). Sembene's *Xala* (1974) is an example of the films that critiqued the new African dreams. The film is set in Dakar, Senegal (Sembene's home country). Xala refers to a curse – in this case of impotence, which strikes the main character (El Hadji) on the night of his wedding to his third wife. This curse also acts as an allegory of the impotence of Senegal's middle class, who have given up wider and more productive goals for easy money and luxurious lifestyles. The failure of the middle class to work to national or other productive goals is crippling Senegal and, by extension, Africa. This is brought home to the viewer after Sembene satirically details the physical impotence of the main character, only slowly are we brought to understand the relationship of the physical impotence with the country's economic impotence. El Hadji and his business colleagues have gotten where they are by cheating their own families, profiteering off of supplies for drought victims, and other unscrupulous means. They live beyond their means and are alienated from their cultural heritage and values – except when it suits them, as with continuing the practice of polygyny (legally marrying more than one woman). Whereas most of the men are self-serving, the women in *Xala* portray various possibilities, from El Hadji's second and third wives who represent a Westernized modernity, to his first wife who represents "traditional" Senegalese values, and finally to his daughter by the first wife who represents the possibilities of an African modernity. Further, the continuing co-optation of Africa by their former colonial powers, in this case France and the French banks that can give out money or not and thereby continue to assert control, is symbolically and sometimes literally running through the film, adding a layer of culpability to El Hadji and his colleagues – they literally sell their country to the neocolonial powers for their own gain. There is much more that Sembene is articulating in the film: complicity of the police with the middle class, the continuing influence of France, the involvement of the government, and the empty promises of "true socialism, African socialism" in the film mirror and therefore implicate the real Senegalese leaders. There is also the song and song style employed by the beggars (who represent the non-middle class Senegalese or Africans betrayed by all of the people mentioned above). These repeated songs weave together popular sayings, proverbs, and metaphors. Senegalese viewers would understand these evocative songs, which would thus act as a form of "co-text" alongside that of the narrative (Ukadike 2000: 135).

Time has passed and a new generation of filmmakers has taken the reins, these filmmakers are less invested in what many of them see as the failed pan-Africanism of the preceding generation of filmmakers (Ukadike 2002). Indeed, some within the Francophone cinema industries are looking at the commercially, rather than critically, successful Nigerian and Ghanaian video film industries and wondering if that is not the model for the way forward (Balogun 2004). But for the generation in question, the form of third cinema they actively and consciously pursued was pursued with vigor and artistry. They had little doubt, even when disillusioned by the real events of post-independence Africa, about what cinema was for them. They continued to argue that cinema had a higher purpose and a wider role and that overlapped with, and gave a voice to, their political beliefs. In *Xala*, as El Hadji's daughter Rama (who, as we are made aware, represents an African modernity) confronts him she is dressed in African-style dress in the colors of Senegal and stands in front of a map of Africa *drawn without national borders.*

escapes, running naked for his life across the ice. Atanarjuat eludes his pursuers with supernatural help, and is nursed back to health by an old couple who had fled the camp prior to the curse years before. After learning to reclaim his spiritual path, and with the guidance of his elder advisor, Atanarjuat returns to rescue his family from both human and supernatural evil. Spurning a chance to continue the cycle of hatred, envy, and killing, he breaks the curse. The film was the first feature film ever to be produced entirely in Inuktitut, the name for Inuit languages. It won many awards at Film Festivals, including the prestigious Camera D'Or at

Cannes, and was the top-grossing film in Canada in 2002 (Bessire 2003: 832). For the filmmakers though, the film's significance could be summed up when one of the producers saw that Inuit children were playing *Atanarjuat*. The goals for *Atanarjuat* were to introduce the new storytelling medium of film to help Inuit communities survive culturally, to show Inuit peoples representing themselves after generations of being represented by outsiders. The film was made primarily for Inuit audiences, for that audience to see positive and accurate images of themselves (Bessire 2003: 835). To date the indigenous feature film remains something of an exception to the rule, largely due to lack of resources and training, but films such as *Ten Canoes* (de Heer and Djigirr 2006), filmed in Australian Aboriginal languages (Gunwinggu and dialects of Yolngu Matha) show that there is potential in this genre of cinema.[6]

CONTEXTS OF DISTRIBUTION AND EXHIBITION

Film studies was in some instances slow to incorporate the context of production into its canon, but particularly since the 1980s there have been an increase in works that look at distinct national traditions in cinemas around the world,[7] as well as works that attempt to locate the various filmmakers within national traditions. Distribution and exhibition, however, have not received quite the same level of interest, though again since the 1980s there has been more work in this area (see, for instance, Lewis 1998). Communications/media studies has been more attuned to this context. Distribution and exhibition are intensely important to the financial health of cinema. It does not matter how good your film is if no one sees it. As we saw in Chapter 1, this is not always as easy as it may seem.

In much of the world, distribution and exhibition preceded production, and in those countries the channels of distribution often formed the contexts of production as either the people who were importing films from Europe and the USA (or China in the cases of Malaysia and Indonesia) began to make films themselves or the types of films being imported helped to develop the audience's expectations and taste for particular types of stories and levels of production quality (see, for instance, Sen 1994: 13–17). The other important factor here is money, as even in the 1920s it took a lot of capital to make a film, and this limited the number (and often type) of people who *could* make films. This put those same groups of people in a powerful position to determine the films being made and influence the success of the industry. For instance, in Indonesia it was a combination of Dutch and Chinese-Indonesian businessmen that made the first locally produced films (Lent 1990: 203–4). These very early ventures were almost entirely aimed at Chinese-Indonesian audiences, and that was a small audience. It was only later that films aimed at the much larger

Indonesian audience were made, although again there films were not made by Indonesians, but by Dutch filmmakers. These films had mixed success – they had the most appeal to the group with the least money, i.e. the working-class audience. As a result, most of the few films produced in Indonesia prior to the Second World War were well attended and popular but not always commercially successful (Lent 1990: 203–4).

In areas of the world where cinema production came first matters were different, although in either case the official channels for a film to be distributed and exhibited are typically strictly controlled. In the USA, Hollywood studios (the producers) also controlled distribution and exhibition until the late 1940s, owning "first run" prestige cinemas and forcing other cinemas to "block book" (i.e. purchase multiple films of varying quality as a set). This meant that studios could parcel B movies and other "filler" in with A list features, which was great for the studios and not nearly so great for the theatres. From the 1930s the American government had been threatening to break up the major studios' monopoly, however, it was not until the Paramount anti-trust case in 1948 that they did so (Parkinson 1995: 155–6). The studios still retained control over international distribution, and this is one of the reasons that international box office grew in importance to USA studios (as mentioned in Chapter 1), but this was not a panacea for the loss of control of US exhibition and distribution. Part of the reason that international box office was only a partial remedy is that, as mentioned above, most countries control what films are allowed in, how many films will be allowed in, and how much the distributor would be taxed for the privilege. Throughout the twentieth century, many countries used taxes and tariffs to limit Hollywood films – either Hollywood's access to that market, or that market's access to Hollywood (Parkinson 1995: *passim*). In other words, there were two distinct arenas of control, an economic arena (usually expressed through taxes and tariffs) and a nationalistic/ideological arena (often, though not always, expressed through censorship), where governments were trying to limit Hollywood's incursion into their country (though the boundary, if there is indeed one, between the two is quite blurred). The British combination of tariff and censorship is an example of one such attempt. It was not only Hollywood films that ran afoul of this particular form of control of distribution and exhibition, however. During the Second World War in Japanese controlled Southeast Asia, all Allied films (USA and Britain in particular) were banned, as were all Axis films (Germany, Italy, Vichy France, and Japan) in Allied controlled territories. A slightly more recent example also comes from Southeast Asia, in particular Indonesia and Malaysia. In this example the economic consequences of government involvement in regulating cinema access had profound effects upon two national cinemas (see the case study on Indonesian film and government ties).

To bring this discussion up to the present, in an increasingly "tight" cinema industry, where profits are to be maximized and risks are to be avoided, independent filmmakers have struggled to get their films distributed and screened within the official networks. Certain filmmakers operating within the system, such as Smith (*Clerks* 1994) or Rodriguez (*El Mariachi* 1992), have managed to break into the Hollywood system via low budget but well made films. Most are not so fortunate and have sought other venues wherein to showcase their work. Film festivals have become very important arenas for young filmmakers, so much so that some of the largest have become de facto interviews for the major studios and producers. This has had a knock-on effect, and getting a film into some of the major festivals (Venice, Berlin, Toronto, or Cannes) is now about as likely as getting a major studio's backing. There has been a proliferation of smaller festivals though, often regionally based or with thematic foci (women filmmakers, gay and lesbian, African American, etc.). Some are held online – "virtual" film festivals. The Internet also provides another platform for prospective filmmakers, namely the increasing ease and accessibility of streaming technologies and sites devoted to exploiting those same technologies. YouTube is probably the most famous, but it has been joined by numerous other variants, Google and Yahoo! have established video sections. On these sites, users can upload short films, which can then be viewed by anyone with a computer and Internet access. On most of the sites the videos can also be rated, commented on, and forwarded to others by viewers. Interesting, well-made or simply trendy videos have huge, though non-fee paying audiences. Arguably more useful to independent filmmakers is the opportunity to post trailers of longer films on these sites and email the link to producers, critics, and fellow filmmakers. While the chances of a YouTube video landing its maker a big Hollywood contract are slim, the filmmaker's work and name are being disseminated. In regards to this last point, as was mentioned in Chapter 1, Hollywood has not missed the "hype" potential inherent in YouTube and social networking sites such as Facebook and MySpace. *Snakes on a Plane* (Ellis 2006) was hyped mercilessly via the Internet, with graphic images "leaked" to spur interest. The engagement of *Cloverfield* (2008) and the Internet has been more sophisticated – pretty much the opposite of *Snakes on a Plane* – with true teasers (the head of the Statue of Liberty crashes onto a New York street, but we do not see what did it, for instance) and an almost unique secrecy as to the film creating huge hype and expectation.

SOCIAL AND CULTURAL CONTEXTS – ANTHROPOLOGY OF THE CINEMA

While ideological approaches to film do take some aspects of the context of production into consideration, this is typically in a Marxist/political economy model, e.g. Hollywood exists in a capitalist state economy, and therefore it will produce safe genre films in order to maximize profits and limit financial risks. While US, French, or Indian economies are important (especially when we look at exhibition and distribution, where the state is generally the most active), there are other contexts that come into play, namely, social and cultural contexts. Of all the various contexts of production we have looked at, the least analyzed has been the socio-cultural. No film is made in a cultural vacuum – even Hollywood, much as it is taken as a culturally unmarked "norm" for filmmaking.[8] To date, there have been very few, and fewer of these well-known, studies of the socio-cultural influence on the context of production in cinema. Of these, only a few have been on Hollywood itself. While the term "culture" is bandied about in some analyses, culture is often used to mean the culture of Hollywood, e.g. the star system and effects of the localized Hollywood political economy on the cinema output. Traube's analysis of *The Secret of My Succe$s* (1994) is one of the few readily available analyses of the influence of wider American society on a particular Hollywood film. Also interesting here are Askew's observations of a Hollywood film shoot in South Africa, and the critical cultural gaps between the filmmakers and the African actors involved in the shooting of a Hollywood film in Africa (Askew 2004). More common is the drawing of links between a film, or the development of a genre of film, and historical events (e.g. Oliver Stone's 1987 *Wall Street* as a comment on 1980s capitalism, or the flood of patriotic films post 9/11). It is in terms of this gap that anthropology could play an important role in furthering our knowledge of the cinema by drawing forth that which is *culturally embedded* – the socio-cultural norms and values that are laden into films as part of the context of their production.

ANTHROPOLOGY

One of the earliest attempts to combine anthropology and the cinema was Powdermaker's study of Hollywood (Powdermaker 2002 [1950]). Powdermaker's study is in many ways a product of its time (for instance, a fairly unproblematic understanding of mass media as a tool of and for manipulation), but is interesting for many reasons other than simply its historic or novelty values. She begins her study with a couple of points that are very important for the current discussion. First of all, Hollywood is not an isolated phenomenon, but a part of the wider society that it takes place within. The second point is the Hollywood industry *is* an industry as well as an art form and that it needs to be understood as both. However, these issues are not actually all given equal weigh in her study:

> The anthropologist sees any segment of society as part of a larger whole; he [*sic*] views Hollywood as a section of the United States of America, and both in the larger frame of Western civilization. The problems of the movie industry are not unique to it. But some characteristics of the modern world have been greatly exaggerated in Hollywood while others are underplayed. *Hollywood is therefore not a reflection, but a caricature of selected contemporary tendencies*, which, in turn leave their imprint on the movies. (Powdermaker 2002: 163–4, emphasis added)

Hollywood, ultimately is not simply a part of society, but is more like an evil industrialist that is a social evil even as they produce things people want. Ultimately, because of her theoretical perspective Powdermaker's study is not really enlightening, it does discuss the context of Hollywood, but that context seems not so much to be in any kind of exchange with Hollywood, rather it seems merely to act as a justification for the Hollywood machine to commit its ideological crimes on "the crowd." In this study, Hollywood is almost entirely understood as an industry and very little as an art form. So, the Powdermaker example illustrates that anthropology per se does not necessarily hold the answer to what cinema is, but we do find some useful hints as to what the discipline and approach might have to offer.

A more useful, and arguably more interesting, combination of cinema and anthropology is Babb's 1981 work on visual interaction in Hindu devotion between devotees and deities. Worshipers wish to see and, importantly, be seen by the gods. Seeing in this understanding allows the viewer to absorb elements of the deity's virtue. In itself, this is an intriguing cultural understanding of sight, but for our purposes here, what is even more interesting is that one of the sources of evidence that Babb employs is a popular religious film *Jai Santoshi Maa* (Sharma 1975). Babb begins his analysis of the film's importance to his argument with the following statement: "The vernacular movie is a rich and greatly underutilized source of cultural data" (1981: 391). This statement is interesting as Babb is really making two arguments: the first is explicit – that anthropologists should be analyzing feature films for their cultural content (he is juxtaposing this against indigenous media) – and the second is more implicit – that cultural content is embedded in feature films. While Babb does not go into great detail about the plot or narrative of the film, he does discuss the content of the film very usefully. In several scenes including the climax of the film, there are exchanges of looking between devotees and the goddess, both the representation of goddess (statues) and the gods themselves, though the exchange is not completely direct in the latter case. The camera is used in the film to represent the subjective position of the looker, so in the scenes mentioned there are many first person point of view shots, from both the worshiper's viewpoint and the goddess's viewpoint. For instance,

> [w]hile they [women] dance they gaze at the goddess, and when the camera turns to the goddess we see what presumably they see, namely, an image of the goddess looking down towards us [...] When the camera shifts to the goddess's perspective, we find ourselves looking downward at the worshipers who, in turn are gazing back at us. (Babb 1981: 392)

Babb goes on to point out that the evil eye is well-known in Hindu life and so the concept of eyes being more than simply a window into the soul, but dangerous objects in themselves, is not outlandish. In the Hindu world, seeing can actually reach out and engage the thing being seen. This particular cultural understanding is firmly embedded within *Jai Santoshi Maa*. In this analysis, Babb is creating a different model for an integration of film and anthropology, namely that he is incorporating *both* context and content. As will be discussed below, this is crucial for an anthropology of the cinema.

Case Study: *The Secret of My Succe$s*

As has been mentioned elsewhere in the text, Hollywood is often treated as if it exists outside of any cultural context whatsoever – a version of the "I don't have an accent – only other people do" idea. This is both disingenuous and also dangerous. Hollywood filmmakers exist in a social and cultural context, one that is partially of their own creation (as the filmmakers are cultural producers on a massive scale) and also in a constant dialogue with a wider American context. Hollywood, as was discussed in Chapter 1, has increasingly come to be dominated by the "blockbuster" – low risk/ high return model – one that depends on attracting the largest number of viewers. The flip side is that you then have to satisfy the largest number of viewers. To do this you must produce something that they both recognize and enjoy. While this seems to contradict the Marxist/Frankfurt School model, in reality it means that a more nuanced approach to this situation is needed. In this case, film producers and wider society are in an unequal but dynamic dialogue. The filmmakers/producers can "tell" their audience what to think, but only in as far as the audience already accepts much or even most of the message already. This long-term plan of persuasion fits more with Gramsci's ideas of *hegemony* and Bakhtin's theory of *dialogism*, making the exchange a more interesting arena of study. An example of an anthropological approach to the exchange of ideology is taken from Traube's analysis of *The Secret of My Succe$s* (Ross 1987). On one hand, the film is an amiable comedy with a likable cast (including Michael J. Fox). On the other, it is a reiteration and extension of the Reagan era socio-political discourse on meritocracy and individual achievement (Traube 1994). The case study will evaluate arguments over the social and cultural context that was both the point of the film, but also the locus of its formation and success.

Traube begins by noting that *The Secret of My Succe$s* is one of a large number of films produced in the mid to late 1980s that promoted similar Reaganite ideals, such as individual socio-economic mobility and personal success (Traube 1994: 557). Along with films like *All the Right Moves* (Chapman 1983), *Ferris Bueller's Day Off* (Hughes 1986) and *Nothing in Common* (Marshall 1986), *The Secret of My Succe$s* re-defines the all-American hero in terms of the (then) contemporary American society – one marked by a consumer-oriented corporate form of capitalism. While the self-made man of Horatio Alger or the stoic cowboy of the westerns are long-established cultural heroes in the American mythos, the America of the 1980s, rocked by the culture wars of the 1960s and 1970s, frightened and threatened by the economic crises of the 1970s and the Cold War, embarrassed by the disillusionment of the Nixon era and the events of Vietnam, needed a new kind of hero – one that was better suited to the jingoism and social *sangfroid* of the new right wing (as exemplified by the governments of Reagan in the USA and Thatcher in the UK). That hero is possibly best articulated by Fox's character in *The Secret of My Succe$s* – Brantley Foster (Traube 1994: 573).

Foster is the Horatio Alger character adapted to a world where, as the infamous Gordon Gekko (Michael Douglas in Stone's 1987 *Wall Street*) states, "Greed is good!" The film opens with Foster leaving his home on a farm and dreaming of his success in New York. His personal abilities and worthiness are already established, as we know he has earned a college degree (I am intentionally using value laden words here to convey the message that the film is imparting to us as we watch). Foster's arrival in New York is interspersed with the back-story exposition. As Traube points out, the imagery of the rural background, the personal toil, and even certain aspects of Foster's character are very economically yet effectively laid out for us: independent, thrifty, hard working, honest, and with strong personal and family values (as we will see, there is a certain irony with that last one). Though, the reality is that Foster's dream is an example of the 1980s' consumerist values of luxury and extravagance (Traube 1994: 573). Foster arrives in New York believing that he has a job and career awaiting him only to find that he is laid off on his first day on the job, before he can even find his desk. Things get worse for Foster, as he is forced to live in a slum apartment, which while he still believes he has prospects seems a lively and colorful place, however, when he is unemployed that same space suddenly degenerates and he is surrounded by poverty and threatened by violence, only marginally controlled by forces of surveillance and authoritarian control. This space of failed capitalism is the context or frame for Foster's struggle to succeed. In contrast is the Gekko-esque world of high-rise buildings and corporate business, to which Foster aspires. This world is not what he has expected though, and his old world values and abilities are not sufficient to get him a job. Here is where the new cultural hero takes a sharp turn away from those previous heroes. Foster falsifies his résumé to match the expectations of the corporate world (Traube 1994: 574). However, even this is insufficient and he is forced to face up to the ultimate reality of 1980s' America (or at least as it is depicted here): Foster cannot be a minority woman. The anti-positive discrimination message here is overt.

Finally, Foster swallows his pride and calls a distant relative to use his family connection rather than his personal skills and abilities to get a job. The relative, Uncle Howard (Richard Jordan), is the CEO of a multinational corporation. Gaining access to Uncle Howard, Foster gets a job. In the mailroom. This is about as far down the corporate ladder as it is possible to be. In the ultra-hierarchical world of big business, this is a no hope, no escape dead end. The mailroom is forever cut off from the corporate hierarchy; the two worlds may inhabit the same space, but they are in all other ways different worlds (Traube 1994: 574). To add to Foster's disillusionment, his immediate supervisor is a tyrant who takes a dislike to Foster and attempts (unsuccessfully) to make his life miserable. However, in the blind bureaucratic control systems, lower or mid-level management is basically impotent as there is little in the way of real authority (or mobility) linked to his position, only responsibility. The upshot of this situation is that apathy and resignation reign supreme except at the upper levels of management. The one area where the mailroom workers do have access to power is in that they control the flow of knowledge, which is typically the province of the most upper levels of management. The mailroom staff, however, cannot act on that knowledge. That is until Foster realizes that what he needs to do is not work his way up the corporate ladder, but simply create a person who belongs on a higher rung of the ladder (Traube 1994: 575–6). Upon discovering an empty office, Foster invents a new executive (his access to knowledge in the mailroom means he can create this identity through getting personalized stationery, a name plate, and other symbols of corporate status) and begins a double life as mailroom clerk Foster and upper echelon executive Carlton Whitfield. This leads to some comedy as Foster must change clothes and personas en route between the two jobs – being caught undressed in his office by his secretary at one point. Foster/Whitfield is, of course, a success – otherwise the film would have a very different title. He saves the company, steals his uncle's mistress, and even has an affair with his uncle's wife (i.e. his "aunt"). This may all sound quite Oedipal, and perhaps on one level is, but the father, or uncle in this situation, also represents an older economic sensibility, one that is no longer relevant in the new fiscal world. There are a few more steps to be gone through, but much of the film is about three relationships: Foster/Whitfield and Uncle Howard, where Foster is the new blood and ideas that are necessary; Foster and Howard's mistress, who Foster is in love with and seeks to extricate from Howard's possession (the film makes it clear that the relationship is on one hand a desire for an authority figure on one hand and a control fetish on the other); and Foster and Aunt Vera, who teaches the young country boy to be a sophisticated aristocrat who can mingle with the elite, as his intelligence and business acumen warrant (Traube 1994: 577). Foster's dual identity is discovered and he is fired from both jobs, while at the same time the corporation is about to be taken over by a speculator. The ending is a wild triumph of excess, as Vera, Foster, Foster's girlfriend (Howard's former mistress), and a couple of other worthies (though not quite as worthy as Foster) sweep in to save the day (Traube 1994: 579–60). Vera it turns out has bought up stock in the company and her banking friends have agreed to finance her acquisition of the speculating company (this is also somewhat ironic given the economic events of the early twenty-first century).

If we disregard any context for this film it is simply a feel good, happy ending comedy, with a particular setting, but otherwise not too special. There is some scope for a psychoanalysis approach to understanding the film, and on the face of it, it seems to make some commentary on bureaucracy. However, if we reinsert that film into the wider context of its production, we gain some important insight into the film, its intended audience, and the social values that are embedded into the story, characters, and narrative. The Reagan era was one where the final nails were hammered into the coffin of a production-led economy. The consumption-led economy is central to Foster's economic plan to save the company and is integral to his own dreams and definitions of success. This might seem somewhat mundane, but there are deeper levels to this, as this consumerist economy profoundly affects other aspects of American society: social control becomes an issue of persuasion and seduction rather than outright repression (at least for the "haves" – for the "have nots," repression works just fine, as the Foster's poor slum dwelling neighbors illustrate); image is at least as important as any substance (this is made clear in several places in the film); and most importantly, the film speaks to an intended audience of young people to assert that this is the world you will live and work in and it may have some problems, but if you possess the right qualities you will succeed – the meritocracy dream held out by Reagan era ideology (Traube 1994: 581). Ultimately, the new cultural hero (Foster) is an updated, not fundamentally changed hero, but one suited to and representative of the time and place.

Perhaps the most obvious area where anthropology has a role in cinema studies comes from its historical emphasis and body of knowledge on non-Western countries. In film studies in particular, non-Western films are much more likely to be "read" in terms of the influence that society or cultural contexts have on cinematic output. Indeed, there is almost an inverse ratio between how well known the particular film/

film industry is and whether that film/industry will be analyzed through some of the film theories discussed in the previous chapter or whether they will be discussed in terms of cultural or sociological specificity. Films from Africa or Indonesia, for instance, are much more likely to be analyzed via the latter, whereas, as we have already seen, Hollywood films are rarely discussed in this manner. Ukadike has written copiously on this point (1994, 2000, 2002), and Freiberg (2000) also comments on this trend within Japanese cinema theorists, mentioning MacDonald and Richie in particular. In the volume they edited, Hill and Church Gibson (2000), present several theorists who articulate different problems that scholars on "world cinema" have both encountered and engendered. The obverse of this is that when those theories are applied to non-Western films, they are applied uncritically without regard for cultural specificity or difference. For instance, if we return to *Jai Santoshi Maa* the subjective position of the goddess's gaze upon her worshipers can not be "real" from a Western perspective, and thus could be read very differently according to different theories, as metaphoric representation, as an ideological commentary or warning on appropriate behavior, or as a voyeuristic fantasy of control. That within the cultural milieu this might be a realistic portrayal is not a usual reading within the film theory canon. Ukadike (2000) gives another example, from the film *Xala* (Sembene 1975), where a psychoanalysis-informed feminist approach has read the pounding of food in a mortar and pestle as being or representing a phallic symbol, whereas Sembene uses the pestle to symbolize the impact of African and Western life, a crucial theme within the film (Ukadike 2000: 190). That may seem like a Catch-22 situation where the Western theorist is damned if they do not use Western theory and damned if they do, but this is an important issue, as it illustrates an important disparity in how different films are treated and conceived of by critics, theorists, and audiences. As mentioned in the second chapter, this double standard is an issue for "Third World" filmmakers and film industries. There are two separate but related issues: Are theories derived for/from Western cinema applicable to non-Western cinema (especially those that may in fact be oppositional to Western filmmaking)? And if these theoretical models are applicable, then why are they not applied equally? A third issue is why it is generally only non-Western cinemas that are regarded as having culture (in the anthropological sense). African filmmakers in particular are sensitive to the assumption that African cinema can only be understood within the context of African oral tradition (Ukadike 2002), rather than through psychoanalysis, structuralism, or literary criticism analyses. What makes matters worse, as McDonald (2006) and Chow (1995) have pointed out separately, is that often the cultural trait or socio-historical specific that the analysts are using is either wrong or inappropriate. Chow mentions how Western theorists focused on the use of space in films such as *Yellow Earth* (Kaige 1984) and *Red Sorghum* (Yimou

1988) to critique the Cultural Revolution, but did not attempt to understand what space means in the local understandings and that the exchange between cinema and audience must be understood in local terms, especially of local constructions of ideology and politics. It is in this regard that Chow calls for an anthropology of the cinema. An approach to cinema that takes seriously the local constructions of meaning, power, and politics (context) *as well as* the actual content of the films being studied, for their analytical value (cultural embeddednesss) and for their dialogue with the audience. It is particularly in regards to providing new and useful ways to address some of these issues that anthropology has so much to offer to the study of the cinema. As we saw with the Powdermaker example, an anthropological approach to the cinema may not have all the answers, but it helps us to begin asking some productive questions.

Figure 3.7   While cineplexes exist throughout Africa, films are also viewed in unexpected places, such as this cinema in Gambia. Photograph by Victor de la Fuente 2008.

SUGGESTED FURTHER READING

GENERAL AND EUROPE/AMERICA

Barker, C. (2000) *Cultural Studies: Theory and Practice*, London and Thousand Oaks: Sage Publications.

Guneratne, A. and Dissanayake, W. (eds) (2003) *Rethinking Third Cinema*, London and New York: Routledge.

O'Sullivan, T. Hartley, J., Saunders, D., Montgomery, M., and Fisk, J. (1994) *Key Concepts in Communication and Cultural Studies*, 2nd edition, London and New York: Routledge.

Traube, E. G. (1994) "Secrets of Success in Postmodern Society," in G. Eley, S. Ortner, and N. Dirks (eds) *Culture/Power/History: A Reader in Contemporary Social Theory*, Princeton, NJ: Princeton University Press, pp. 557–84.

Vitali, V. and Willemen P. (2008) *Theorising National Cinema*, London: British Film Institute.

AFRICA[9]

Diawara, M. (1992) *African Cinema: Politics and Culture*, Bloomington, IN: Indiana University Press.

Ukadike, N. F. (1994) *Black African Cinemas,* Berkeley: University of California Press.

Ukadike, N. F. (2002) *Questioning African Cinema: Conversations with Filmmakers*, Minneapolis: University of Minnesota Press.

INDONESIA

Heider, K. (1991) *Indonesian Cinema: National Culture on Screen*, Honolulu: University of Hawai'i Press.

Sen, K. (1994) *Indonesian Cinema: Framing the New Order*, London and New Jersey: Zed Books.

4 CONTEXT OF RECEPTION

Figure 4.1   Cathay Cinema in Shanghai, China. Photograph by Shun-che (Mark) Chang 2006.

In the late 1980s [in Thailand] there was no legitimate space for public discussion of such matters, no forum at which people might express their opinions openly or hear others do so. Although newspapers were able to print what they liked, any direct mention of individuals or groups was likely to result in a hand grenade thrown through the bedroom window of an editor or journalist. On television there were no investigative shows or commentary, on radio no call-in show. The restriction and circumspection [of public discussion of political, economic or religious issues in Thailand] resulted in the creation of a para-discourse, where something could be discussed only by referring to something else – notably, television or short stories. Narratives could be interpreted as being "about" something else – for example, a wealthy eldest son in a current Chinese drama who was having marital problems could be coded as a subject for conversation about the Crown Prince. Current events and television and film narratives could take their place within a vast signifying chain of Thai history and destiny, meaning much more that they would seem to do at a literal level.

Hamilton The National Picture: Thai Media and Cultural Identity.

INTRODUCTION

As the initial theoretical approaches to cinema were attempts to validate it and making sense of it as an art form, it is possibly no surprise that it took a while for questions of audience to enter the equation. That is not to say that no one thought about the audience, but that between arguments over legitimacy on the one hand (formalism), and the cinema being somewhat of a subset of wider concerns with new (popular) visual media technology on the other (Frankfurt School), understanding what the actual viewers of cinema thought or understood took somewhat of a backseat for some time. For the approaches in this chapter any definition of cinema is incomplete unless it includes the audience and what the audience "makes" of the films being consumed.

FILM THEORY

Arguably the first to discuss the audience, even if in a limited way, and certainly the first to publish on the audience were the Marxist-influenced Frankfurt School theorists, although as mentioned above cinema was largely part of a wider argument on capitalism and manipulation of the masses through populist media (Barker 2000: 44–5). It is interesting to speculate to what extent this position vis-à-vis cinema came about as a result of the audience for early cinema (i.e. pre-1920s) being largely working class and (in the USA) immigrant. Certainly the audience changed when films became more narrative oriented, though by this time the Hollywood studio and star systems were in force and this is when much of the critical writing took place, but was it to the earlier period of shabby nickelodeon and carnival attractions that the Frankfurt School theorists were reacting? Either way, the argument is that media (as part of the wider culture industry) are tools by which the elite subjugate the masses. As cheap, popular entertainment, a medium such as cinema helps control the masses by dulling their senses to the inequalities inherent in the capitalist system, which in turn depends on the quiet compliance of the masses. Popular media do this in a couple of ways: shallow entertainments "pacify" the audience by pandering to base pleasures; fantasies aid the audience to forget the unpleasant realities of their lives; and aspirational films/television depicting "the good life" persuade the working class that their lot in life can be improved through hard work and compliance with the system. This argument should be fairly familiar as a version of it gets resurrected whenever there is a discussion of the potential harmful effects of the media, for instance that violent films (video games, death metal music, etc.) promote – in a straightforward and uncomplicated manner – violence in viewers/listeners. Before I leave you with the idea that film theory ignored the audience outright, there were approaches within film theory that tried to make sense of the audience. Foremost among these were the psychoanalysis approaches to cinema, as discussed in Chapter 2.

One of the questions that had been, in one way or another, taken for granted in earlier approaches to cinema was what the audience "got" out of it. Why do people go to and, seemingly, enjoy the cinema? Formalist arguments appear to assume that audiences would not only appreciate, but also enjoy issues such as artful

Figure 4.2   Cinema-goers at the entrance of the Elgin Talkies cinema in Bangalore, India. Photography by Paul Keller 2008.

use of lighting, skillful composition, and artful *mise en scène*. The mass audience of the Marxist approaches enjoyed the cinema because they were supposed to. Policy studies showed whether audiences went to a particular film (or genres of films), or what the demographics (gender, age, income, etc.) of a particular film audience was. None of these approaches explained why people enjoy cinema either in general or in particular. Psychoanalysis approaches to film begin with that question (see, for instance, the section on Mulvey in Chapter 2). If you think about it, sitting in a dark room surrounded by strangers watching a progression of two-dimensional images that your brain interprets as a continuous three-dimensional image is a strange thing to do. Investigating why we should not only do this, but also enjoy doing it, has been an important aspect of psychoanalysis approaches to cinema. These approaches, as discussed in more detail in Chapter 2, argue that film "taps" into our subconscious – in ways both good and not so good. As we saw in the second chapter, the issues raised by this arena of criticism highlighted the audience (even if in a reductive way), the subject, and "identification." One thing that you may have noticed in the above argument is that the audience being discussed does not consist of real people, but is an idealized or theoretical audience. An issue that has been a point of criticism of this approach is that the thoughts and ideas of real viewers seldom concern these theorists (see Barker 2000). Further, when the views of real audiences are not in agreement with the theory, this discrepancy is simply dismissed as showing how successful the media have been in promoting a false consciousness in the audience.

RECEPTION AND AUDIENCE STUDIES

COMMUNICATION STUDIES

Media/communication studies was probably where the first systematic attempts to get to the "real" audience occurred. However, there are two issues with those early attempts to understand how audiences received the media they were consuming: the models that were employed and the methods that were employed. As was mentioned in the previous chapter, the early model of reception was the *Transmission* or *Hypodermic Needle Model*, which was a one-way, direct transmission from producer to consumer (O'Sullivan et al. 1994: 137). This model made way for a more nuanced version – the *Two Step Model*, which as the name suggests argued that there was more than a straight line between producer and consumer. In this case consumers who either had more access or were more media savvy would act as transmitters to those with less access or who were less attuned to the messages being produced (O'Sullivan et al. 1994: 322–3). The other issue with early communications approaches to the audience was that they were arrived at via quantitative (statistical) methods, e.g.

surveys, questionnaires, etc. The results of these analyses were often of use in policy studies, for instance finding out if changing censorship or film classification codes affected audience numbers or composition. Quantitative studies are also very useful for finding broad demographic trends in audiences. Grenfell's work (1979) on media in Malaysia is an example of this approach; while he does theorize on what his data suggests and draws some conclusions for differences in viewership numbers, for the most part his work is compiling figures on the use levels of various media. However, quantitative studies are not so good at helping in understanding *why* the changes happen. For instance, when I was conducting fieldwork on Malay-language cinema, an explanation that was presented to me several times as to why audiences for Malay-language films were typically poor was that Malay people have families relatively young and so it becomes too expensive. Malay people with children do not, as a rule, leave the children at home when they go out (this is at least true of most Malays aside from the elite – the upper middle classes and above), except for work. So, going to the movies would entail taking all of the children with them – and paying for them. This was a nice quantitative explanation that had been arrived at via some of the methods mentioned above, but it does not explain why cinema should be a luxury to be dropped. Families still have disposable income, so it is a *choice* not to go to the cinema, and the basis for this choice is not explained by the statistical answer. For that answer we need other approaches.

Case Study: Watching People Watch TV

This case study will focus on one of the first approaches to audience studies that adopted a qualitative methodology, namely television audience studies. Scholars from a range of disciplines, including cultural studies, communications, and anthropology, conducted these studies. Besides the content of Louise Spence's analysis of viewership and pleasure in watching daytime soap operas (1995), in this case study the general approach and methodology will be highlighted. While not without critics, the studies that came out of this approach were beneficial in changing the way audiences were conceptualized and, in turn, researched. This case study will address those benefits, in particular the question as to the difference that methodology makes to audience reception studies. The case study will also contrast the approach of media studies with that of anthropology. One of the benefits mentioned in this chapter is that anthropological research is long-term and as much as possible involves participating in the daily life of the people. Does this difference have any effect on the outcome of the research? Aside from providing students with an example of a reception study, the case study will also lead to some basis for comparing different methods and theories regarding the audience.

Building on work going back to the 1980s, Spence has written about the pleasures involved for female spectators of American daytime soap operas. In particular, in this case study, her article "They Killed off Marlena, but she's on another show now" (1995) takes its title from a conversation between her mother and grandmother, both of whom were familiar with a particular soap opera, *Days of Our Lives*. As the grandmother had not seen the show lately, the mother was catching her up by telling the grandmother "They [the people who made the show] killed off Marlena [name of major character], but she [the actress who played Marlena] is on another show now" (Spence 1995: 182). The grandmother asks who did it, meaning which character in the show, and the mother tells her which character did it. This one conversation was the catalyst for Spence to analyze more deeply the relationship between fantasy and reality in soap opera viewing. Specifically, the way that her mother and grandmother could flip between reality (the makers of the show and the actress having another job) and the television show (the character Marlena being killed by another character) opened the exchange to analysis in terms of soap opera viewership. I had a similar experience not long after reading Spence's account. I was on a bus in London, England and two women in the seat ahead of me were talking about their families and the British soap opera *Eastenders*. What caught my attention was that they were talking about these two interchangeably – to such an extent that it took several minutes for me to realize that this is what they were doing. I should hasten to add that the two women were speaking very loudly and the exchange was much more annoying than illuminating until I heard a particular exchange where one woman was speaking about family members (in those terms, i.e. "my nephew") and the other woman answered by discussing events among *Eastenders* characters. I found the exchange fascinating, as it seemed to reaffirm the stereotype of people who watch soap operas as unable to distinguish between the fantasy of the show and the reality of their real lives. As Spence points out, there have been many stories about people who have actually attacked "bad" characters or sent wedding presents to characters married on a show (Spence 1995: 182). The examples, particularly the one I overheard, seem to back up that stereotype, but as Spence goes on to argue, if we actually engage with the viewers it is clear that this is not the case, but that the viewers have quite clear ideas of "reality" that they employ in viewing and making sense of the shows in question. However, being well versed in the "reality" of the soap opera world, which overlaps with but is also quite different from the "real" world, they judge issues like the plausibility of certain storylines or plot devices (the "Bill isn't your father, John is…" storyline, or characters who "die" but come back to life later) employing a sophisticated mix of these two realities. Fact and fiction are subtly intertwined in a world that is both recognizable and strange at the same time. The characters, the situations, and the locales are familiar, but by the very fact that they are on television they are also extraordinary. Added to that is the assumption, particularly by American soap opera makers as opposed to British and Australian soap operas, that real life would not be interesting enough, hence the exaggerated, even outrageous storylines. Soap opera viewers factor this unreal reality into their discussions of plausibility (Spence 1995: 183–4). Further, the publicity and promotion of soap operas and their stars likewise plays with the unreal reality of the soap worlds, often mixing events from the lives of the real actor or actress with the lives of their character. Storylines are frequently adjusted to incorporate real world events in the actors' or actresses' lives into their soap lives. Spence gives examples of face-lifts and in one case an actress's medical condition was worked into the script.

When talking with the people who are the viewers of these shows, Spence found that there was a high level of expectation that the stories would be believable, that they would fit with aspects of the viewer's experiences and expectations of the world. One viewer speaking of a particular soap commented negatively "Nobody lives with their parents; everyone has been married to somebody else. I don't think that real life is as mixed-up as this show is" (Spence 1995: 187–8). The viewer expects the makers of the show to know what life is like, and to depict that reality. That reality might not be exactly what the viewer knows, but it has to make sense enough that they can make some personal connection with it – that we the viewers are getting to know about people and life. In other words, we expect that we can identify with and empathize with the characters and situations. We also know that this is not the "real" real world and so there is some play in what "real" means and just how much the "real" life of the soaps must conform to our expectations and experiences. This balancing act is further complicated by the viewers' understandings about how the show works, something else that the makers often promote through magazines and other media devoted to following the complicated stories and characters. As one of Spence's informants says in referring to a particular character "He's a bastard. But then you give him credit for good acting, so you don't really dislike him!" (Spence 1995: 190–1). As with the quote that acted as the catalyst for the article this case study is focused upon, there are multiple levels of "reality" going on in this one sentence. This makes perfect sense to anyone who knows the character, who understands that this is not the real world, but still expects the soaps to be "real" – in other words, anyone who watches soap operas. As another informant states of an outlandish event in one of the shows "It *does* happen but it doesn't happen in – in every day form of life, you know. It happens to someone else, not to me" (Spence 1995: 192).

Even just with this snippet of Spence's work, in this piece she also looks at issues such as whether there is a reciprocal influence from the viewers to the makers (yes) and why extravagant and outrageous storylines would be pleasurable (they are like mirrors to affirm that our own lives are good ones and therefore reinforce the values of the viewers), we can see certain aspects of the audience study approach that are discussed in the text – the agency of the viewers is foregrounded throughout the article, these are not the voiceless masses of the Frankfurt School, in fact that kind of viewer is expressly pointed out to be a stereotype (the viewer that attacks the actor who plays a villain character). However, an issue with many of the earlier audience studies is that methodologically they had some weaknesses. As noted in the main text, a criticism is that they often involved a small number of respondents. For critics of the approach, this meant that the findings were also based on a small data set, and any claims were therefore suspect. For many of the studies, this criticism has a certain validity, though the strength of a qualitative study is the *depth* of knowledge gained rather than simply the *breadth*. To this point we might also look as to what depth of knowledge there is. As Spence does not give any details as to the length of time she spent conducting the research, the number of informants she interviewed, or the length of time she spent with the informants – all information that would give some idea of the depth of her work. This is not to insinuate that she did "bad" research, but to point out some of the expectations of qualitative research. I would, however, say that overall there is in general a lack of depth to her representation of her informants. In her longer work this information is available (e.g. Spence 2005), but as an illustration of some of the criticisms of the approach, her shorter article works very well. Her informants come onstage, speak their lines, and retreat until they are called again. To keep with the soap opera métier, even her mother and grandmother are plot devices rather than characters to be engaged with. We gain no sense of the women that she is interviewing, the length of time she spent with them, or any aspect of their lives. They are more real than the hypothetical audience of Marxism, but there is little depth to them beyond the words they utter. For that depth, the audience study had to move beyond acting as a rebuttal to the mass audience approaches to spending more time with the audiences they were studying. As we will see in the following case studies, this happened both within the various media studies and cultural studies disciplines, and especially within anthropological studies of the audience.

Communication/media studies did engage with qualitative audience studies, and some important studies came out of this discipline. Further, qualitative communication studies audience studies were also some of the first to tackle non-Western audiences. Lopez's look at the *telenovela* (television serial melodrama) in Latin America (1995) is a good example. The *telenovela* is effectively a limited-run soap opera, sharing many characteristics, particularly, but not exclusively, a penchant for melodrama. Lopez begins her work by noting the history of writing on the Latin American *telenovela*: in the 1970s the mass media approach ruled, with many Latin American scholars especially arguing that these entertainments were the creation of

US interests with the aim of "dumbing down" the populace and alienating them from their own culture (Lopez 1995: 256). Scholarship in the 1980s went in the opposite direction, in this case to an extreme level, claiming that the *telenovela* was actually the savior of Lain American culture and a weapon against American cultural hegemony (Lopez 1995: 256–7). *Telenovelas* went in a decade from being an alien other to a cultural hero. Both of these positions were overblown, and part of Lopez's work sought to navigate between these two positions. The *telenovela* is a site of negotiation for viewers, particularly of modernization and the relationship between viewer and producer. Lopez argues that the *telenovela* needs to be understood as an agent in the complex sets of relationships and processes of modernization and nation building (Lopez 1995: 257). In terms of the latter, *telenovelas* have been enormous money spinners, which has allowed the stations and industry a degree of freedom and power in regards to the US culture industry. Unlike film production, which has not been very successful compared to Hollywood, the *telenovela* reinforced television industry has been successful. In terms of the latter, national identities are readily and easily read into the *telenovelas* themselves, with easily characterized differences between the products of various countries: Mexican *telenovelas* are marked by extreme pathos and very rigidly drawn divides between good and bad. Brazilian *telenovelas* are characterized as more realistic and having higher production values. The *telenovelas* of other Latin American countries fall in between, but often add touches of comedy – in Columbia this is a focus of their *telenovelas* (Lopez 1995: 261–2). In this way, the *telenovela* provided Latin American audiences with an obvious and recognized presentation of self that the viewer could identify with and so confirm their national identity. In the 1990s, as pan-Latin American interests began to dominate local and interregional discourses, the *telenovelas* also began to show a certain contraction of difference. Further, with large audiences in the USA, the *telenovela* has come to be influential in the cultural giant itself (Lopez 1995: 266–7).

CULTURAL STUDIES

Qualitative studies of the cinema have not existed for as long as other approaches, essentially beginning with the rise of cultural studies as a discipline.[1] While communication studies was early to engage in studies of the audience, as mentioned above, these were often quantitative-based and, furthermore, in the early stages of audience studies, they worked on a fairly restricted model. This model did become much more sophisticated over time, not least with the realization that the "receivers" played a role beyond passively receiving (Barker 2000: 32–3). However, by this time the cultural studies approach – especially Stuart Hall's *Encoding-Decoding Model* – had already hit its stride. Cultural studies combines ideas from a diverse range of theoretical approaches such as political economy, sociology, literary theory, philosophy, and art criticism to study culture – usually, though not always, popular culture (Barker 2000: 3–34). Cultural studies concentrates on the relationships between particular forms of popular culture (cinema, television, advertising, for instance) and wider issues such as political ideology, class, or gender. While there is more than one branch of cultural studies, the acknowledged birthplace is The Centre for Contemporary Cultural Studies (CCCS) in the 1960s (Barker 2000: 6). CCCS was founded at the University of Birmingham, and is also sometimes known as the Birmingham School of Cultural Studies. From the start, the focus of CCCS was overtly political and aimed towards developing some of the ideas of the Frankfurt School, especially in terms of the latter's critique of popular culture as capitalism-affirming mass culture (Barker 2000: 10). Through the later 1960s and 1970s, the CCCS began to address the relationship between culture and power along new lines and to develop a new form of critical theory.

Under Stuart Hall, CCCS began to analyze media as a form of text. Text in this case is not limited to written or printed texts, but extends the idea of text to include cultural products like cinema (Barker 2000: 11). The text exists between the producer and the consumer/audience. What is crucial here is that texts are "read" by the audiences for those texts. Reading is an active, rather than passive, method of engaging with the text. In other words, the reader was now understood as having *agency* – a capacity for active and critical engagement. The idea of agency, particularly in some branches of cultural studies has been put into opposition with ideas of groups of people as either limited or nonexistent. The concept of agency has led to further analyses of ways in which groups may resist, accept, or assimilate the ideologies and policies of the dominant groups. To return to our reader, he or she will interpret the meaning of the text, accepting or rejecting the "message," based upon many factors, one of the most important being the cultural background of the reader. Therefore, Hall's encoding-decoding model promotes the agency of audiences – taking it away from the Frankfurt School model. Using this model, cultural studies scholars began to produce empirically based research on the relationship between cultural texts and audiences. Ien Ang produced arguably one of the most important audience studies in the agency model – *Watching "Dallas:" Soap Operas and the Melodramatic Imagination* (1985). David Morley (1980, 1996) and Marie Gillespie (1995) are other researchers who produced important research on film and television audiences.

Cultural studies was not the only discipline to engage in qualitative audience studies, but it was cultural studies that popularized the endeavor. The approach (with some differences I will explain later) was to spend time with real people watching (or consuming – another name for these types of studies was *consumption studies*)

Case Study: How an Indian Devotional Film is "Read" outside of India

One of the most important of the elements that audience studies have to add to the entire field of film study is the wealth of information they provide on the ways in which real people accept, reject, assimilate, or appropriate the messages intended by the film producers. This dynamic is even more interesting when the message in question is being consumed far outside of its intended locale (which is not necessarily only spatial). In this case study, Gillespie's audience study of Indian television and film consumers in Southall, west London will be used to address just this issue (Gillespie 1995). While Gillespie's audience is still "Indian," it is an expatriate audience that is no longer immersed in the national, political, or cultural sphere that the filmmakers inhabit. What effect does this have on the reception of the films in question? Does this question even matter when we are dealing with real audiences? Can we still talk about audience studies or should we be discussing *audiences* studies? This case study will provide interesting information with which to rethink some of the various claims vis-à-vis the relationship between the film producers and their audiences. The implications for global cinemas such as Hollywood or anime are profound.

Gillespie argues quite strongly for a truly ethnographic audience study, arguing that it would get media studies out of the Frankfurt School versus agency approaches to the audience (Gillespie 1995: 360). She goes on to chide anthropologists for having ignored the media. From my own experience, I have to agree fully with Gillespie that taking visual media and those media audiences seriously can be extremely productive and rewarding. Gillespie also demonstrates the difference, even in her shorter articles, between an approach that uses the audience to back up the theory, as with many of the earlier audience studies, and one that looks at the situation starting from the audience (at least as much as possible, all researchers will work within theoretical paradigms and other influences). This is made evident from the first page of her work "Sacred Serials, Devotional Viewing and Domestic Worship" (1995), which begins with excerpts from her field diary:

> 6:00 p.m. I arrive at the Dhani's three-bedroom terraced house in old Southall. Shoes are removed in the hallway. The smell of incense hangs heavily in the air. Mother, father, and seven children (aged 11 to 21 years old) are seated in the living room. We greet each other from a distance. Malati, a bright-eyed, smiling 14-year-old girl (and an ex-pupil of mine) ushers me to the sofa where I sit cushioned between the younger children and we chat. (Gillespie 1995: 354)

With economy Gillespie sets the stage for her interaction with the Dhani family and for the media encounter they are all about to embark upon. Further, she provides information on how she is connected with the family. She goes on to outline more about the encounter, providing the reader with further details about the family and the household, such as that they are devotees of the god Krishna and that they are familiar with British television – as the family engages with the television program *Blind Date*, the mother encouraging the female contestant to pick number two (Gillespie 1995: 354). Gillespie gives some details about the program that she has gone to the house to view, the British televised theatrical production of *The Mahabharata* (one of the major Hindu religious epics). Gillespie's interest was to find out this Hindu family's reception of a non-Indian production of such an important cultural and religious text. Almost immediately, she has an answer:

> 7:30 *The Mahabharata* begins. The international casting has the immediate effect of rendering their dearly beloved gods unrecognizable. The confusion is expressed in a loud barrage of repartee:

> Ranjit: That's Ganesha!
> Sefali: No it isn't, be quiet!
> Lipi: That's Vishnu!
> Malati: Don't be silly, it's Vyasa!
> […]
> The room was filled with a sea of noise. The children appeal to their mother for help but she could not recognize the gods either. (Gillespie 1995: 355)

The father and oldest son soon leave, and shortly afterwards the children tell Gillespie that she should see the film *Sita's Wedding* (probably *Sita Swayamvar*, Bapu 1976), which is an episode from *The Ramayana* (another of the major Hindu religious epics). Eventually, at around 10.25 p.m., alarmed and confused by what they perceive as a morally ambiguous representation of the god they particularly venerate, the family turns off the television and perform a *puja* (a ritual prayer) at a shrine in their house. The children convince Gillespie to watch *Sita's Wedding* with them. As this is a three-hour film that the family will likely watch in its entirety, this takes some convincing. Gillespie notes that even as the children suggest the other film, the atmosphere in the house changes, becoming more relaxed. And when Krishna appears in the film "a joyful atmosphere reigns for the first time in the evening" (Gillespie 1995: 356). Gillespie begins her analysis of the events by asking if the reason for the two very different reactions to the television show and the film are down to a simple dichotomy such as one being seen as sacred (*Sita's Wedding*) and the other profane (the Western produced version of *The Mahabharata*), or Indian versus Western contexts of production and reception, or even the targeting of a particular audience for *The Mahabharata* – middle class and Western rather than a popular Indian (Gillespie 1995: 357). Perhaps by chance, a different British television company showed the Indian version of *The Mahabharata* quite soon afterwards, allowing Gillespie and her informants to compare the two versions directly. The way that the family and especially the children, born in the UK, reacted to all three of these programs gave Gillespie the opportunity to come to some conclusions about issues relevant to this book – namely the cultural specificity of the ways that the audience makes sense of what they are watching, how a particular ethnic group's consumption may tap into both local (as with *Blind Date*) and global media networks (the video of *Sita's Wedding*), and also the local interpretations of that global media.

What Gillespie suggests is somewhat contrary to both the mass audience and agency-oriented approaches. The audience, in this case the Dhani family, is navigating two worldviews – one pragmatic and the other religious. And these two worldviews are mutually informing; they affect one another (Gillespie 1995: 359). I would suggest that we could usefully substitute other terms like ethnic identity or national identity in place of religious. For instance, in viewing a television program like the popular Australian soap opera *Neighbours*, the two worldviews are negotiated differently by the parents and the children. For the parents and the local Indian community, *Neighbours* is somewhat transgressive, as the program displays social values that are counter to those of the older community members. For the children, *Neighbours* provides them with a framework from which to negotiate with their mother (and by extension the wider Indian community) about changing ideas of gender or other important social values (Gillespie 1995: 361–2). The viewing of Indian media promotes the Indian identity and values, even promoting Indian nationalism or religious fundamentalism. For the children, like the Dhani children, they are more able to translate the two worldviews when watching the Indian media. For the older members of the Indian community, the Indian films and television shows can provide comfort and certainty in a world that can be quite alien, or in times of problems like family illness (Gillespie 1995: 362–78). However, crucially, the viewing of the different media also allows the Dhanis to explore and develop their religious worldview as well. In the example of the Dhanis, Gillespie is referring to religion, but again we could discuss ethnicity or national identity here usefully. Because of the context of the viewing, an Indian family in London, there is a dynamic to the viewing that is different as their context is different. The different global (*Sita's Wedding*, *Neighbours*) and local (*Blind Date*) media all provide a different set of viewpoints from which to take solace, push boundaries, and affirm beliefs in a particular ratio that is linked to the context of reception.

television, going to the cinema, or using the Internet. As the case studies suggest, the most work has been done on television and the results of this variant in particular have been extremely influential in studies of media in general, whether that be within cultural studies, communication studies, anthropology, or sociology. The results of these studies have largely contradicted the presumptions of the Frankfurt School-oriented theories, in that audiences show a great deal of agency and are quite media-savvy when consuming television shows, that they can engage with aspirational shows like *Dallas* or *Dynasty* in complex ways – aspiring to wealth and lifestyle, while simultaneously commenting on the impracticality of that aspiration (Barker 2000: 32–3). Again, Ang's analysis of *Dallas* (1985) is seminal in this regard. As mentioned, the focus on agency in many of these studies has meant that they are often in direct conflict with "mass audience"-oriented approaches, to such an extent that within media studies there is a dichotomy between the two approaches, and while there are some analysts who use the ideas of both quite productively, there is a great deal of argument between the two positions. While this dichotomy makes for a certain frisson within media studies, the polarization is also damaging. One of the strengths of anthropology in this regard lies in its attempts at *holism* (the idea that a particular system or phenomenon cannot be understood in terms of its component parts, but only as a complete entity). In other words, it is not enough just to understand what audience X makes of a television show, we also need to know how that understanding fits into the wider cultural and social context of the viewing. It

Figure 4.3   Films are not only watched in cinemas, the Special Video Club, Gambia. Photograph by Victor de la Fuente 2008.

would be disingenuous to fail to point out that many sociology, cultural studies, and communication studies researchers also do this, and many anthropologists do not do it, but for anthropology this is expected, and as we will see in some of the case studies, with extremely informative results.

ANTHROPOLOGY

Anthropologists have been more hesitant to become involved with media, and cinema in particular, than some other disciplines. Indeed, as has been pointed out in different places in this book, scholars from outside the discipline have chided anthropologists for neglecting the media (e.g. Gillespie 1995: 360). However, one area in which anthropology has engaged with mass media has been reception studies (see, for instance, several of the chapters in either Ginsberg, Abu-Lughod, and Larkin (2002) or Askew and Wilk (2002)). There are a couple of reasons for this: historically, socio-cultural anthropologists have focused on village-level communities rather than cities (though since the 1960s this has changed); anthropologists have also concentrated on societies and cultures from what would be classified as the "Third World" – often former colonies – and cinema-going is a semi-regular event at best as opposed to television watching, which is a daily occurrence. Indeed, I remember a discussion as an anthropology undergraduate with a professor who said (regarding fieldwork) that you better get used to watching a lot of television, as that is what your informants will be doing most of the time you are with them. I have to add that this was not meant as positive, though media now is increasingly an important subfield within the discipline, and within anthropology as a whole is studied as one element that makes up the society in question. The formation of the Media Anthropology Network, for instance, has been a positive step for many anthropologists whose work has come to encompass new media technologies such as the Internet.

At the moment, however, audience studies are where anthropology has had the most intersection with film. Taking Dickey's work on south Indian cinema audiences as an example, her interest lies in "what the audience makes of the medium" (1993: 5). Investigating the specificities of life among the urban poor in south India, she analyzes Tamil language films, their genres, the fan clubs that surround actors in Tamil films, and the impact they have upon their audience, from the perspective of that audience. To give a sense of the importance of cinema in south India, Dickey states:

> In the city of Madurai, cinema is everywhere. Glittering billboards advertise the latest films, and smaller posters are slapped on to spare inches of wall space. Movie songs blare from horn speakers and cassette players at weddings, puberty

> rites, and temple and shrine festivals. Tapes of movie dialogues play at coffee
> stalls, while patrons join in reciting them. Rickshaws and shop boards are
> painted with movie stars' pictures. Young men and women follow dress and
> hairstyle fashions dictated by the latest films. Younger children trade movie star
> cards, learn to disco dance like the film actors, and recreate heroic battles in
> imitation of their favourite stars. Fan club members meet in the streets to boast
> about their star and make fun of his rival. (Dickey 1993: 3)

Dickey's work is in many ways an analysis of the juncture that may occur between
cultural producers and consumers when the media is successful in satisfying the
demands/needs/wishes of its consumers (even when those needs may have been
created, at least in part, by that same media). In this case, as opposed to the middle
class, which frequently looks down upon popular Indian cinema, the working classes
enjoy and participate actively in their consumption of the media. The films serve
different needs for their audiences, and as the audience numbers suggest, as does the
quote above, the films satisfy these needs very well.

Case Study: Cinema-Going in Nigeria

Following on from the previous case study, we turn to another question for the
audience study approach – namely whether there is a different relationship between
the audience/producer in different locations and with different types of films around
the world. There are many differences in the physical experience of cinema-going
around the world. There are very different expectations of behavior and standards of
conduct. In the Netherlands and Myanmar, audiences are quite boisterous. In the UK
and USA, audiences tend to be attentive and quiet, unless there are a lot of teens or
if it is culturally appropriate *not* to be respectful – e.g. at a midnight showing of *The
Rocky Horror Picture Show* (Sharman 1975). How do these differences affect the way
the audience relates to the film and the film message – or does it have an effect? Do
the different ideological meanings in different cinemas, such as Hollywood, Japanese
film, or in this case Indian cinema, or the stylistic or technical differences also make
a difference in the audience's reception? This case study will focus on cinema-going
in Nigeria to address some of these questions (Larkin 2002). Again, this will have
implications for our understanding of the audience/media relationship.

One of the definitions of cinema that was raised in the Introduction but has not
really been dealt with too much since is the definition of cinema as a physical space.
Although the physical space of the cinema and in the cinema can have a profound
effect upon the audience's viewing pleasure (or lack thereof), this aspect of the cinema
is little talked about. If the physical space of the cinema is combined with different

cinema-going practices and attitudes, there is even more scope for effects upon the viewing public (Larkin 2002: 320–1). The possibilities for watching a film in a cinema are varied. The cover of this book depicts a cinema, still operational, from a different era – and vastly different physical space entirely – from the shopping center multiplex. The possibilities for watching films range from the old "picture palaces" that still exist in different parts of the world, to the art house cinema-devoted screen in a multiplex that may uncomfortably seat 20 people at most, to almost limitless variations in between. This is even before bringing up watching films at home or in home theatres. Beyond the physical space of the cinema is the physical space of the cinema itself and how that space fits into the surrounding landscape, whether that landscape is spatial or social. The cinema is more than just a building that films are shown in (Larkin 2002: 320). They are located within many layers of social and moral discourse. The cinema can be seen as a place of wonder, a place of leisure, and it can be seen as a place of immorality. In different parts of the world with different ideas of morality, and especially public morality, the cinema will take on very different connotations.

In northern Nigeria, the cinema is caught up not only in the moral/immoral landscape, but also a landscape fashioned by and located in the colonial period (Larkin 2002: 319–20, 322, 326, and *passim*). Cinema-going in Nigeria is diverse, with a mixture of Nigerian video films, Bollywood films, and Hollywood films. The locales for the viewing of these different films are also diverse, including home viewing on VCRs, televised, or in a cinema. The attendance at and reception of the films at these different venues is mixed with different social relations and the meanings that can be attached to the different films at different spaces and different audiences. Who gets to go to the cinema is related to issues such as class, gender, ethnicity, and even religious belief. This interaction has a crucial effect upon the meanings given to and taken from the media consumption (Larkin 2002: 323). The British colonial government introduced the cinema in Nigeria, and as was the case in their colonies, the cinema was initially intended for the elite, particularly the European elite. For Muslim Nigerians who make up the majority of the population in northern Nigeria, this link to the colonial period along with Islamic prohibitions on the creation of images meant that the cinema had a doubly "bad" connotation. In the city of Kano, the first cinema was established outside the traditional Muslim center of the city, which immediately lent an air of depravity to the establishment (Larkin 2002: 327). As it was in an area where drinking and other illicit activities took place, the cinema as a social space has a negative connotation to this day. In this part of Nigeria, cinema attendance is principally a lower class male activity (this does not mean small audiences, however, as we shall see shortly). Any woman that goes to the cinema is regarded as a prostitute, with the further result that the cinema is also linked to sexual desire and reinforcing the impression of immorality. Watching Indian films then takes on a different dynamic in northern Nigeria than that more typical of cinema-going in India itself for instance. The cinema space is regarded as an area where, because of its inherent immorality, social conventions do not have to be upheld, and so activities that would be deemed anti-social outside the confines of that space are allowed. Alongside the general prohibition for women in Muslim Nigeria from entering mixed gender spaces, the immorality of the cinema space means that women are basically denied access to this social space (Larkin 2000: 225). Television and video, however, are domestic media and, therefore, very important to women. Indian cinema is extremely popular on television and video, so much so that in northern Nigeria Indian films are spoken of as women's films. One of the effects of this is that young Hausa women (the main ethnic group in this part of Nigeria) wear jewelry fashioned after that worn by Indian actresses. The experience of spectatorship is also shaped by these factors:

> Watching the image of Indian actress Sridevi dancing across a twenty-foot-high screen in an arena with thousands of other men, many whistling and shouting sexual comments, is a visceral experience. This sensuality is only heightened by the sexual availability of *karuwai* (prostitutes), wandering from row to row. (Larkin 2000: 227)

The same film watched at home on the television takes on a different meaning and experience.

The different meaning and codes of behavior that these different media spaces have has also affected the development of the other major cinematic media: the Hausa version of the Nigerian video film. The different experiences of cinema, and the different meanings that it takes on, form one aspect of the background to the development of Hausa video films. Indian cinema for Nigerian consumers provides a non-Western model of modernity, one that is not exactly synonymous with Muslim Hausa expectations and values, but again provides an alternative to the Western model (Larkin 2000: 228–33). The diversity of possible readings and experiences of different media has also allowed the Hausa video filmmakers different models for their productions. While the song and dance routines in Indian cinema are extremely popular, they would not be appropriate for a Hausa to perform, so the routines are amended. In one instance the main character sings his love song into a cassette recorder and sends the tape to the woman he is in love with – allowing for singing of love songs while retaining sexual segregation (Larkin 2000: 236). A point that comes out quite powerfully in this case study is that Indian popular cinema, once accused of being purely imitative of Western cinema, is now recognized as offering a different model for cinema audiences, one that shows up as an influence in films made on a different continent. The Nigerian video films that have come out of the Hausa area share certain key elements with Indian cinema, particularly a social commentary on the erosion of social values under the influence of Western materialism. The Hausa video films often focus on love, but in a culturally specific manner – negotiating the tensions between the traditional arranged marriages with love marriages, for instance. The films also borrow from the video films of other Nigerian ethnic groups such as the Yoruba and Igbo, as well other cultural aspects of these groups, but, as with the example from Indian cinema, translate them into culturally appropriate or acceptable versions (Larkin 2000: 233). How the development of Hausa video films is changing, or not, the social space of the cinema in northern Nigeria is not known as yet as the social and cultural effects of this developing media form are still very much in production.

Perhaps the most important aspect that anthropology has to contribute to audience studies (or, as was suggested in the Chapter 3, the study of film in general) is that anthropology, almost uniquely, has focused upon non-Western peoples and their media. As was mentioned above, there have been studies within cultural studies and

Figure 4.4   Nollywood VCDs on display at a stall at the multicultural Kwakoe festival in the Bijlmermeer district of Amsterdam, the Netherlands. Photograph by Paul Keller 2006.

Figure 4.5   Close-up of Nollywood VCDs on display at a
stall at the multicultural Kwakoe festival in the Bijlmermeer
district of Amsterdam, the Netherlands. Photograph by
Paul Keller 2006.

other disciplines of non-Western audiences, but these are almost always expatriate audiences, for example Indian audiences in London watching Indian movies or television (Gillespie 1995). These studies are intriguing and informative, but are of limited use in understanding the relationship between, say, Indian cinema and Indian filmgoers, as Dickey has done. As we saw with the example of Deepa Mehta and the reception of her film *Fire*, the differences between the two can be extreme. What analyzing the audience "at home" adds is an awareness of the social and cultural context in which viewing takes place. Abu-Lughod's analysis of Egyptian melodrama (2002), for instance, is an intriguing look at Egyptians' negotiations with modernity, and how television has played a role in that negotiation. More like the *telenovela* than a British or American soap opera, Egyptian melodramas are fixed run serials. Further, they are both more morally unambiguous and more emotional than European or American soap operas. As well as representing a national identity, as Lopez argued for Latin American *telenovelas* (1995), the Egyptian melodramas are reproducing middle class values. The emotion that the Egyptian melodramas demonstrate, therefore, are actively creating new senses and discourses of selfhood and identity, one that is geared more towards a middle class understanding of and relationship to modernity (Abu-Lughod 2002: 115–16). In particular, what is being created is an increasing sense of individualism, often seen as one of the most important markers of a Western modernity: extended sense of self, an autonomous, bounded, and self-activating modern subject. To illustrate her argument Abu-Lughod provides the reader with the example of Amira, a domestic worker (Abu-Lughod 2002: 122–7). Amira watches the serials ever night and seldom watches foreign television programs. The manner in which Amira demonstrates most powerfully her engagement in this identity creation via the serials is through accounts of her life history. When recalling events like her arrival in Cairo, Amira's account takes on the trappings of a melodrama serial one in which she starred – people she encountered were either good or bad. As Abu-Lughod puts it:

> Like the television dramas, the themes of her story are money, with the villain trying to cheat her out of hers, and the secret, with the truth of her sinister husband discovered too late. The melodramatic heroine, innocent and good, is wronged and victimized. Seeking a better life, symbolized by her sisters' good clothe and gold, she leaves the village and home to find herself overworked, underpaid, and hungry in a house where the food is locked up. Seeking love, companionship, or respectability – whatever it is that marriage is supposed to bring-she finds herself betrayed. (2002: 124)

Abu-Lughod argues that Amira's casting of herself as the star in her own melodrama positions her as a modern citizen, what the people making the shows intend

(Abu-Lughod 2002: 124). So far this sounds like a straightforward Transmission Theory or Frankfurt School analysis, but there is a catch: Islam. Islam is also an important part of Amira's life and conception of self, and Islam has its own (not Westernized middle-class) model of modernity. This alternative and competing vision of modernity in fact leads to Amira negotiating the two. The everyday social worlds that people are living within also affect their understanding of self. Thus, as with kin ties, religious identities and the "modern" identity of the middle class are being combined in people like Amira to create a very different "modern" Egyptian (Abu-Lughod 2002: 128–9). The example is also a case where the rigid dichotomy of mass audience versus agency approaches was also navigated productively – for good reason, the social worlds of real audiences are more complex than either of the two approaches acknowledges. Approaches that move between the two, ones that attempt to make connections between the media and the social understand this.

As the example of Amira illustrates and as has been discussed in previous chapters, viewing does not occur in a socio-cultural vacuum any more than production does. This is a significant difference as the specific historical, social, or religious contexts of India, Japan, Indonesia, or Nigeria are read into cinema, and it is through these contexts that the audience makes sense of the cinema. To return to a previous point, expatriate audiences are only partially reading these cinemas through these elements. For instance, if those audiences are second or third generation, or are political or religious dissidents, they will be reading those cinemas through different sets of cult-ural "filters." Further, as they are engaging with those cinemas at a remove, their responses are often much more as the agency theorists argue – namely more nuanced and overtly thought-out (see the Gillespie case study in this chapter for an instance). These audiences will be much more "active" in their engagement with the media – accepting, even glorying in certain aspects and reacting critically to others. The dynamics of non-expatriate audience reactions is often more complex, with nuances depending on age, class, and other more esoteric factors, such as nostalgia. A further complication on this issue is when we bring diasporic production back into the picture. As we saw earlier in the book with Deepa Mehta's film *Fire*, diasporic media can have an uneasy relationship with the different groups who do not share the new sensibilities of the diasporic media maker. When that diasporic community begins to span generations, other complications arise. Schein's look at Hmong diasporic media production and consumption illustrates some of these problems (Schein 2002). The Hmong are an ethnic group originally from China, where they are referred to as Miao, now living throughout much of Southeast Asia and, since the Vietnam War and events following it, have emigrated to the United States, Canada, France, and Australia. Hmong diasporic media is of a different level of media from that of the films and television produced by exiled Iranians, discussed by Naficy (1993, 2001).

The media produced by the Hmong diaspora is diverse, with newspapers, photography, music CDs, television and radio shows, and videos. The content of the videos is wide ranging: dramas, melodramas, war stories, martial arts, beauty pageants, and other public events of concern to Hmong, both in the diaspora as well as in Southeast Asia (Schein 2002: 230). With regard to the videos, they are produced solely for consumption within the Hmong ethnic group, both emigrant and home. The videos are made without corporate sponsorship such as advertising, though they are often produced for profit. Probably the largest genre is that of videos set in Laos (the birthplace of most USA-based Hmong), Thailand (where many spent time in refugee camps), and China (the original homeland of the Hmong). The stories and representation of these different places are also very different. As mentioned, USA-based Hmong media is consumed both in the USA and in Laos. Among the issues to understand when studying exile or diasporic media is that there are at least two very different desires at play (Schein 2002: 230–1; Naficy 1993). This is certainly true in the creation of Hmong media. Hmong media is in a dialogue with Hmong senses of identity, which for the emigrant community is one that is formed partially by an *imagining* of Southeast Asian Hmong identity, one that is not based on experiential knowledge for many, but through media such as the videos (Schein 2002: 231). This is especially true of videos that celebrate Hmong culture and their Chinese ancestral home. These representations of ethnic pride and achievement are important when a group is culturally and economically marginalized, such as the Hmong are in their diaspora. There are generational differences, for instance older Hmong who do remember Laos have a different understanding of and relation to the videos that celebrate Hmong culture than do younger members. The videos are important for another reason in that they allow the diasporic Hmong to communicate with the homeland Hmong, even if at a distance and in a very mediated manner. These types of videos are usually documentary style, with personal messages mixed in:

> In another documentary-style piece, the roving tourist eye of the camera suddenly takes on a brokering function. After introducing the landscape, villages, and lifestyles of the local Miao people, it turns to a more instrumental function. Three rural young women are arrayed on a hilltop, colorfully dressed before a backdrop of panoramic scenery. The cameraman asks: "Will you sing a song for me to take back to America to find you a man?" And then: "Are you girls still young and unmarried?" [...] They proceed to sing, not knowing where to cast their eyes, They appear disoriented at the staging of what, in face-to-face courtship, would have been a dialogue, but now has been rendered as a one-way self-marketing opportunity about which their faces convey primarily ambivalence. (Schein 2002: 239)

The example, and others that Schein gives, points out another significant difference in the way this medium of exchange is understood, namely that it is the diasporic Hmong that are the ones in control of the representations, even of the voices of the homeland Hmong. The tapes and what they depict ultimately are for the consumption desire of the diaspora, who watch and listen to the content in very particular ways.

There are problems with the audience study approach – for instance, there is a danger of over-generalization. Qualitative approaches by their very nature are small-scale endeavors. A researcher simply cannot have the degree of personal contact necessary to the approach and have the same number of contacts as a quantitative approach. For proponents of the latter, that a qualitative researcher cannot make general statements based on such a limited data set is a failing of qualitative studies (Gillespie 1995: 359). Unfortunately, some early audience studies fulfilled this criticism only too well. The other main criticism that the audience study approach faces is one that many *subaltern* (bottom up) approaches share, namely that they do not always acknowledge the power and control of the establishment upon their respondents (O'Sullivan et al. 1994: 110). They are so focused on proving the agency of the viewers and consumers that they fail to acknowledge when, where, and why this is not the case. However, there are some important lessons that should be taken from audience studies: one of the most important is helping to understand how film "works." For theorists, the benefits of understanding how film works for the audience includes having a more nuanced set of tools for analyzing film, and for filmmakers and film students this means making better/more successful films. From my experience, this aspect of film theory/study faces the most initial resistance from film students (including ethnographic film students). However, the context of reception is or should be important for a filmmaker – for selfish reasons if no other – understanding how a film "works" for an audience means that you can make films that "work" better, and in theory at least films that are more enjoyable or hit more of a chord with the audience will be more successful (whether that success is critical or commercial). This entails not only an understanding of the "nuts and bolts" of filmmaking (e.g. how to frame a close-up successfully), but why those "nuts and bolts" work (e.g. using a close-up appropriately engages the viewer with the character's subjective position and thus creates empathy or identification with that character). The explanation for why this works will change depending on who the theorist is: for instance, from a psychoanalytic perspective film taps into subconscious human interaction; from a textualist approach the audience understands the film "grammar" in which a close-up signals an important emotional portrayal. Pragmatically, from the filmmaker's perspective as long as she or he understands the result and can employ it successfully, the reason may *seem* secondary, but either way understanding how film works for the audience is critical.

At a different level though, this still does not answer some of the criticisms, and here is where anthropology can have a crucial role to play. The anthropological examples and case study show that, by taking into account the larger social world in which the media consumption is talking place, this gets us beyond at least some of these problems mentioned above. As we saw with the Hmong, both agency and global forces are involved in understanding what the Hmong diasporic media *means* to the consumers of that media (Schein 2002: 242). Larkin's case study in this chapter shows us how the physical spaces and social attitudes can impact upon the way the audiences engage with particular media and even genres of media. As noted in the previous chapter, an anthropological approach to cinema has much to offer and this is certainly true for the context of viewing. The long-term engagement with peoples' daily lives that the anthropological methodology insists upon gives scope to both deepen and broaden the audience that is being analyzed. Spending a year or more with a group of people allows for a range of information collection that simply is not possible with short-term research: experiencing different life cycle events, such as births; the chance to meet a wider range of informants that will expand that data pool; experiencing and analytically incorporating wider events such as elections; or even just the opportunity to see changes within the group being worked with over time, are all benefits that add significantly to the analytical depth available, particular when combined with the understanding that a medium of expression, such as cinema, is an integral part of society – not a reflection of it, but part of a network of relationships that need to be understood in terms of one another – cinema is embedded in society just as cultural values and social knowledge is embedded in the cinema. To return to the question of definition raised in the Introduction, for an anthropology of the cinema, the answer is all of the above.

SUGGESTED FURTHER READING

GENERAL AND EUROPE/AMERICA

Barker, C. (2000) *Cultural Studies: Theory and Practice*, London and Thousand Oaks, CA: Sage Publications.

Hay, J. Grossberg, L. and Wartella, E. (eds) (1996) *The Audience and its Landscape*, Boulder, CO: Westview Press.

O'Sullivan, T. Hartley, J., Saunders, D., Montgomery, M., and Fisk, J. (1994) *Key Concepts in Communication and Cultural Studies*, 2nd edition, London and New York: Routledge.

INDIA

Derné, S. (2000) *Movies, Masculinity, and Modernity: An Ethnography of Men's Filmgoing in India*, Westport, CT: Greenwood Press.

Dickey, S. (1993) *Cinema and the Urban Poor in South India*, Cambridge: Cambridge University Press.

NIGERIA

Haynes, J. (ed.), (2000) *Nigerian Video Films*, Ohio Center for International Studies.

Larkin, B. (2002) "The Materiality of Cinema Theaters in Northern Nigeria," in F. Ginsburg, L. Abu-Lughod, and B. Larkin (eds) *Media Worlds: Anthropology on New Terrain*, Berkeley: University of California Press, pp. 319–36.

CONCLUSION

Figure C.1   Cineplex in Japan. Photograph
by Yukari Yoshitake 2009.

> The value of anthropological approaches lies in a shared understanding of media as simply one aspect of contemporary social life, no different in essence from law, economics, kinship, social organization, art, and religion. All these categories of thought and behavior are socially conceived and socially enacted. Anthropologists categorically reject the common tendency to treat media as separate from social life and in ethnographic case after case highlight the interconnections between media practice and cultural frames of reference.
>
> Askew, *The Anthropology of Media: A Reader*

Studying cinema is one of the most interesting and rewarding activities I have engaged in as an academic. Feature films have the ability to relate to our daily life in ways that are almost frighteningly accurate, and yet can also be wondrous flights of fantasy that free us from the stresses and strains of our daily lives. They can reinvigorate our interest in the world around us by reminding us just how astonishing it can be. They can make us laugh or cry, make us angry or happy. When they are done well they take us out of ourselves (suspension of disbelief) and wrap us up in their stories. Conversely, when they are not done well it is doubly disappointing, like losing out twice – once for the time and money and then again for the loss of that transport. Film has almost limitless potential for ways to tell stories and engage the viewer. Even "throwaway" films like many Hollywood blockbusters have levels of depth and meaning that may not be apparent on first glance. In fact, studying films like *Transformers* (Bay 2007) or *Friday the 13th* (Nispel 2009) can be enlightening in its own right, though not necessarily for the same reasons as studying classics like *Citizen Kane* (Welles 1941) or *The Third Man* (Reed 1949). Even more enlightening, again for vastly different reasons, is to study "bad" movies like *Robot Monster* (Tucker 1953) or *Plan 9 from Outer Space* (Wood Jr. 1959), as understanding what is happening when films do *not* work is also important. For these reasons, and many more, it is worth understanding how film can be made to have these profound effects on us, the viewers. In other words, to understand how film works. I am sometimes asked if studying film does not spoil some of that magic I just described, if knowing the secret behind the magician's trick does not in fact spoil the trick. It does not. If anything, I feel that I enjoy the cinema now more than I ever did when I was just "going to the movies." Knowing the magician's trick only "spoils" the illusion when the magician is inept – in which case the magic is usually gone anyway. Part of the rationale for this book is to make anthropology and non-anthropology students aware that there is much going on beneath the surface story, and also to give students some tools to begin excavating those deeper levels.

The book begins by setting out a seemingly simple task, to provide a definition of *cinema*. As we went through different historical events in cinema around the world it began to become clear that cinema has a very complex history, especially if we understand cinema beyond the normal boundaries of Hollywood, Europe, and maybe Japan and India. By incorporating a broader history of the development of cinema, some interesting issues come to the fore. One is the extraordinary success and rapid spread of cinema across the globe, which is especially interesting as cinema is often held to be the most Western and technologically driven of all media. This is important for both anthropology and non-anthropology film students to understand. Cinema has been, and remains to this day, very popular because of its ability to affect people in many ways. Further, different cinemas began to develop in different parts of the world. These cinemas both intersect with audiences *as cinema* (a German film, for instance, still functions as a film), and also as particular local expressions of a particular culture. Understanding both of these aspects of cinema is important for any study of that medium. This understanding of the complex connections and disconnects between various times, genres, national endeavors, and events did not help us with a definition, but did perhaps warn us that a definition could be more difficult than might be imagined. The history of cinema, beyond any use or uselessness regarding the definition of cinema, is extremely important in getting us past certain long-standing assumptions about the cinema, however. Principally, cinema is a *global* phenomenon and although some aspects of that phenomenon have relatively more power, the relationship is at heart dialogic.

In terms of our search for a definition, the second chapter outlining the developments in film theory certainly aided in providing one working definition, that, for many who theorize about film, cinema is understood as content and filmmaker (especially the auteur). While there is certainly some attention to context, the principal interest is what is on screen or in the intention of the filmmaker. From some of the earliest practitioners, there has been a close link between the cinema and theories about the cinema, as some the most important early filmmakers were also some of the earliest theorists of the cinema. Early cinema was not universally appreciated despite, or possibly because of, its rapid success, and some of the early theoretical models (e.g. Frankfurt School) were highly critical. Conversely, other early theoretical models were attempts to legitimize the new media/art form (e.g. formalism). While many of the early theories were interested in film as an art form, with the academicization of film theory in the late 1960s and 1970s, new models began to be promoted, models that looked at film's ideological function and how film "works." Some of the numerous models and theories that are available to contemporary film theorists include Marxist, structuralist, semiotic, psychoanalysis, and literary theory approaches. Again, it is vitally important for both anthropology and non-anthropology students of film to know and appreciate the rich history of film theory. Understanding how film works is also vital to any study that seeks to understand either the medium's effect on its viewers, or the medium in itself. This focus on how film works does bring the wider context of film production into the analysis, but with the exception of approaches like national cinema and third cinema this context was and is not the main focus.

While film theory has covered a wide range of issues relating to cinema, it has also left certain arenas relatively understudied. The context of production, distribution, and exhibition is one of those areas. The approaches that investigate these elements of cinema provide yet another definition, namely, that cinema is more than the pictures on the screen, but involves a network of relationships that stretch from local sites of exhibition to global political and economic maneuvering. In Chapter 3 some of the wider environments that filmmaking takes place within were discussed. Those environments include the national context, and several different approaches and disciplines within and outside of film theory have investigated that arena, including the Frankfurt School, communication studies, and, within film theory itself, national cinema and third cinema. A further context, and one even less studied is that of the social and cultural context in which films are produced. It is important for both anthropology and non-anthropology students to appreciate how crucial these contexts are to cinema. As is argued throughout this book, an anthropological approach would have a significant amount to offer our attempt to understand the contexts in which cinema is created. And in this chapter were some of the first suggestions for what that approach might entail.

There is another context relevant to the cinema that traditional approaches to film have perhaps not paid sufficient attention to: that of the audience. In other words, we have yet another differing opinion about the definition of cinema, namely, that a definition or understanding of cinema needs also to incorporate the reception of the medium. While several elements of traditional film theory do analyze the effects of cinema on its audience, that audience is often a "model" audience, i.e. a theorized audience rather than an audience of real living and breathing people. For example, while psychoanalysis approaches did seek to understand what audiences "got" out of cinema – why the audiences enjoyed the experience or what cinema did to them – these approaches were not basing their theories on empirical studies of actual people. Several approaches outside of classic film theory, such as communication studies, cultural studies, and anthropology, do base their understanding of audience responses to media on real people. In this regard, anthropology's focus on context and use of participant-observation are important arguments for an anthropological approach to the study of audiences, as the levels of information that long-term qualitative research can provide offer new insights and understandings of the relationship between the cinema and its audiences articulated throughout this chapter (and in different ways throughout the book): interpellation, agency, subjectivity, and negotiation of the message among many, many others.

So, to return to the suggestion raised in the Introduction, that anthropology might have significant value in our understanding the cinema. This suggestion is fundamental to the entire book, and I want to spell out the various reasons that anthropology indeed has great value to film study. As was mentioned in Chapter 3, there are some key features of anthropology that would be useful in furthering the ways we attempt to understand the cinema. First of all is one of the most important rationales for incorporating an anthropological approach to cinema, which is anthropology's history of experience working with non-Western peoples. Too often within classic film theory it has been assumed that the models and theories employed are universal, that issues like interpellation, agency, and subjectivity – as well as many others mentioned throughout the book – are the same everywhere, or that the ways that the audiences make sense of those issues are the same everywhere. Anthropology's knowledge of and experience with making sense of local understandings and worldviews is of immense help in overcoming at least to some degree these issues. It has also too often been assumed that the social or cultural contexts of production and reception can be taken for granted, especially regarding Hollywood films. Perhaps even worse is the assumption that Hollywood is somehow "culture free." As has been pointed out, the obverse of the unwarranted universal application of Western developed and oriented theories, is the omission of non-Western films from any analytical framework outside of a "cultural" analysis. Hollywood films on the other hand are often regarded as somehow developing outside of any context besides its own context. The focus on non-Western cinema in Chapter 3 was both intentional, but also to an extent necessary, as there are far fewer studies that seriously attempt to link American film output to the wider social and cultural context that it takes place within, and when it does occur, is usually of a facile nature. This becomes increasingly the case when the focus is on a particular director – as if the auteur-ness of said director may be called into question. While there are studies that do take the context of American cinema and cinema makers seriously, they are not representative of the majority. All of which is especially dangerous when considered along with the presumption that the theories (usually based upon Western cinema) are universal. While these assumptions *are* gradually changing, it is in facilitating that change and furthering our understanding of cinema that an anthropological approach to fiction film has so much to offer.

This historical expertise with different understandings of the world is not the only area where anthropology has much to offer cinema studies, though. Another area is the discipline's focus on context – it is no accident that chapters 3 and 4 use the word "context" in their titles. As the quote that opens this chapter states, anthropologists regard a phenomenon like cinema as part of society, one that cannot usefully be understood apart from that partnership. The more holistic approach of anthropology may help to overcome some the problems that result when aspects of that partnership are analyzed in isolation, such as was discussed in several places in the book. Pulling cinema out of its context and analyzing it as separate from its place in society *has* resulted in knowledge of cinema, which has been of fundamental importance in our understanding of cinema, but ultimately such an inherently partial approach leaves almost as many questions and criticisms as it does answers. The complaints of many non-Western film scholars about the treatment of the films of their countries, for instance, would be an example where the tendency to analyze cinema in isolation, combined with the aforementioned misplaced expectation of a universal applicability for said theories, might be at fault. This means understanding the wider contexts in which films are produced and consumed. An appreciation of the wider contexts that production, distribution, exhibition, and viewing take place within can productively bridge theory, the international level (globalization, the influence of other cinemas and media), the local (government policies and aesthetics), and the audience. All media, but film perhaps especially, is where the "grand discourses" – political economy and globalization, class and gender, and internationalism versus nationalism – intersect with the lives of everyday people. The diasporic Hmong media production and consumption example or the cinema-going in Nigeria case study both illustrate how productive this contextualization can be. Turning to the methods of anthropology, participant-observation in particular, with its emphasis on long-term and engagement in the daily lives of people, is a powerful tool in helping to understand how people negotiate those discourses in their daily lives, what the local constructions of meaning are, and what sense they make of the messages of the cinemas they are consuming. As has been mentioned, too often ideological approaches and other theoretical paradigms that sought to understand how films affect people based their theories on hypothetical audiences, rather than empirical evidence from actual people. An anthropological approach to film can help us in terms of understanding how the aforementioned discourses and their intersections with daily life are represented to the viewer, but also what sense the audience makes of that representation. This is especially true in non-Western contexts of film production and consumption – cinema industries and audiences that are usually less well researched by Western theorists, and somewhat problematically when they are.

While anthropology has much to offer the study of cinema, the reverse is also true. Anthropologists' historical aversion to cinema (and to a lesser extent popular culture and mass media in general) has diminished the discipline. As was mentioned in the Introduction, fiction film can act as a historical document on fashion, tastes, and styles. Studying it can tell us about the ideas and prejudices of a particular time and place, and can also act as a guide to cultural constructions of everyday life, to symbolic and metaphoric communication, and to political and economic forces. These and other cultural artifacts are embedded in the films produced in that context, and as various commentators have suggested have been sadly under-researched by anthropologists. Fiction film can also give us insight into reactions to issues and events, either in the past or among groups that are difficult to access otherwise. As anthropology increasingly moves away from its traditional sites and interests, its practitioners will also need to engage with some new aspects of the societies and peoples in question. Media, and cinema being an important medium in this regard, is one of those aspects. One result of this is that anthropologists can no longer ignore media, but should be actively engaging with it in their research. To do this, anthropologists need also to take more seriously the content of the media they are investigating. In particular, anthropologists need to familiarize themselves with the existing film theories. Speaking from personal experience, incorporating film theory into anthropology was not only interesting in its own right, but also opened vistas of meaning and analytical depth to my own research. This is in many ways just an extension of something anthropologists already do, which is to attempt to gain as holistic a viewpoint of their research topic as possible. Just as bringing anthropological knowledge into the study of film would be extremely beneficial, so too would it benefit anthropologists to take on board attempts to understand how film (and other forms of popular culture and media) work. Understanding how these powerful influences in people's lives actually affect people is crucial.

Anthropology's lengthy relationship with cultural relativism and the goal of attempting as much as possible to understand another culture in its own terms, the focus on the daily lives and experiences of the people that anthropologists work with, the endeavor to take a holistic approach to the subject of study, and anthropology's traditional focus on the non-Western are important, it could be argued even critical, elements that anthropology has to offer to the study of cinema. If those benefits were combined with a deeper awareness of and appreciation for the content and a richer theoretical background from which to make sense of that content, we have the powerful tools that an anthropology of the cinema would bring to the study of cinema. And that can only be a good thing.

NOTES

Introduction

1. I have not provided suggested readings for introductory texts to anthropology as the discipline is very broad and I feel that it would be of more benefit to a student wishing to investigate further to read ethnographies, such as Lee's *The Dobe Ju/'hoasi* (1993) for a classic example, or Bourgois' *In Search of Respect: Selling Crack in El Barrio* (1995) for a more contemporary example. I would also heartily recommend Raybeck's *Mad Dogs, Englishmen, and the Errant Anthropologist* (1996) for a humorous take on doing fieldwork. If an introductory text is desired, Robbins's *Cultural Anthropology: A Problem-based Approach* (2001) or Peacock's *The Anthropological Lens: Harsh Light, Soft Focus* (2002) are both useful introductions. In terms of the theories of anthropology, Barnard's *History and Theory in Anthropology* (2000) is one of the better guides to the development of theory in anthropology. For students interested in visual anthropology, Banks and Morphy's *Rethinking Visual Anthropology* (1997) is a good starting point.

2. Often the terms ethnographic film and anthropological film are used interchangeably. However, there is also pressure to distinguish the two terms. Though the terminology is (very much) debated, ethnographic film is understood as a form of documentary that concentrates more upon depicting the lifeways of a particular group of people. It may focus upon a specific aspect of their cultural practices, such as a specific ritual, or more widely on social institutions, such as kinship. However, the depiction is as much as possible not arguing a particular theory or attempting to prove a particular anthropological point of view. The term anthropological film is used to refer to cases where there is a more active involvement by the filmmaker(s) in articulating a particular anthropological theory, position, or viewpoint.

3. To paraphrase Barker's "health warning" at the beginning of his excellent introduction to cultural studies, "Any book about [cinema] is necessarily selective and likely to engender debate, argumentation and even conflict" (Barker 2000: 3). The scope of this book is such that I will touch upon the various aspects discussed, such as cinema history, rather than attempt to provide a definitive analysis. The Suggested Readings at the end of each chapter are intended to be guides to further and more in-depth reading. These lists are in themselves partial, and some worthy texts have been left off for various reasons. Salim Said's book on Indonesian cinema, for instance, is out of print and only available at exorbitant prices (e.g. around US$100 used).

1 The History of Cinema

1. Video is shot and displayed at a higher fps than film, one of the reasons that a movie shot on video looks different than one shot on film.

2. This was also made possible by the introduction of faster exposure times.

3. There was a short film that predates this time, *Bridge in Leeds* (1888), shot by a French photographer Louis Le Prince. However, Le Prince mysteriously disappeared and his work was never completed (Cousins 2004: 17).

4. One of the most serious problems for any research on the early days of cinema is that, due to factors such as chemical composition of the film stock itself and improper storage, many of the films from this time no longer exist intact. This is particularly true for less commercially successful films and films made outside of Hollywood.

5. Another disputed term. Critics argue that a linguistic term such as grammar cannot be usefully imported to describe the way elements of cinema are combined. As the term is still used widely in the literature, for clarity I have continued to use it, though with quotation marks to note the dispute.

6. Crosland's 1926 feature *Don Juan* was the first film to feature synchronized sound, but not for dialogue – it was essentially a silent film with the music and sound effects already added. It was commercially successful and likely persuaded the Warner studio to continue the experiment with sound.

7. Several film historians and theorists claim that sound destroyed the "pure" cinema of the silent era. Their argument is that with the coming of sound the visual artistry necessary to tell the story became of secondary importance – if not disappeared from the cinema altogether.

8. As Universal did not have their own theatre chain, they concentrated on independent rural theatres, providing an affordable "package deal" combining three levels of film (low budget, mainstream, and prestige). *Dracula* and the other monster films were not initially intended as prestige offerings.

9. Auteur is a term used to refer to when a film displays the director's personal artistic vision. Directors who consistently create films that embody their vision are called auteurs. This idea will be discussed in the next section and again in Chapter 2.

10. Also discussed in more detail in Chapter 3, the British government put in place policies to ensure the exhibition of British-made films to try and spur film production – cheaply made poor-quality films (i.e. quota quickies) were the result.

11. I am not going to discuss pornography in this book, though it is a form of cinema and commercially at least a very successful form of cinema. I have chosen to do this for several reasons – not least of which is that pornography works differently from other fiction film genres, with different expectations of how the audience will relate to the film and its characters, and vice versa (how film works will be discussed Chapter 2). For a scholarly analysis of pornography, Williams (1989) is a classic work on the genre.

12. The plot of a high concept movie is easily understood by audiences, and can often be described in a sentence or two, and succinctly summarized by the movie's title. High concept movies feature relatively simple characters and a heavy reliance on conventions of film genre.

13. Not forgetting *Ocean's Thirteen* (Soderbergh 2007), *Rush Hour 3* (Ratner 2007), *Evan Almighty* (Shadyac 2007), and *Live Free or Die Hard* (Wiseman 2007).

14. There are numerous viable alternative books on the history of cinema: Slide (1989), Thomson and Bordwell (1994), and Stam (2000) are just three of many others.

2 Film Theory

1. Classic writings on film theory include Andrew's *The Major Film Theories: An Introduction* (1976) and Mast and Cohen's edited volume of readings *Film Theory and Criticism* (1979). As is suggested by the dates of these two publications, they are better suited to the early theories, such as formalism, up to semiotics. For later theories, Lapsley and Westlake's *Film Theory: An Introduction* (1988) is an excellent source.

2. Edvard Munch's famous painting *The Scream* is regarded as an inspiration for expressionism.

3. Irising is a cinematic technique popularized by D. W. Griffith, usually used to open or end a scene. If at the beginning of a scene, the shot appears inside a small circular vignette surrounded by black screen. The vignette gradually gets larger till it expands beyond the frame, and the whole shot is then clear. If the irising is at the end of scene, the reverse of the above occurs.

4. This is an *extremely* condensed synopsis of a very important and influential set of theories. Not to mention the thousands of works that have been written based upon these ideas. I would strongly suggest anyone unfamiliar with Marx's ideas to take the time to investigate them further than I have space to develop here.

5. *Cinéthique* took a more hard-line Marxist approach than did *Cahiers du cinéma*, and the two journals were often in conflict, though ideologically they were working from very similar principles (Lapsley and Westlake 1988: 8–10).

6. Freud used the term "Oedipus complex," taken from the Greek story of Oedipus who unknowingly kills his father and marries his mother, to explain a male child's subliminal desire for the exclusive love of his mother and jealousy towards the father, which may take the form of an unconscious wish for the father's death.

7. This rule has to do with camera movement. If two characters are being depicted, the camera must not move around them more than 180°. This ensures that the two characters do not reverse on the screen for the audience.

8. Dwyer's *100 Bollywood Films* (2005) provides synopses of, as the name suggests, 100 Bollywood films. This book is a very good starting point for anyone wishing to investigate Indian popular cinema further.

3 Context of Production, Distribution, and Exhibition

1. The title and translation of this film are also given as *Terang Boelan* [Full Moon] elsewhere.

2. The Philippines under Marcos is another example of a country where the cinema was mobilized by government for its own ends (David 1995).

3. See also Hatta Azad Khan (1997) or Crofts (2000) for a further example of and a discussion on national cinema respectively.

4. I have not discussed female filmmakers separately. As Parkinson points out, outside of the avant-garde film scene, "the need to demonstrate commercial potential to secure funds for further independent projects, let alone break in to the mainstream, has meant that Kathryn Bigelow, Lizzie Borden, Martha Coolidge, [...] and others have usually been forced to sublimate their feminist concerns" (Parkinson 1995: 230). In other countries and times, this has not necessarily been the case, as the examples of Deepa Mehta or Mira Nair demonstrate.

5. The film was also released as *Atanarjuat: The Fast Runner* and even just *The Fast Runner*.

6. Though the director is white, he regards the film as being an Aboriginal production that he merely facilitated the making of.

7. Wallflower Press in particular has introduced a series of books on national cinemas. See, for instance, Beumers (2006), Falicov (2006), and McFarlane (2006).

8. In an earlier note, I mentioned the series of books on national cinemas that Wallflower Press is publishing – none of them are on the USA. Hollywood is seen as somehow not a national cinema.

9. Gugler (2003) provides useful synopses for the films from African directors mentioned in this book, as well as many others. This would be a useful starting point for anyone wishing to investigate African cinema.

4 Context of Reception

1. Machor and Goldstein's edited volume (2000) is another good source regarding the relationship between cultural studies and reception studies.

BIBLIOGRAPHY

Abel. R. (ed.) (1996) *Silent Film*, New Brunswick, NJ: Rutgers University Press.

Abel. R. (1999) *The Red Rooster Scare: Making American Cinema, 1900–1910*, Berkeley: University of California Press.

Abel. R. (2006) *Americanizing the Movies and "Movie-mad" Audiences, 1910–1914*, Berkeley: University of California Press.

Abu-Lughod, L. (2002) "Egyptian Melodramas – Technology of the Modern Subject?," in F. Ginsburg, L. Abu-Lughod, and B. Larkin (eds), *Media Worlds: Anthropology on New Terrain*, Berkeley: University of California Press, pp 115–33.

Adesanya, A. (2000) "From Film to Video," in J. Haynes (ed.), *Nigerian Video Films,* Athens, OH: Center for International Studies, pp 37–50.

Andrew, J. D. (1976) *The Major Film Theories: An Introduction*, New York: Oxford University Press.

Anderson, B. (1991) *Imagined Communities: Reflection on the Origin and Spread of Nationalism*, London and New York: Verso.

Ang, I. (1985) *Watching "Dallas:" Soap Operas and the Melodramatic Imagination*, London: Methuen.

Arnheim, R. (1979) "From Film as Art," in G. Mast and M. Cohen (eds), *Film Theory and Criticism: Introductory Readings*, 2nd edition, New York and Oxford: Oxford University Press, pp. 28–32.

Askew, K. (2002) Introduction, in K. Askew and Wilk, R. (eds), *The Anthropology of Media: A Reader*, Oxford: Blackwell Publishing, pp. 1–13.

Askew, K. (2004) "Striking Samburu and a Mad Cow. Adventures in Anthropollywood," in A. Shyrock (ed.), *Off Stage/On Display: Intimacy and Ethnography in the Age of Public Culture*, Stanford, CA: Stanford University Press, pp. 31–68.

Askew, K. and Wilk, R. (eds) (2002) *The Anthropology of Media: A Reader*, Oxford: Blackwell Publishing.

Babb, L. (1981) "Glancing: Visual Interaction in Hinduism," *Journal of Anthropological Research* 37(4): 387–401.

Bakari, I. (2000) "Introduction: African Cinema and the Emergent Africa," in J. Givanni (ed.), *Symbolic Narratives/African Cinema: Audiences, Theory and the Moving Image*, London: British Film Institute, pp. 3–24.

Balázs, B. (1979) "From *Theory of the Film*" in G. Mast and M. Cohen (eds), *Film Theory and Criticism: Introductory Readings*, 2nd edition, New York and Oxford: Oxford University Press, pp. 288–98.

Balogun, F. (2004) "Booming Videoeconomy: The Case of Nigeria," in F. Pfaff, (ed.), *Focus on African Films*, Bloomington, IN: Indiana University Press, pp. 173–81.

Banks, M. and Morphy, H. (eds) (1997) *Rethinking Visual Anthropology*, New Haven and London: Yale University Press.

Barker, C. (2000) *Cultural Studies: Theory and Practice*, London and Thousand Oaks: Sage Publications.

Barnard, A. (2000) *History and Theory in Anthropology*, Cambridge and New York: Cambridge University Press.

Barthes, R. (1977) *Image, Music, Text*, trans. S. Heath, New York: Hill and Wang.

Baudry, J.-L. (1985) "Ideological Effects of the Basic Cinematographic Apparatus," in B. Nichols (ed.), *Movies and Methods Volume II: An Anthology*, Berkeley: University of California Press, pp. 531–42.

Baudry, J.-L. (1986) "The Apparatus: Metapsychological Approaches to the Impression of Reality in Cinema," in P. Rosen (ed.), *Narrative, Apparatus, Ideology: A Film Theory Reader*, New York: Columbia University Press, pp. 177–98.

Bazin, A. (1967–1971) *What is Cinema?* Berkeley: University of California Press.

Belton, J. (1996) "New Technologies," in G. Nowell-Smith (ed.), *The Oxford History of World Cinema*, Oxford: Oxford University Press, pp. 483–90.

Bessire, L (2003) "Talking Back to Primitivism: Divided Audiences, Collective Desires, *American Anthropologist* 105(4): 832–8.

Bergstrom, J. (1996) "Friedrich Wilhelm Murnau: (1888–1931)," in G. Nowell-Smith (ed.), *The Oxford History of World Cinema*, Oxford: Oxford University Press, pp. 146–7.

Beumers, B. (2006) *The Cinema of Russia & the Former Soviet Union (24 Frames)*, London and New York: Wallflower Press.

Bordwell, D. (1996) "Sergei Eisenstein: (1898–1948)," in G. Nowell-Smith (ed.), *The Oxford History of World Cinema*, Oxford: Oxford University Press, pp. 168–9.

Bourgois, P. (1995) *In Search of Respect: Selling Crack in El Barrio*, Cambridge and New York: Cambridge University Press.

Bracht Branham, R. (1995) "Inventing the Novel," in C. Emerton (ed.), *Bakhtin in Contexts: Across the Disciplines*, Evanston, IL: Northwestern University Press, pp. 79–89.

Burch, N. (1979) *To the Distant Observer: Form and Meaning in Japanese Cinema*, Berkeley: University of California Press.

Cascardi, A. (1992) *The Subject of Modernity*, Cambridge: Cambridge University Press.

Charney, L. and Schwartz, V. R. (1995) "Introduction," in L. Charney and V. R. Schwartz (eds), *Cinema and the Invention of Modern Life*, Berkeley: University of California Press, pp. 1–12.

Chow, R. (1995) *Primitive Passions: Visuality, Sexuality, Ethnography, and Contemporary Chinese Cinema*, New York: Columbia University Press.

Collier, P. and Geyer-Ryan, H. (1992) "Introduction: Beyond Postmodernism," in P. Collier and H. Geyer-Ryan (eds), *Literary Theory Today*, Cambridge: Polity Press, pp. 1–9.

Comolli, J.-L. (1985) "Technique and Ideology: Camera, Perspective, Depth of Field," in B. Nichols (ed.), *Movies and Methods Vol. II: An Anthology*, Berkeley and London: University of California Press, pp. 40–57.

Cousins, M. (2004) *The Story of Film,* New York: Thunder's Mouth Press.

Crary, J. (1990) *Techniques of the Observer: On Vision and Modernity in the Nineteenth Century*, Cambridge, MA: MIT Press.

Crofts, S. (2000) "Concepts of National Cinema," in J. Hill and P. Church Gibson (eds), *World Cinema: Critical Approaches*, New York: Oxford University Press, pp. 1–10.

Das Gupta, C. (1991) *The Painted Face: Studies in India's Popular Cinema*, New Delhi: Roli Books.

David, J. (1995) *Fields of Vision: Critical Applications in Recent Philippine Cinema*, Manila: Ateneo de Manila University Press.

Derné, S. (2000) *Movies, Masculinity, and Modernity: An Ethnography of Men's Filmgoing in India*, Westport, CT: Greenwood Press.

Derrida, J. (1976) *Of Grammatology*, trans. G. S. Spivak, Baltimore: Johns Hopkins University Press.

Diawara, M. (1992) *African Cinema: Politics and Culture*, Bloomington, IN: Indiana University Press.

Dibbets, K. (1996) "The Introduction of Sound," in G. Nowell-Smith (ed.), *The Oxford History of World Cinema*, Oxford: Oxford University Press, pp. 211–20.

Dickey, S. (1993) *Cinema and the Urban Poor in South India*, Cambridge: Cambridge University Press.

Dwyer, R. (2005) *100 Bollywood Films: BFI Screen Guides*, London: British Film Institute Publishing.

Dwyer, R. and Patal, D. (2002) *Cinema India: The Visual Culture of Hindi Film,* New Brunswick, NJ: Rutgers University Press.

Editors of *Cahiers du Cinéma* (1979) "*John Ford's* Young Mr. Lincoln," in G. Mast and M. Cohen (eds), *Film Theory and Criticism: Introductory Readings*, 2nd edition, New York and Oxford: Oxford University Press, pp. 778–831.

Eisenstein, S. (1979) "From *Film Form*," in G. Mast and M. Cohen (eds), *Film Theory and Criticism: Introductory Readings*, 2nd edition, New York and Oxford: Oxford University Press, pp. 85–122.

Erhat, J. (2005) *Cinema and Semiotic: Peirce and Film Aesthetics, Narration, and Representation*, Toronto: University of Toronto Press.

Falicov, T. (2006) *The Cinematic Tango: Contemporary Argentine Film*, London and New York: Wallflower Press.

Foucault, M. (1972) *The Archaeology of Knowledge*, trans. A. M. Sheridan Smith, New York, Pantheon Books.

Foucault, M. (1974) *The Order of Things: An Archaeology of the Human Sciences*, London: Tavistock Publications.

Freiberg, F. (2000) "Japanese Cinema," in J. Hill and P. Church Gibson (eds), *World Cinema: Critical Approaches*, New York: Oxford University Press, pp. 178–84.

Fujii, A. (1993) *Complicit Fictions: The Subject in Modern Japanese Prose Narrative*, Berkeley: University of California Press.

Ganti, T. (2002) "'And Yet My Heart is Still Indian': The Bombay Film Industry and the (H)Indianization of Hollywood," in F. Ginsburg, L. Abu-Lughod, and B. Larkin (eds), *Media Worlds: Anthropology on New Terrain*, Berkeley: University of California Press, pp. 281–300.

Ganti, T. (2004) *Bollywood: A Guidebook to Popular Hindi Cinema,* New York: Routledge

Giannetti, L. (1990) *Understanding Movies,* Englewood Cliffs, NJ: Prentice Hall.

Gillespie, M. (1995) "Sacred Serials, devotional viewing and domestic worship: A case study in the interpretation of two TV versions of *The Mahabharata* in a Hindu family in west London," in R. D. Allen (ed.), *To Be Continued…: Soap Operas around the World*, London and New York: Routledge, pp. 354–81.

Ginsburg, F. Abu-Lughod, L. And Larkin, B. (eds), (2002) *Media Worlds: Anthropology on New Terrain*, Berkeley: University of California Press.

Gokulsing K. M. and Dissanayake, W. (2004) *Indian Popular Cinema: A Narrative of Cultural Change*, revised edition, Sterling, VA: Trentham Books.

Gomery, D (1996) "The New Hollywood," in G. Nowell-Smith (ed.), *The Oxford History of World Cinema*, Oxford: Oxford University Press, pp. 475–82.

Gramsci, A. (1973) *Letters from Prison,* trans. L. Lawner, New York, Harper & Row.

Grenfell, N. (1979) *Switch On: Switch Off: Mass Media Audiences in Malaysia*, Kuala Lumpur: Oxford University Press.

Grieveson, L. (2004) *Policing Cinema: Movies and Censorship in Early-Twentieth-Century America*, Berkeley: University of California Press.

Gugler, J. (2003) *African Film: Re-Imagining a Continent,* Bloomington, IN: Indiana University Press.

Guneratne, A. (2003) "Introduction: rethinking Third Cinema," in A. Guneratne and W. Dissanayake (eds), *Rethinking Third Cinema*, New York: Routledge.

Guneratne, A. and Dissanayake, W. (eds), (2003) *Rethinking Third Cinema*, New York: Routledge.

Gunning, T. (1991) *D. W. Griffith and the origins of American narrative film: the early years at Biograph*, Urbana, IL: University of Illinois Press.

Gunning, T. (1995) "An Aesthetic of Astonishment: Early Film and the (In)Credulous Spectator," in L. Williams (ed.), *Viewing Positions: Ways of Seeing Film*, New Brunswick, NJ: Rutgers University Press, pp. 114–31.

Gunning, T. (2000) "'Animated pictures': tales of cinema's forgotten future, after 100 years of films," in C. Gledhill and L. Williams (eds), *Reinventing Film Studies*, London: Arnold Publishing, pp. 316–31.

Hamilton, A. (2002) "The National Picture: Thai Media and Cultural Identity," in F. Ginsburg, L. Abu-Lughod, and B. Larkin (eds), *Media Worlds: Anthropology on New Terrain*, Berkeley: University of California Press, pp. 152–70.

Khan, H. A. (1997) *The Malay Cinema*, Kuala Lumpur: Penerbit Universiti Kebangsaan Press.

Hay, J., Grossberg, L. and Wartella, E. (eds), (1996) *The Audience and its Landscape,* Boulder, CO: Westview Press.

Haynes, J. (ed.) (2000) *Nigerian Video Films,* Athens, OH: Center for International Studies.

Haynes, J. (2000) "Introduction," in J. Haynes (ed.), *Nigerian Video Films,* Athens, OH: Center for International Studies, pp. 1–36.

Haynes, J. and Okome, O. (2000) "Evolving Popular Media: Nigerian Video Films," in J. Haynes (ed.), *Nigerian Video Films,* Athens, OH: Center for International Studies, pp. 51–88.

Heider, K. (1991) *Indonesian Cinema: National Culture on Screen,* Honolulu: University of Hawai'i Press.

Hill, J. and Church Gibson, P. (eds) (1998) *The Oxford Guide to Film Studies,* New York: Oxford University Press.

Hill, J. and Church Gibson, P. (eds) (2000) *World Cinema: Critical Approaches*, New York: Oxford University Press.

Holquist, M. (1990) *Dialogism: Bakhtin and his World,* London and New York: Routledge.

Jaikumar, P. (2006) *Cinema at the End of Empire: A Politics of Transition in Britain and India,* Durham, NC: Duke University Press.

Jarvie, I. C. (1987) *Philosophy of the Film: Epistemology, Ontology, Aesthetics,* New York: Routledge.

King, R. (2008) *The Fun Factory: The Keystone Film Company and the Emergence of Mass Culture,* Berkeley: University of California Press.

Komatsu, H. (1996) "Akira Kurosawa: (1910–)", in G. Nowell-Smith (ed.), *The Oxford History of World Cinema*, Oxford: Oxford University Press, pp. 716.

Kracauer, S. (1947) *From Caligari to Hitler: A Psychological History of the German Film,* Princeton, NJ: Princeton University Press.

Kracauer, S. (1979) "From *Theory of Film,*" in G. Mast and M. Cohen (eds), *Film Theory and Criticism: Introductory Readings,* 2nd edition, New York and Oxford: Oxford University Press, pp. 7–22.

Lapsley, R. and Westlake, M. (1988) *Film Theory: An Introduction,* Manchester: Manchester University Press.

Larkin, B. (2000) "Hausa Dramas and the Rise of Video Culture in Nigeria," in J. Haynes (ed.), *Nigerian Video Films,* Ohio Center for International Studies, pp. 209–241.

Larkin, B. (2002) "The Materiality of Cinema Theaters in Northern Nigeria," in F. Ginsburg, L. Abu-Lughod, and B. Larkin (eds), *Media Worlds: Anthropology on New Terrain*, Berkeley: University of California Press, pp. 319–36.

Lee, R. B. (1993) *The Dobe Ju/'hoansi,* Fort Worth, TX: Harcourt Brace College Publishers

Lent, J. A. (1990) *The Asian Film Industry*, London: Christopher Helm.

Lévi-Strauss, C. (1982) *The Way of the Masks,* Seattle, WA: University of Washington Press.

Lewis, J. (ed.) (1998) *The New American Cinema,* Durham, NC: Duke University Press.

Lewis, J. and Smoodin, E. (eds) (2007) *Looking Past the Screen: Case Studies in American Film History and Method,* Durham, NC: Duke University Press.

Lodge, D. (1990) *After Bakhtin: Essays in Fiction and Criticism*, London and New York: Routledge.

Lopez, A. M. (1995) "Our Welcomed Guests: Telenovelas in Latin America," in R. C. Allen (ed.), *To Be Continued…: Soap Operas Around the World*, London and New York: Routledge, pp. 256–75.

McDonald, K. (2006) *Reading a Japanese Film: Cinema in Context,* Honolulu: University of Hawai'i Press.

McFarlane, B. (ed.) (2006) *The Cinema of Britain and Ireland (24 Frames)*, London and New York: Wallflower Press.

McKeon, M. (1987) *The Origin of the English Novel 1600–1740,* Baltimore, MD: John Hopkins University Press.

Machor, J. and Goldstein, P. (eds), (2000) *Reception Study: From Literary Theory to Cultural Studies,* New York: Routledge.

Marks, M. (1996) "Music and the Silent Film," in G. Nowell-Smith (ed.), *The Oxford History of World Cinema*, Oxford: Oxford University Press, pp. 183–92.

Mast, G and Cohen, M. (1979) *Film Theory and Criticism: Introductory Readings*, New York and Oxford: Oxford University Press.

Morandini, M. (1996a) "Italy from Fascism to Neo-Realism," in G. Nowell-Smith (ed.), *The Oxford History of World Cinema*, Oxford: Oxford University Press, pp. 353–61.

Morandini, M. (1996b) Italy: Auteurs and After," in G. Nowell-Smith (ed.), *The Oxford History of World Cinema*, Oxford: Oxford University Press, pp. 586–96.

Morley, D. (1980) *The "Nationwide" Audience: Structure and Decoding,* London: British Film Institute.

Morley, D. (1996) "The Geography of Television: Ethnography, Communication, and Community," in J. Hay, L. Grossberg, and E. Wartella (eds), *The Audience and Its Landscape*, Boulder, CO: Westview, pp. 317–42.

Mulvey, L. (1975) "Visual Pleasure and Narrative Cinema," *Screen* 16(2): 6–18.

Munsterberg, H. (1979) "From *The Film: A Psychological Study*," in G. Mast and M. Cohen (eds), *Film Theory and Criticism: Introductory Readings*, 2nd edition, New York and Oxford: Oxford University Press, pp. 349–58.

Naficy, H. (1993) "Exile Discourse and Televisual Fetishization," in H. Naficy and T. Gabriel (eds), *Otherness and the Media: The Ethnography of the Imagined and the Imaged*, Langhorne, PA: Harwood Academic Press, pp. 85–116.

Naficy, H. (2001) *An Accented Cinema: Exilic and Diasporic Filmmaking*, Princeton, NJ: Princeton University Press.

Newman, K (1996) "Exploitation and the Mainstream," in G. Nowell-Smith (ed.), *The Oxford History of World Cinema*, Oxford: Oxford University Press, pp. 509–16.

Nichols, B. (2000) "Film theory and the revolt against master narratives," in C. Gledhill and L. Williams (eds), *Reinventing Film Studies*, London: Arnold, pp. 34–53.

Nowell-Smith, G. (ed.) (1996a) *The Oxford History of World Cinema: The Definitive History of Cinema Worldwide,* New York: Oxford University Press.

Nowell-Smith, G. (1996b) "The Post-War World: After the War," in G. Nowell-Smith (ed.), *The Oxford History of World Cinema*, Oxford: Oxford University Press, pp. 436–43.

O'Neill, E. (1996) "Alfred Hitchcock: (1899–1980)," in G. Nowell-Smith (ed.), *The Oxford History of World Cinema*, Oxford: Oxford University Press, pp. 310–11.

O'Sullivan, T., Hartley, J., Saunders, D., Montgomery, M., and Fisk, J. (1994) *Key Concepts in Communication and Cultural Studies*, 2nd edition, London and New York: Routledge.

Parkinson, D. (1995) *History of Film*, London: Thames and Hudson.

Peacock, J. L. (2002) *The Anthropological Lens: Harsh Light, Soft Focus*, Cambridge: Cambridge University Press.

Pearson, R. (1996a) "Early Cinema," in G. Nowell-Smith (ed.), *The Oxford History of World Cinema*, Oxford: Oxford University Press, pp. 13–23.

Pearson, R. (1996b) "Transitional Cinema," in G. Nowell-Smith (ed.), *The Oxford History of World Cinema*, Oxford: Oxford University Press, pp. 23–42.

Pearson, R. (1996c) "David Wark Griffith: (1875–1948)," in G. Nowell-Smith (ed.), *The Oxford History of World Cinema*, Oxford: Oxford University Press, pp. 30–1.

Petrie, D. (1996) "British Cinema: The Search for Identity," in G. Nowell-Smith (ed.), *The Oxford History of World Cinema*, Oxford: Oxford University Press, pp. 604–14.

Pines, J. (1996) "The Black Presence in American Cinema," in G. Nowell-Smith (ed.), *The Oxford History of World Cinema*, Oxford: Oxford University Press, pp. 497–509.

Pfaff, F. (ed.) (2004) *Focus on African Films*, Bloomington, IN: Indiana University Press.

Powdermaker, H. (2002) "Hollywood and the USA," in K. Askew and R. Wilk (eds), *The Anthropology of Media: A Reader*, Oxford: Blackwell Publishing, pp. 161–71.

Propp, V. (1968) *Morphology of the Folktale*, Austin, TX: University of Texas Press.

Pudovkin, V. (1979) From Film Technique," in G. Mast and M. Cohen (eds), *Film Theory and Criticism: Introductory Readings*, 2nd edition, New York and Oxford: Oxford University Press, pp. 77–84.

Alauddin, R. A. (1992) "A Brief History of The Development of Indonesian Films in Malaysia," in S. Burhanuddin and Wosmen Pasaribu Moch Jufry (eds), *Indonesian Film Panorama*, Jakarta: Permanent Committee of the Indonesian Film Festival, pp. 83–87.

Rajadhyaksha, A. (1996) "Satyajit Ray: (1921- 1992)," G. Nowell-Smith (ed.), *The Oxford History of World Cinema*, Oxford: Oxford University Press, pp. 682–3.

Rajadhyaksha, A. and Willemen, P. (eds), (2002) *Encyclopedia of Indian Cinema*, revised edition, London: British Film Institute Publishing.

Raybeck, D (1996) *Mad Dogs, Englishmen, and the Errant Anthropologist: Fieldwork in Malaysia*, Prospect Heights, IL: Waveland Press.

Richie, D. (1990) *Japanese Cinema: An Introduction*, New York: Oxford University Press.

Richie, D. (2005) *A Hundred Years of Japanese Film: A Concise History, with a Selective Guide to DVDs and Videos*, New York: Kodansha International.

Robbins, R. (2001) *Cultural Anthropology: A Problem-based Approach*, Itasca, IL: F. E. Peacock Publishers, Inc.

Roof, M. (2004) "African and Latin American Cinemas: Contexts and Contacts," in F. Pfaff, (ed.), *Focus on African Films*, Bloomington, IN: Indiana University Press, pp. 241–70.

Ruby Rich, B. (1998) *Chick Flicks: Theories and Memories of the Feminist Film Movement*, Durham, NC: Duke University Press.

Said, S. (1991) *Shadows on the Silver Screen: A Social History of Indonesian Cinema*, Jakarta: The Lontar Foundation.

Schatz, T. (1996) "Hollywood: The Triumph of the Studio System," in G. Nowell-Smith (ed.), *The Oxford History of World Cinema*, Oxford: Oxford University Press, pp. 220–35

Schein, L. (2002) "Mapping Hmong Media in Diasporic Space," in F. Ginsburg, L. Abu-Lughod, and B. Larkin (eds), *Media Worlds: Anthropology on New Terrain*, Berkeley: University of California Press, pp. 229–44.

Sen, K. (1994) *Indonesian Cinema: Framing the New Order*, London and New Jersey: Zed Books.

Sen, K. and Hill, D. (2007) *Media, Culture and Politics in Indonesia*, Jakarta: Equinox Publishing.

Shaka, F. O. (2004) *Modernity and the African Cinema: A study in Colonialist Discourse, Postcolonialty, and Modern African Identities,* Trenton, NJ: African World Press, Inc.

Shohat, E. and Stam, R. (1994) *Unthinking Eurocentrism: Multiculturalism and the Media*, London and New York: Routledge.

Slide, A. (1989) *The International Film Industry: A Historical Dictionary*, London: Greenwood Press.

Solanas, F. and Getino, O. (1976) "Towards a Third Cinema," in B. Nichols (ed.), *Movies and Methods: An Anthology*, Berkeley: University of California Press, pp. 44–64.

Spence, L. (1995) "'They killed off Marlena, but she's on another show now': Fantasy, reality and pleasure, in watching daytime soap operas," in R. C. Allen (ed.), *To Be Continued…: Soap Operas Around the World*, London and New York: Routledge, pp. 182–98.

Spence, L. (2005) *Watching Daytime Soap Operas: The Power of Pleasure*, Middletown, CT: Wesleyan University Press.

Stam, R. (2000) *Film Theory: An Introduction*, Malden, MA: Blackwell.

Standish, I. (2005) *A New History of Japanese Cinema; A Century of Narrative Film*, New York: The Continuum International Publishing Group Inc.

Thompson, K. and Bordwell, D. (1994) *Film History: An Introduction*, New York: McGraw-Hill.

Traube, E.G. (1994) "Secrets of Success in Postmodern Society," in G. Eley, S. Ortner, and N. Dirks (eds), *Culture/Power/History: A Reader in Contemporary Social Theory*, Princeton, NJ: Princeton University Press, pp. 557–84.

Ukadike, N. F. (1994) *Black African Cinemas,* Berkeley: University of California Press.

Ukadike, N. F. (2002) *Questioning African Cinema: Conversations with Filmmakers*, Minneapolis: University of Minnesota Press.

Ukadike, N. F. (2000) "African Cinema," in J. Hill and P. Church Gibson (eds), *World Cinema: Critical Approaches*, New York: Oxford University Press, pp. 185–91.

Usai, P. C. (1996) "The Early Years: Origins and Survival," in G. Nowell-Smith (ed.), *The Oxford History of World Cinema*, Oxford: Oxford University Press, pp. 6–13

Vasudevan, R. (ed.) (2000) *Making Meaning in Indian Cinema*, New York: Oxford University Press.

Vasey, R. (1996) "The World-Wide Spread of Cinema," in G. Nowell-Smith (ed.), *The Oxford History of World Cinema*, Oxford: Oxford University Press, pp. 53–62.

Vincendeau, G. (1996) "The Popular Art of French Cinema," in G. Nowell-Smith (ed.), *The Oxford History of World Cinema*, Oxford: Oxford University Press, pp. 344–53.

Vincendeau, G. (2000) "Issues in European Cinema," in J. Hill and P. Church Gibson (eds), *World Cinema: Critical Approaches*, New York: Oxford University Press, pp. 56–64.

Vitali, V. and Willemen P. (2008) *Theorising National Cinema,* London: British Film Institute.

Whissel, K. (2008) *Picturing American Modernity: Traffic, Technology, and the Silent Cinema*, Durham, NC: Duke University Press.

Willemen, P. (1995) "Regimes of Subjectivity and Looking," *The UTS Review*, 1(2): 101–29.

Williams, L. (1989) *Hard Core: Power, Pleasure, and the "Frenzy of the Visible,"* Berkeley: University of California Press.

INDEX

Note: *italic* page numbers denote references to figures.

1408 (2007), 32
42nd Street (1933), 17

Abel, R., 77
Abu-Lughod, L., 129–30
Adorno, Theodor, 41, 50, 77
aesthetics, x, 11
Africa
    Askew's work, 75–6, 99
    cinemas in, *106*
    cultural analysis of films, 105
    further reading, 107
    national cinema, 86
    third cinema, 90–1, 92–5
agency, 118, 119, 121–2, 130, 132, 133, 138
Akira (1988), 67, 68
Allen, Woody, 26
All Quiet on the Western Front (1930), 18
All the Right Moves (1983), 102
Althusser, Louis, 50–1
amateur films, xv, 76
And God Created Woman (1956), 49
Ang, Ien, 118, 122
Angels with Dirty Faces (1938), 19
anime, 67–8
anthropology, x, xi–xii, xvi–xvii, 76–7, 139–41
    audiences, xv–xvi, 113, 122, 123–33, 138,
      140
    contexts, xii, 99–106, 138, 139–40
    definition of, xii
    value of, 136
apparatus theory, 70
Appledon, Richard John, 6
Argentina, xvi

Arnheim, Rudolf, 37
The Arrival of a Train at La Ciotat Station
    (1895), 5
art cinema, 24, 26, 35, 80, 89
Asia, 82
Askew, K., 75–6, 99, 136
The Assassination of the Duke of Guise (1908),
    8–11
Astaire, Fred, 17
Atanarjuat- The Fast Runner (2001), xii, 91–6
audiences, xv–xvi, 109–34, 138–9
    anthropology, xv–xvi, 113, 122, 123–33,
      138, 140
    colonies, 6
    communication studies, xv, 112–17, 119,
      122
    cultural studies, 117–23
    diasporic cinema, 130–2
    dynamic dialogue with, 101
    expatriate, 119–21, 129, 130
    film theory, 72, 110–12, 138
    Indians in the UK, 119–21, 129
    Latin America, 116–17
    Nigeria, 124–7
    non-Western, 127–9
    semiotic analysis, 56
    television, 113–16
    Use and Gratification Model, 81
Australia, 8, 96
auteur theory, 46, 47–8, 60–1, 77, 144n9
authority, 63–4

Babb, L., 76, 100–1
Bakhtin, Mikhail, xiv, 65–70, 101

Balázs, Béla, 37
Balink, Albert, 83
Barbaro, Umberto, 46
Barker, C., 143n3
Barthes. Roland, 71
Barton Fink (1991), 18
Battleship Potemkin (1925), 44, 45
Bazin, André, 47–9
Beineix, Jean-Jacques, 30, 38
Benjamin, Walter, 37, 40, 41
benshi, 14–15, 22
Bergman, Ingrid, *19*, 61
Berkeley, Busby, 17
Besson, Luc, 30
Betty Blue (1986), 30
The Bicycle Thieves (1948), 21, 47
Bigelow, Kathryn, 145n3
Billy Liar (1963), 25
Biograph, 9, 10
The Birds (1963), 62
Birmingham School of Cultural Studies, 118
The Birth of a Nation (1915), 8, *8*, 9, 10–11
Bitzer, Billy, 8, 9
Blade (1998), 30
Blade Runner (1982), 55
blaxploitation films, 26
"block booking", 23, 97
"blockbuster" films, 17, 28–32, 101
B movies, 28, 97
Bogart, Humphrey, 19, *19*
Bogdanovich, Peter, 26
Bollywood, 17, *57*, 66–7, 87, 90, 125, 145n8
Borden, Lizzie, 145n3
The Bourne Ultimatum (2007), 32
Brazil, xvi, 117
Breathless (1959), 24–5
Bride and Prejudice (2004), 17, *18*
Bridge in Leeds (1888), 144n3
Britain, *see* Great Britain
Buena Vista Social Club (1999), 30

The Cabinet of Dr. Caligari (1919), 11, 38–9
Cahiers du cinéma (magazine), 47–9, 50, 52–3, 60, 61, 79
Camera D'Or, 95–6
camera obscura, 4
Cameron, James, 26

Cannes Film Festival, 95–6
capitalism, 40, 50, 99, 102, 110
Captain Blood (1935), 19
Casablanca (1942), 18–19, *19*
Cathay Cinema, Shanghai, *109*
CCCS, *see* Centre for Contemporary Cultural Studies
censorship, 82, 97
    Great Britain, 86
    Indonesia, 84, 85
    Russia, 44
Centre for Contemporary Cultural Studies (CCCS), 118
Chabrol, Claude, 35, 49
Chan, Jackie, 30
Channel Four Films, 30
character types, 54–5
child development, 58–9
China, xvi, 30
    Cathay Cinema, *109*
    Hmong diaspora, 130–2
Chow, R., xi–xii, 76, 105–6
Church Gibson, P., 105
Cimino, Michael, 27–8
Ciné-Art, 38, 39, 46, 47
cinema
    anthropology of the, xi–xii, 76–7, 99–106, 139–41
    definitions of, x, 136–7
    hegemony, 72
    as ideological apparatus, 51–2, 78–9
    institutional/sociological role of, 48
    physical space of, 124–6
    power of, x–xi
    structuralist approach to, 55
    see also early cinema; film theory; history of cinema
cinéma du look, 30
Cinématographe, 5
cinéma vérité, 20, 24
Cine Oriente, Santiago de Cuba, *91*
Cineplex, Japan, *135*
Cinéthique (magazine), 52, 145n5
Cissé, Souleymane, 92, 93
Citizen Kane (1941), 47, *48*, 136
Clerks (1994), 98
Clooney, George, 24

close-ups, 9, 56, 62, 132
Cloverfield (2008), 32, 98
codes, 56
Coen Brothers, 18
Cold War, 94
Colonial Film Units, 92–3
colonialism, 6, 88
    Africa, 92–3
    India, 87
    Nigeria, 125
Columbia, 117
communication (media) studies, 79–83, 96
    audiences, xv, 112–17, 119, 122
    ideological values, 77–8
composition, 36, 37
consumerism, 102, 104
consumption studies, 118–22
content, xiii–xiv, 46
    anthropology of the cinema, 100, 101
    Marxist film theory, 52
    Transmission Model, 79–80
context, xiv–xv, 72, 75–107, 138
    anthropology, xii, 99–106, 138, 139–40
    audiences, 122, 130, 133
    Bakhtin, 70
    communication studies, 79–83
    distribution and exhibition, 76, 96–8, 140
    film theory, 46
    Frankfurt School, 77–9
    Hollywood, 101
    Marxism, 52, 53
    national cinema, 86–8
    Nigerian video films, 69
    The Secret of My Succe$s, 102, 104
    socio-cultural, 99–106, 139
    third cinema, 88–91, 92–5
Coolidge, Martha, 145n3
Coppola, Francis Ford, 26, 28
Corman, Roger, 26
corporatization, 29
Cousins, M., 4, 60, 86
Crary, J., 72
Crosland, Alan, 16, 144n6
cross-cutting, 6–7, 9
The Crying Game (1992), 30
Cuba, 90, *91*
cultural relativity, xii, 141

cultural studies, xv–xvi, 72, 77–8, 79, 117–23, 127–9
culture
    African, 93–4
    Frankfurt School, 40–1
    non-Western film analysis, 104–5, 139

Dallas (TV show), 118, 122
Days of Our Lives (TV show), 114
decolonization, 92
The Deer Hunter (1978), 27
Delluc, Louis, 38, 39
Del Toro, Guillermo, 29
Demme, Jonathan, 26
De Niro, Robert, *27*
Derrida, Jacques, 71–2
Dial M for Murder (1954), 61
dialogism, 66, 70, 101
dialogue, 46–7
diasporic cinema, 88, 130–2, 133
Dibbets, K., 17
Dickey, S., 123–4, 129
Dickson, William, 5
Disney, 67
distribution, xv, 3, 29
    contexts of, 76, 96–8, 140
    government policy, 82
    third cinema, 89–90
Diva (1981), 30
Djamaluddin Malik, 84
documentary cinema, xii–xiii, 14, 49
    Hmong diaspora, 131
    Nigeria, 68
    realism, 47
    third cinema, 89
Doniol-Valcroze, Jacques, 47
Don Juan (1926), 144n6
Douglas, Michael, 75–6
Dracula (1931), 12, 18, 144n8
dubbing, 46
Duca, Lo, 47
DVD market, 30

early cinema, 5–15, 64
    audiences, 110
    cross-cutting, 6–7, 9
    film theory, 37–45, 137

France, 8–11
Germany, 11–14
Great Britain, 14
Griffith, 7–8, 9–11
Italy, 11
Japan, 14–15
Murnau, 12–13
United States, 6
Eastenders (TV show), 114
Eastwood, Clint, 26
Eco, Umberto, 57
Edison, 9
Edison, Thomas, 5, 16
editing techniques, 6–7, 9, 10, 37, 42–5
Egypt, 129–30
Eisenstein, Sergei, xiv, 10, 37, 42–5, 47
Elgin Talkies movie theatre, Bangalore, *71, 80, 87, 111*
El Mariachi (1992), 98
Encoding-Decoding Model, 117, 118
enculturation, xi
Enter the Dragon (1973), 29
ethnographic film, xii–xiii, 143n2
Europe
    communication studies, 79
    further reading, xviii, 73, 107, 133
    "Second Cinema", 89
    social changes, 63
exhibition, xv, 3
    contexts of, 76, 96–8, 140
    government policy, 82
    third cinema, 89–90
exile cinema, 88
    see also diasporic cinema
expressionism, 13, 38–9, 41–2, 60, 145n2

fairy tales, 54
The Fall of Troy (1910), 11
Family Plot (1976), 60
Fantastic Four: Rise of the Silver Surfer (2007), 32
Farewell My Concubine (1993), 30
Fatal Attraction (1987), 2
feminism, 52, 59, 70, 105, 145n3
Ferris Bueller's Day Off (1986), 102
fetishism, 59, 62
film-as-art theorists, 37–8, 46, 50, 77

film festivals, 32, 98
    Atanarjuat, 95–6
    independent, 76
    Kwakoe, *65, 127, 128*
film noir, 24, 56
film studies, 77, 79, 96
    audiences, 132
    non-Western films, xi, 104–6
film theory, xiii–xiv, 35–73, 137–8
    academicization of, 45–6, 47, 60, 77, 137
    audiences, 110–12, 132, 138
    expressionism, 38–9
    formalism, 37–8
    French New Wave, 47–9
    incorporation into anthropology, 141
    Italian neo-realism, 46–7, 49
    Kracauer, 39–42
    literary theories, 63–70
    Marxism, 50–3
    montage and editing, 42–5
    non-Western films, xi, 105, 139
    psychoanalysis, 58–60
    semiotics, 55–7
    structuralism, 53–5
Fire (1996), 88, 129, 130
"First Cinema", 89
A Fistful of Dollars (1964), 22, 26
Ford, John, 22, 55, 88
formalism, 36, 37–8, 46, 110, 111–12
Foucault, Michel, 71
Four Daughters (1938), 19
framing, 36, 56
France
    African colonies, 92, 93, 95
    backlash against Hollywood, 20, 45
    early cinema, 8–11
    film theory, 38
    New New Wave, 30, 38
    New Wave, 24–5, 38, 47–9
    student/labor unrest, 90
    wartime censorship, 97
Frankenstein (1931), 18
Frankfurt School, 40–1, 50, 77–9, 81
    audiences, 110, 119, 121, 130
    cultural studies, 118
Fred Ott's Sneeze (1894), 5
Freiberg, F., 105

Freudianism, 58, 145n6
Friday the 13th (2009), 136
fusil photographique, 4–5

Gambia, *106, 122*
Gandhi, Indira, 22
Ganti, T., 2
gaze, 59
gender, 59, 140
    see also women
Germany
    early cinema, 11–14
    expressionism, 38–9, 41–2
    Kracauer's critique, 41, 42
    wartime censorship, 97
Getino, Octavio, 89
Ghana, 66–7, 68, 69, 92, 93, 95
Gillespie, Marie, 118, 119–21
Gish, Lillian, *8*
globalization, xi, 29, 66, 140
Godard, Jean-Luc, 24–5, 49
gods, 100–1
The Gold Diggers of 1933 (1933), 17
Good Night, and Good Luck (2005), 24
government intervention
    Indonesia, 83–5, 97
    national cinema, 86
    policy studies, 81–2
    United States, 23, 97
    see also politics
"grammar" of films
    African cinema, 93–4
    early cinema, 7, 9
    Godard, 25
    Ray/Kurosawa, 23
    textualist approach, 132
    Western focus, 70
Gramsci, Antonio, 72, 101
Grant, Cary, 61
Great Britain
    African colonies, 92–3
    Channel Four Films, 30
    cinema audiences, 124
    communication studies, 79
    early cinema, 14
    Indian audiences in, 119–21
    protectionist policies, 14, 86–7, 97
    "quota quickies", 87, 144n10

social realism, 24, 25, 49
    wartime censorship, 97
The Great Train Robbery (1903), 6, 7
Grenfell, N., 83, 113
Griffith, D. W., xiii, 7–8, 9–11, 64, 145n3
Guneratne, A., 90
Gunning, T., 72
Gutiérrez Alea, Tomás, 90

Hairspray (2007), 32
Hall, Stuart, 117, 118
Halloween (1978), 39
Halloween (2007 remake), 32
Hamilton, A., 109–10
A Hard Day's Night (1964), 49
Harry Potter: The Order of the Phoenix (2007), 32
Hausa, 126–7
Hawks, Howard, 55
Heath, S., 57
Heaven's Gate (1980), 27–8, 29
hegemony, 72, 101
Hellboy (2004), 29
Hill, D., 85
Hill, J., 105
Hinduism, 100–1
history of cinema, xiii, 1–33, 137
    "blockbuster" era, 28–32
    British social realism, 24, 25
    early cinema, 5–15
    French New Wave, 24–5
    "Golden Era", 15–28
    Internet, 32–3
    New Hollywood, 26–8
    precursors to, 3–5
    resistance to Hollywood, 20–4
    sound, 15–17
    studio system, 17–20, 24, 25–6
    technological developments, 4–5, 16–17, 24
Hitchcock, Alfred, xiv, 19, 39, 55, 56, 58, 60–2
Hmong diaspora, 130–2, 133
holism, xii, 122, 140, 141
Hollywood
    anthropological analysis, 99–100
    cultural context, 101, 139
    distribution and exhibition, 97

expressionism, 39
as "First Cinema", 89
globalization of, 29
"Golden Age", 17, 19–21
psychoanalytical theory, 58
resistance to, 20–4, 45
sound, 16
studio system, xiii, 17–20, 24, 25–6, 45, 110
see also United States
homosexuality, 88
Hondo, Med, 93, 94
Hopper, Peter, 26
Horkheimer, Max, 50, 77
The Hunchback of Notre Dame (1923), 18
Hypodermic Needle Model, 79–80, 112

identification, 59, 62, 112
identity
Egyptian, 129, 130
Hmong diaspora, 131
Indian, 121
interpellation, 51
Lacanian child development, 58–9
ideology, 44, 46, 65
Frankfurt School, 77–8
Indonesia, 84, 85
Marxism, 50–2, 53
The Secret of My Succe$s, 101–2
independent films, xv, 26, 32, 76, 98
India
audience studies of British Indians, 119–21, 129
Bollywood, 17, *57*, 66–7, 87, 90, 125, 145n8
British colonial policies, xvi, 14, 87
diasporic cinema, 88
early cinema, 6, 14
Elgin Talkies theatre, *71, 80, 87, 111*
Eros Cinema, *20*
further reading, xviii, 33, 73, 134
Hindu devotion, 100–1, 120
importance of cinema in, 123–4
Indian films in Nigeria, 125–6
Palace Talkies theatre, *51*
popular vs artistic cinema, 80
Ray, 21–2, 23
indigenous film, xii, xv, 91–6

Indonesia, xvi, *82*
cultural analysis of films, 105
film production, 96–7
further reading, xviii, 107
government intervention, 82, 83–5, 97
I Now Pronounce You Chuck and Larry (2007), 32
Internet, 32–3, 76, 98
interpellation, 51, 52, 65, 138
Intolerance (1916), 11
Inuit, 91–6
irising, 145n3
Islam, 125, 130
Italy
backlash against Hollywood, 20, 45
early cinema, 11
neo-realism, 20, 46–7, 49
student/labor unrest, 90
wartime censorship, 97
Ivan the Terrible Part I (1944), 44
Ivan the Terrible Part II (1958), 44

Jai Santoshi Maa (1975), 100–1, 105
Japan
anime, 67–8
art-house cinema, *35*
Cineplex, *135*
early cinema, 14–15
further reading, xviii, 33, 73
Kurosawa, 22–3
local cinema, *ix*
wartime censorship, 97
Jarvie, I. C., ix, 76
Jaws (1975), 28
The Jazz Singer (1927), 16
JCVD (2008), *78*
Judith of Bethulia (1914), 10
Ju Dou (1990), 30
Jules et Jim (1961), 24

Kaboré, Gaston, 92
kabuki, 14, 15
Kagemusha (1980), 23
Kaige, Chen, 30
Kelly, Grace, 61
Kill Bill films (2003/2004), 68
Kinetograph, 5
Kinetoscope, 5

"kitchen sink" dramas, 24, 25, 49
Knocked Up (2007), 32
Kracauer, Siegfried, 37, 39–42, 47
Kubrick, Stanley, 49
Ku Klux Klan, 10–11
Kuleshov, Lev, 42
Kurosawa, Akira, xi, 21, 22–3, 26, 88
Kwakoe festival, *65*, *127*, *128*
Kyo, Machiko, *1*

Lacan, Jacques, 58–9
Lang, Fritz, 11, 39
language, 58–9
Laos, 131
Lapsley, R., 62
Larkin, B., 126, 133
The Last Days of Pompeii (1908), 11
The Last King of Scotland (2006), 30
The Last Laugh (1924), 13
Latin America
    national cinema, 86
    telenovelas, 116–17
    third cinema, 90
Lee, Bruce, 29
Lenin, Vladimir, 45
Lent, John, 82–3
Leon (1994), 30
Leone, Sergio, 22, 26, 35
Le Prince, Louis, 144n3
Lester, Richard, 49
Lévi-Strauss, Claude, 55
The Life of an American Fireman (1902), 6, 7
lighting, 36, 37, 39, 56
literary theories, xiv, 63–70, 71
Look Back in Anger (1959), 25
Lopez, A. M., 116–17
The Lord of the Rings trilogy (2001-3), 30
Lorre, Peter, 19
Lucas, George, 28
Lucrezia Borgia (1910), 11
Lumet, Sidney, 49
Lumière brothers, xiii, 2, 4, 5

magic lantern shows, 3–4
The Magnificent Seven (1960), 22, 88
The Mahabharata (TV show), 120
Malaya, 6, 14, 84
Malaysia, 87, 97, 113

Mamoulian, Roubert, 16
The Man Who Knew Too Much (1956), 61
The Man with the Movie Camera (1929), 42
Marey, Etienne Jules, 4–5
Marrakesh, *75*
martial arts films, 29–30
Marxism, xiv, 36, 50–3, 71, 99
    audiences, 110, 112
    Cinéthique, 145n5
    hegemony, 72
    literary theory, 63
    oppositional art, 78–9
"master antimony", 55
The Matrix (1999), 30, 67
McCabe, C., 57
McCarthyism, 24
McDonald, K., 105
McLuhan, Marshall, 80–1
meaning, 46, 53, 56, 57
media (communication) studies, 79–83, 96
    audiences, xv, 112–17, 119, 122
    ideological values, 77–8
Media Anthropology Network, 123
media effects, 79
Mehta, Deepa, 88, 129, 130, 145n3
Méliès, Georges, 6, *7*
Memorias del subdesarrollo [Memories of
    Underdevelopment] (1968), 90
Metropolis (1927), 11, 41
Metz, Christian, 56–7, 71
Mexico, 90, 117
Meyers, Russ, 26
middle classes
    Egypt, 129, 130
    Indian audiences, 120, 124
    Kracauer on, 39
    Senegal, 94, 95
Mifune, Toshiro, *1*
Million Dollar Baby (2004), 42
mise en scène, xiv, 8, 11, 36
    anime, 67
    Bazin, 47
    expressionism, 39
    French cinema, 38
    Griffith, 10
    Italian neo-realism, 46
modernity, 63, 64, 126, 129, 130
Monsoon Wedding (2001), 88

montage, xiv, 10, 42–5, 46
Moonlight (1938), 82
Moore, Michael, xiii, 45
morality, 125
Morley, David, 118
Morocco, *75*
Mr. & Mrs. Smith (1941), 60
"MTV style", 28–9
Mulvey, Laura, 59, 70
The Mummy (1932), 18
Munsterberg, Hugo, ix, 37
Murnau, F. W., xiii, 10, 11, 12–13, 39, 60
music, 16
musicals, 17, 66
Muybridge, Eadweard, 3, 4

Nair, Mira, 88, 145n3
narrative function, 64
national cinema, xv, 86–8
national identity, 117, 121, 129
  see also identity
nationalism, xv, 76, 94, 140
nation building, 93, 117
Nazism, 39, 41
Neighbours (TV show), 121
neo-realism, 50, 79
  film noir, 24
  French New Wave, 49
  Italian, 20, 46–7, 49
  Ray, 21, 23
  see also realism
New Hollywood, 26–8
New New Wave, 30, 38
New Order (Indonesia), 83, 85
New Wave, 24–5, 38, 47–9
Nias Island, Indonesia, *82*
Nicholson, Jack, 26
nickelodeons, 15, 110
Nigeria
  Bollywood influence on, 66–7
  British colonial policies, xvi, 87
  cinema-going in, xvi, 124–7
  further reading, xviii, 134
  Nollywood, 69, *127*, *128*
  video films, *65*, 68–9, 92, 93, 95, 125,
    126–7
Nikita (1990), 30

noh, 14, 15
Nollywood, 69, *127*, *128*
North by Northwest (1959), 58, 61, 62
Nosferatu (1922), 11, 12–13, *12*
Nothing in Common (1986), 102
Notorious (1946), 61

October (1928), 44
Oedipal issues, 58, 62, 145n6
Oklahoma (1955), 17
The Old and the New (1929), 44
Once Upon a Time in the West (1968), 26
One from the Heart (1982), 28
oppositional cinema, 78–9, 89–90
Ouedraogo, Idrissa, 92

Palace Talkies theatre, Mumbai, *51*
pan-Africanism, 90–1, 92, 93, 94, 95
Paramount, 97
Pareh (1936), 82, 83
Parkinson, D., 2, 5, 24, 42, 145n3
participant-observation, xii, 138, 140
Pather Panchali (1955), 21–2
Peckinpah, Frank, 49
Peirce, C. S., 71
Pereira dos Santos, Nelson, 90
The Phantom of the Opera (1925), 18
photography, 3, 4
"picture palaces", 15, 16, *20*, 125
Pirates of the Caribbean: At World's End (2007),
  32
Plan 9 from Outer Space (1959), 136
pleasure, 59
point of view (POV) shots, 62, 64, 101
policy studies, 81–2, 112
political economy, 46, 81, 99, 140
politics
  African cinema, 92, 93, 94
  communication studies, 81
  India, 22
  Indonesia, 83–5
  Marxist film theory, 52–3
  Reaganite ideals, 102
  see also government intervention
popular culture, 35, 48, 110–11, 118
Porter, Edwin, 6, 9
Powdermaker, H., 76, 99–100

pre-modernity, 63, 64
propaganda
    African Colonial Film Units, 92
    communication studies, 79, 81
    Indonesia, 82, 83, 85
    Soviet, 44, 45
Propp, Vladimir, 54
protectionism, 84, 85, 86–7, 97
Psycho (1960), 39, 60, 61, 62
psychoanalysis, xiv, 58–60, 71, 132
    audiences, xv, 111, 112, 138
    Hitchcock's films, 61, 62
Pudovkin, V. I., 45

qualitative studies, 113–16, 117, 118–22,
        132, 138
    see also participant-observation
quantitative studies, 112–13
Queen Elizabeth (1912), 11
Queen Victoria's Diamond Jubilee (aka
    *Diamond Anniversary Celebrations of Queen
    Victoria*) (1897), 6
queer theory, 70
quotas, 86–7, 144n10
Quo Vadis? (1913), 11

race
    The Birth of a Nation, 10–11
    blaxploitation films, 26
Rai, Aishwarya, *18*
Rains, Claude, 19
Raise the Red Lantern (1991), 30
Raja Harischandra (1913), 87
Ramlee, P., 84
Ran (1985), 23
Rashomon (1951), ix, *1*, 22, 23
Ray, Satyajit, 21–2, 23
Reagan era, 102, 104
realism
    Bazin, 47, 48–9
    French New Wave, 49
    Kracauer, 41
    Kurosawa, 23
    New Hollywood, 26
    Ray, 21, 22
    social, 24, 25, 49
    see also neo-realism

Rear Window (1954), 58, 61, 62
reception, *see* audiences
Red Sorghum (1987), 30, 105–6
Reed, Carol, 13, 39
religion, 120, 121
Renoir, Jean, 21
representation, politics of, 70
Republican Party, 53
Resnais, Alain, 49
Reville, Alma, 61
Reynaud, Emile, 4
The Rice/Irwin Kiss (1896), 5
Robot Monster (1953), 136
Rocha, Glauber, 90
Rocky (1976), 42
The Rocky Horror Picture Show (1975), 124
Rodriguez, Robert, 98
Roger & Me (1989), 45
Rogers, Ginger, 17
Rope (1948), 61
Roselyn and the Lions (1989), 38
Rossellini, Roberto, 47
Russia, 42–5

Saussure, Ferdinand de, 53
Scary Movie, 10
Schein, L., 130–2
Scorsese, Martin, 26
Screen Magazine, 52
"Second Cinema", 89
Second World War, 97
The Secret of My Succe$s (1994), 99, 101–4
Sembène Ousmane, 92, 93, 94–5, 105
semiotics, xiv, 55–7, 71
Sen, K., 85
Senegal, 94–5
sequels, 29, 32
sets, 8–11
The Seven Samurai (1954), 22, 88
sexploitation films, 26
Shohat, E., xi, 76
Shoot 'Em Up (2007), 30
Siegmann, George, *8*
signification, 56, 57
signs, 55
silent film, 45
The Simpsons Movie (2007), 32

Singapore, 6, 84
Siodmak, Robert, 39
Sita Swayamvar (1976), 120
Slumdog Millionaire (2008), 67
Smith, Kevin, 98
Smokin' Aces (2006), 29
Snakes on a Plane (2006), 32, 98
Snow White (1937), 67
soap operas, 113–16, 121, 129
social commentary cinema, 24, 25, 126
socialization, xi, 58–9
social networking sites, 98
social realism, 24, 25, 49
socio-cultural context, 99–106, 139
Solanas, Fernando, 89
sound, 15–17, 44, 45, 144n6, 144n7
South Pacific (1958), 17
Soviet Union, 42–5
spaghetti westerns, 26, 35
special effects, 27, 28
specialization, 89
Special Video Club, Gambia, *122*
Speed Racer (2008), 67–8
Spellbound (1945), 61, 62
Spence, Louis, 113–16
Spider-Man 3 (2007), 32
Spielberg, Steven, 26, 28
Stachka (1925), 43, 44
Stalin, Joseph, 44
Stallone, Sylvester, 26
Stam, R., xi, 76
Standish, I., 14
Stardust (2007), 41
Star Wars (1977), 28, 41, 53–4
Stewart, James, 61
Stone, Oliver, 99
The Story of the Kelly Gang (1906), 8
structuralism, xiv, 52, 53–5, 63, 71
Sturges, John, 22
style, x, 49
subjective camera, 10, 11, 13, 39, 101
subjectivity, 58, 63, 64, 138
Subway (1985), 30
Suharto, President, 83, 85
Sukarno, President, 82, 83, 84, 85
Sundance film festival, 32
Super Size Me (2004), xiii

Surf's Up (2007), 32
Suspicion (1941), 61
Svilova, Elizaveta, 42
symbolism, 57

Tait, Charles, 8
Tarantino, Quentin, 68
tariffs, 84, 85, 86, 97
Tati, Jacques, 35
Taxi Driver (1976), 26, *27*
technology, 4–5, 16–17, 24
Technology Model, 80–1
telenovelas, 116–17
television, 113–16
    cultural studies, 118–22
    Egypt, 129–30
    Indian audiences in the UK, 120–1
    Latin America, 116–17
    Nigeria, 126
Ten Canoes (2006), 96
Terminator (1984), 29, 68
Terminator 2: Judgement Day (1991), *31*
Terra em transe [Earth Entranced] (1967), 90
texts, 118
Tezuka, Osamu, 67
Thailand, 109–10, 131
theatre, 3, 14
third cinema, xv, 88–91
    Africa, 92–5
    oppositional focus, 78–9, 89–90
The Third Man (1949), 13, 39, *40*, 136
This Sporting Life (1963), 25
Thunderbolt and Lightfoot (1974), 27
To Catch a Thief (1955), 61
Tokyo, *ix*
Toland, Gregg, *48*
Top Hat (1935), 17
Trainspotting (1996), 30
Transformers (2007), 32, 136
Transmission Model, 79–80, 112, 130
Traube, E. G., 99, 102
A Trip to the Moon [Le Voyage dans la Lune] (1902), 6, *7*
Truffaut, François Roland, 24, 49
truth, 63–4
20th Century Fox, 52, 53
Two Step Model, 112

Ukadike, N. F., 76, 105
Under Capricorn (1947), 61
Underdog (2007), 32
United Artists, 27–8
United Kingdom, *see* Great Britain
United States
  anti-Americanism in Indonesia, 84–5
  cinema audiences, 124
  communication studies, 79
  distribution and exhibition, 97
  early cinema, 6
  "First Cinema", 89
  French imports, 77
  further reading, xviii, 73, 107, 133
  government intervention, 23
  Hmong diaspora, 131
  Marxist film theory, 52–3
  McCarthyism, 24
  New Hollywood, 26–8
  Reagan era ideology, 102, 104
  sound, 16
  student/labor unrest, 90
  telenovelas, 116–17
  wartime censorship, 97
  see also Hollywood
Universal, 18, 144n8
Use and Gratification Model, 81
Usmar Ismail, 84

Van Cleef, Lee, 26
Van Damme, Jean-Claude, *78*
Vertigo (1958), 56, 61, 62
Vertov, Dziga, 36, 42, 45, 47, 93
Vidas secas [Barren Lives] (1963), 90
video films
  Hmong diaspora, 131
  Nigerian, *65*, 68–9, 92, 93, 95, 125, 126–7
Vincendeau, G., 35
violence, 79–80, 81, 111

viral marketing, 32–3
voyeurism, 59, 61, 62

Wall Street (1987), 99, 102
Wanted (2008), 30
Wedlock of the Gods (2007), 69
Week End (1967), 25
Welles, Orson, *40, 47, 48*
westerns, 22, 26, 35, 77, 88
Western theory, xi, 72, 105–6
Westlake, M., 62
Wiene, Robert, 11
Wilder, Billy, 39
Willemen, P., 57, 72
Wollen, Peter, 55
women
  filmmakers, 145n3
  Hitchcock's films, 62
  male gaze, 59
  Nigeria, 125–6
Woo, John, 30
working classes
  audience studies, 110, 111
  British social realism, 25
  early cinema, 6
  Indian audiences, 124
  Indonesia, 97
  Italian neo-realism, 46
  Marxism, 50

Xala (1974), 94–5, 105

Yellow Earth (1984), 30, 105–6
Yojimbo (1961), 22, 26
Young Mr. Lincoln (1939), 52–3
YouTube, 98

Zavattini, Cesare, 46
Zhang, Yimou, 30